Globalisation & Indian Small Scale Industries

Technology & Competitiveness

Globalisation & Indian Small Scale Industries

Technology & Competitiveness

T.A. Bhavani

Ane Books Pvt Ltd.
New Delhi ♦ Chennai

Globalisation & Indian Small Scale Industries

T.A. Bhavani

Published by

Ane Books Pvt. Ltd.

4821, Parwana Bhawan, 1st Floor, [illegible]

Darya Ganj, New Delhi - 110 002, [illegible]

Tel.: +91(011) 23276843-44, Fax: [illegible]

e-mail: [illegible]

Branch Office

Avantika Niwas, 1st Floor, [illegible]

Chennai - 600 017, Tel.: [illegible]

e-mail: [illegible]

Disclaimer

Please be informed that the author and the publisher have put in their best efforts in producing this book. Every care has been taken [illegible] of the contents. However, we make no warranties for the same [illegible] be responsible or liable for any loss or any commercial damages [illegible] the author and the publisher in providing services [illegible] be responsible for any incidental, consequential, special or any other damages [illegible] where appropriate.

ISBN : 978-81-8052-044-0

Printed at : R. K. Offset Process, New Delhi

Globalisation & Indian Small Scale Industries

Technology & Competitiveness

T.A. Bhavani

Ane Books Pvt Ltd.

New Delhi ◆ Chennai

Globalisation & Indian Small Scale Industries

T.A. Bhavani

Published by

Ane Books Pvt. Ltd.
4821, Parwana Bhawan, 1st Floor, 24 Ansari Road,
Darya Ganj, **New Delhi** - 110 002, India
Tel.: +91(011) 23276843-44, Fax: +91(011) 23276863
e-mail: kapoor@anebooks.com,

Branch Office :

- Avantika Niwas, 1st Floor, 19 Doraiswamy Road, T. Nagar,
Chennai - 600 017, Tel.: +91(044) 28141554, 28141209
e-mail: anebookschennai@gmail.com, rathinam@anebooks.com

ISBN : 978-81-8052-044-0

Printed at : R. K. Offset Process, New Delhi

Dedicated to my Mother

Sandhyavali

Whose continuous strive against odds has been a great source of inspiration for me.

Preface

This book is an outcome of the IDPAD project entitled "Technological Change in the Small Scale Units in Northern India" carried out by me at the Institute of Economic Growth, New Delhi in collaboration with the Erasmus University Rotterdam, The Netherlands. I am highly grateful to IDPAD/ ICSSR for funding the study. But for the resources provided by the IDPAD, it could not have been possible for me to interact with the numerous agencies in the area and to conduct primary survey that has added value to the study.

I could not have completed the study without support of my parent organization—the Institute of Economic Growth. My sincere thanks to the former directors professors (late) Pravin Visaria and B.B. Bhattacharya and the current director professor Kanchan Chopra for their encouragement and cooperation. The support of the administrative, computer and library staff of the Institute is duly acknowledged. I would like to express my special thanks to Mr. Sridharan, computer centre of the Institute, who is always ready to help even at odd hours.

The paper covering the main theoretical framework relating to the causes of firm-level technological change and the empirical results pertaining to the auto component industry was presented at the Global Development Network (GDN, Washington) Annual Conference held at Cairo in January, 2003 and won GDN research medal. Theoretical frame and empirical results relating to the impact of technological change on competitive strength were presented at UNU-WIDER Conference on 'New Economy and Development' held in May 2002 at Helsinki, Finland and subsequently published under WIDER discussion paper series. My thanks are also due to the participants of these two conferences whose comments helped in the revision of the text.

I wish to express my sincere gratitude to professors J.G. Waardenburg of Erasmus University Rotterdam and N.S. Siddharthan of Institute of Economic Growth for their constant encouragement and guidance. But for the tireless efforts of professor Waardenburg, the study could not have been materialised. Expert advice of professor Siddharthan helped me in improving the quality of the study. I owe to my Dutch research collaborator Mr. Walter Samplonius who worked on the other part of the study for his critical comments on the earlier draft.

I am highly grateful to Professor K.L. Krishna for his expert comments especially on the econometric methodology used in the study. But for his encouragement and expert advice, I could not have completed this book. I am also thankful to Prof. Charan Wadhwa for Policy Research and to many other participants of the seminar organised to discuss findings of the study for their comments and suggestions.

My special thanks goes to the numerous organisations involved in the promotion of small-scale industrial units. These are: Development Commissioner, Small Scale Industries (Dr. Prasad, Additional Development Commissioner and Mr. Sambhu Singh Dy. DC, Technology), Directorate of Industries, Delhi (especially Mr. Reddy), Small Industries Service Institute, Delhi, Small Industries Development Bank, Delhi, National Small Industries Corporation, Delhi, Haryana and U.P., Technology Bureau for Small Enterprises, Automotive Component Manufacturers Association, Electronic Component Industries Association, Garment Exporters Association, Apparel Exporters and Manufacturers Association, Okhla Industries Association, Faridabad Association of Small Scale Industries, and Noida Small and Tiny Industries Association. These organisations not only helped me to understand small units but also facilitated the primary survey. Special thanks are also due to the owners of numerous small and tiny industrial units who have given their valuable time not only in answering my questions but also teaching me the nuances of their operations. Indeed these interactions have added practical knowledge about the Indian small units. Otherwise, my knowledge would have confined to academic research findings only.

I owe the greatest debt to my guru Professor Suresh Tendulkar, my husband, Gopal Krishna Murty and my daughters Natya and Kavya without whose moral support this book would not have been possible.

T.A. Bhavani

Contents

Preface vii
List of Tables xv
List of Figures xvii

CHAPTER 1 **Introduction 1**

1.1 Introduction 1
1.2 Dynamic Global Business Environments 2
1.3 Protective Local Business Environment 6
1.4 The Research Questions 8
1.5 Overview of the Book 9

CHAPTER 2 **Indian Small Scale Industries : Stagnant Units in the Dynamic Business Environment? 21**

2.1 Introduction 21
2.2 Village and Small Scale Industries: Composition and Characteristics 21
2.3 Business Environment in the Pre-Reform India 25
2.4 Policy Reforms of the 1990s and Changes in Business Environment 31
2.5 Summary 33

CHAPTER 3 **Firm-Level Technological Change : What Does Theory Say? 39**

3.1 Introduction 39
3.2 Evolutionary Economics 40
3.3 Economics of Technological Change 49
3.4 Technological Capabilities 52
3.5 Structure of Economic Organisations 54

CHAPTER 4 **An Eclectic Approach to Study Technological Change 63**

4.1 Introduction 63
4.2 Firm and Business Environment 63
4.3 Process of Technological Change and Factors Affecting It 67
4.4 Empirical Approaches to Study Firm Level Technological Change 72
4.5 Field of Enquiry 73

CHAPTER 5 **Selected Industries, Questionnaire and Sample 77**

5.1 Introduction 77
5.2 The Selected Region 77
5.3 The Selected Industries 79
5.4 Factors Influencing Technological Change 94
5.5 The Questionnaire and the Sample 97

CHAPTER 6 **Empirical Analysis: Methodology 111**

6.1 Introduction 111
6.2 Field Impressions Regarding Small Units 112
6.3 Remarks on Empirical Analysis 114
6.4 Specification and Estimation of Technology Functions 116
6.5 Estimation of the Impact of Technological Change 116

CHAPTER 7 **Empirical Analysis of Technological Change: Auto Components 123**

7.1 Introduction 123
7.2 Field Impressions 123
7.3 Basic Features of the Survey Units 125
7.4 Determinants of Technological Change: Empirical Evidence 141
7.5 Estimation of the Impact of Technological Change 146
7.6 Summary 148

CHAPTER 8 **Empirical Evidence for Technological Change: Electronics Industry 151**

8.1 Introduction 151
8.2 Field Impressions 151
8.3 Salient Features of the Sample Units 152
8.4 Empirical Evidence for the Determinants of Technological Change 168

8.5 Impact of Technological Change 171
8.6 Summary 173

CHAPTER 9 **Technological Change in the Garments Industry 175**

9.1 Introduction 175
9.2 Field Impressions 175
9.3 Basic Characteristics of the Garments Sample 176
9.4 Determinants of Technological Change 193
9.5 Impact of Technological Change 197
9.6 Summary 199

CHAPTER 10 **Summary Findings and Policy Suggestions 201**

10.1 Introduction 201
10.2 Analytical Features 201
10.3 General Characteristics of the Selected Industries 205
10.4 Causes and Consequences of Technological Change 208
10.5 Implications for the Industry and Policy 210

Appendix A 213
Appendix B 225
References 243
Index 259

List of Tables

4.1 Factors Affecting the Process of Firm-Level Technological Change 70

7.1 Descriptive Statistics for output, Inputs and Their Ratios: Auto Components Industry 126

7.2 Marginal Coefficients of Technology Functions: Auto Components Industry 143

8.1 Descriptive Statistics for output, Inputs and Their Ratios: Electronics Industry 159

8.2 Marginal Coefficients of Technology Functions: Electronics Industry 170

8.3 Estimates of Production Function: Electronics Industry 172

9.1 Descriptive Statistics for output, Inputs and Their Ratios: Garment Industry 183

9.2 Marginal Coefficients of Transformation and Organisation Technology Functions: Garment Industry 195

9.3 Marginal Coefficients of Information Technology Functions: Garment Industry 196

9.4 Estimates of Production Function: Garments Industry 198

List of Tables

List of Figures

4.1 Firm and Business Environment 65
7.1 Size Groups of Sales: Auto Components Industry 127
7.2 Investment Size Classes: Auto Components Industry 127
7.3 Employment Size Classes: Auto Components Industry 128
7.4 Size Distribution of Wage Share: Auto Components Industry 129
7.5 Size Groups of Material Share: Auto Components Industry 129
7.6 Range of Capital Intensity: Auto Components Industry 130
7.7 Size Groups-Labour Productivity: Auto Components Industry 131
7.8 Size Groups-Capital Productivity: Auto Components Industry 132
7.9 Level of Mechanisation: Auto Components Industry 133
7.10 Changes in Machinery: Auto Components Industry 133
7.11 Work Allocation: Auto Components Industry 134
7.12 ISO 9000: Auto Components Industry 134
7.13 Business Organisation: Auto Components Industry 135
7.14 Means of Communication: Auto Components Industry 135
7.15 Changes in Communication: Auto Components Industry 135
7.16 Record Keeping: Auto Components Industry 136
7.17 Product Market: Auto Components Industry 137
7.18 Market Competition: Auto Components Industry 137
7.19 Impact of Market Competition: Auto Components Industry 137
7.20 Demand Problem: Auto Components Industry 138
7.21 Education of Owners: Auto Components Industry 138
7.22 Experience of Owners: Auto Components Industry 139
7.23 Use of Professional Labour: Auto Components Industry 139

7.24 Information Problem: Auto Components Industry 140
7.25 Finance Problem: Auto Components Industry 140
7.26 Sources of Finance: Auto Components Industry 140
7.27 Labour Behaviour: Auto Components Industry 141
7.28 Labour Attitudes: Auto Components Industry 141
8.1 Sales Turnover: Electronics Industry 154
8.2 Plant and Machinery: Electronics Industry 154
8.3 Employment Size Groups: Electronics Industry 155
8.4 Wage Share Groups: Electronics Industry 155
8.5 Material Share Groups: Electronics Industry 156
8.6 Capital Intensity: Electronics Industry 157
8.7 Labour Productivity: Electronics Industry 157
8.8 Capital Productivity: Electronics Industry 158
8.9 Level of Mechanisation: Electronics Industry 160
8.10 Changes in Machinery: Electronics Industry 160
8.11 Business Organisation: Electronics Industry 161
8.12 Work Allocation: Electronics Industry 162
8.13 Means of Communication: Electronics Industry 162
8.14 Changes in Communication: Electronics Industry 162
8.15 Record Keeping: Electronics Industry 163
8.16 Product Market: Electronics Industry 163
8.17 Brand Name: Electronics Industry 164
8.18 Market Competition: Electronics Industry 164
8.19 Impact of Competition: Electronics Industry 164
8.20 Education of Owners: Electronics Industry 165
8.21 Experience of Owners: Electronics Industry 165
8.22 Use of Professional Labour: Electronics Industry 166
8.23 Information Sources: Electronics Industry 166
8.24 Sources of Finance: Electronics Industry 167
8.25 Finance Problem: Electronics Industry 167
8.26 Labour Behaviour: Electronics Industry 167
8.27 Labour Attitudes: Electronics Industry 169
9.1 Sales Turnover: Garments Industry 178
9.2 Percentage of In-house Production: Garments Industry 178
9.3 Plant and Machinery: Garments Industry 179
9.4 Total Employment: Garments Industry 179
9.5 Wage Share: Garments Industry 180

9.6 Share of Materials: Garments Industry 180
9.7 Capital Intensity: Garments Industry 181
9.8 Capital Productivity: Garments Industry 182
9.9 Labour Productivity: Garments Industry 182
9.10 Level of Mechanisation: Garments Industry 184
9.11 Changes in Machinery: Garments Industry 184
9.12 Presence of Foreign Machinery: Garments Industry 185
9.13 Means of Communication: Garments Industry 186
9.14 Changes in Communication: Garments Industry 186
9.15 Record Keeping: Garments Industry 186
9.16 Business Organisation: Garments Industry 187
9.17 Type of Management: Garments Industry 187
9.18 Product Market: Garments Industry 188
9.19 Demand Problem: Garments Industry 189
9.20 Market Competition: Garments Industry 189
9.21 Impact of Market Competition: Garments Industry 189
9.22 Education of Owners: Garments Industry 190
9.23 Professional Labour: Garments Industry 190
9.24 Experience of Owners: Garments Industry 190
9.25 Information Problems: Garments Industry 191
9.26 Information Sources: Garments Industry 191
9.27 Sources of Finance: Garments Industry 191
9.28 Finance Problem: Garments Industry 192
9.29 Labour Behaviour: Garments Industry 192
9.30 Labour Attitudes: Garments Industry 193

Chapter 1 Introduction

1.1 INTRODUCTION

Small-scale industries occupy an important place in the Indian economy especially in terms of creation of employment opportunities that provide a source of income to millions of people, and their regional dispersal. In order to continue to play this role, small industries have to be competitive and commercially viable. The general observation, since the beginning, had been that majority of the small-scale industries were not competitive and there was a need for their improvement in this respect. Consequently, numerous policies were initiated by the Government of India to enable small industries to improve their competitive strength.[1] Although these policies emphasised technological upgradation of small-scale industries taking it as crucial for their competitive strength, they created a paradoxical situation by protecting these units indiscriminately. Continuous policy protection not only discouraged these industries from going in for technological upgradation to grow in size but also encouraged them to get into the production areas characterised by scale economies.[2] As a result, even after the policy support for more than four decades, they remained too small and technologically backward to be competitive.[3] But the rapid technological developments and changing business environments due to globalisation and liberalisation policy reforms in the recent decade increased the role of technology and scale in enhancing the competitive strength. It is in this context that a study of technological change and its determinant factors such as scale of operation in the Indian small-scale industries assumes significance.

Industrial units[4] undertake changes, technological or other, as a reaction to the movements (actual or anticipated) in their business environments. In this respect, although the changes in global business environment create pressures as well as incentives for industrial units to go for technological change, it is the local environment that provides the units with an immediate need to go for the changes along with its specific conditions and constraints. Hence, the next section discusses briefly the changes in global business environment which are becoming highly integrated thus influencing the local environments to a great extent. Section 1.3 describes the local context, i.e. the salient features of small-scale industries in India and the conditions responsible for their survival so far. Against this background, section 1.4 specifies the research questions of the study. The final section presents the overview of the book.

1.2 DYNAMIC GLOBAL BUSINESS ENVIRONMENTS

The phenomena of liberalisation, globalisation, and rapid technological developments are changing business environments world over for the past two decades. There has been a shift from 'policy regulation' to 'market orientation' all over the world through liberalisation of the state controls on economic transactions. Globalisation is taking place in the sense that all the economies are becoming highly integrated. There have been rapid technological developments that are drastically changing the methods of doing business. The recent liberalisation and globalisation policies are not only exposing industrial units to market competition to a greater extent but also making markets more and more competitive. These two phenomena are together posing significant challenges to individual enterprises. Technological developments, on the other hand, are providing opportunities to the industrial units to improve their competitive strength so as to deal with these challenges.

Since the beginning of the 1980s, there has been a remarkable shift in the policies of many developing countries towards 'market oriented' economic policies from their earlier policies of state intervention.[5] In the Indian economic policy regime, a major reform process is underway since July 1991 to liberalise the regulations on domestic economic transactions in order to make the economy more market-oriented (important policy reforms are discussed in section 2.4). These liberalisation measures have intensified the competition by removing the entry barriers to domestic market that were created by past policies.

Globalisation, whether taken in a limited way in terms of 'multilateral trade liberalisation'[6] or in the broader sense of 'increasing internationalisation of production, distribution and marketing of goods and services,'[7] is taking place resulting in the opening of world economies and intensifying competition in the domestic markets. For example, the World Trade Organisation (WTO) that regulates multilateral trade started enforcing its member countries not only to remove various restrictions on imports and to reduce tariffs but also to impart national treatment to multinational corporations thereby prohibiting any preferential treatment for local firms. In addition, countries (especially the developing countries) are asked to cut subsidies to exports as well as to domestic goods. In all these respects, time limits are prescribed and strictly enforced by the WTO.

As per the GATT agreement, India has to bring down its tariff rates to 40 percent for finished products and 25 percent for intermediate goods. In addition, India was to remove quantitative restrictions on imports by 2001 and all export subsidies by 2003.[8] As a result, every enterprise in India, small or large, whether exporting or serving the domestic market, is exposed to competition. There is a direct competition in the domestic market with the import of high quality goods from the developed countries and cheap products from the other developing countries. The process has already started for the small-scale units with the placement of 586 of the 812 items reserved for production by these units exclusively, in the open general license (OGL) list that makes these easier to import. Competition in the domestic market is intensifying further with the arrival of multinational companies (MNCs). To be able to compete with imports or MNCs in the domestic market, or to export successfully without any external support, Indian enterprises, small or large, need to improve their productivity and quality, reduce costs, go for higher performance products and better services—all to be delivered simultaneously.[9]

In addition, there are non-trade issues of WTO such as sanitary, environment and labour standards, TRIPS (Trade Related Intellectual Property Rights), and TRIMs (Trade Related Investment Measures). For example, sanitary and phyto-sanitary measures (SPS) empower countries to deny imports from certain regions for reasons like spread of diseases. Under this, the United States has already banned the import of Indian Beedies.[10] TRIPS does not allow industrial units to produce patented products without authorisation. This has immediate and important implications for the small units as most of these units get technologies through unauthorised imitation of products than by formal technology transfers.[11] Multilateral agreement on TRIMs forces the member governments to remove some of the earlier policies such as local content requirements (mandates a proportion of the input requirements of companies, domestic as well as multinationals, to be procured locally) and trade balancing requirement (mandates that the imports of industrial units should be a proportion of their exports) and thus intensifies competition further. India has already removed some of the measures like phased manufacturing programme (i.e. local content requirements). Now, Indian input supplying units like that of auto component units (as a set) do not automatically get their share. These units have to compete in the open market for their market shares. Whatever be the status of multilateral agreements on environment and labour standards, importers are already enforcing these standards in the case of exports from India.[12] All these measures are taking away the comparative advantage of Indian enterprises especially that of the small-scale units (i.e. advantages of cheap labour) and giving instead higher importance to the competitive advantage of the latest technologies.

Internationalisation of production, distribution and marketing has given rise to global commodity chains. These chains are the networks of business units of different sizes involved in various stages of a product beginning from the supply of raw materials and components to production, marketing and retailing spread across the countries. These commodity chains can either be producer-driven or buyer-driven. Producer-driven commodity chains exist for the capital and technology-intensive products where the manufacturers of the final product will be the key economic agents. More advanced products like automobiles fall in this category. In contrast, buyer-driven commodity chains exist for the design and marketing-intensive products that are labour-intensive in the manufacturing stage such as garments. Retailers and brand merchandisers control these chains.[13] It is easier for an enterprise to access technologies and markets if it is a part of these international production and trade networks. However, to get into these chains, individual enterprises have to meet, to start with, the buyers' standards in terms of price, quality and delivery schedules.[14]

In effect, globalisation has been intensifying market competition thereby creating pressures on firms to pay more attention to quality, price and delivery considerations rather than profitability. All these require substantial improvement in various dimensions of technology, i.e. transformation, organisation and information.[15]

Major changes in the past few decades both in the basic sciences and in applied fields like technology have drastically altered the manufacturing processes as well as the nature of inputs and outputs. Mechanical devices have been replaced initially by electrical, later by electronic and very recently by computerised machines. Microelectronics-based technologies permit increased automation of a wide range of operations in many industries.[16]

Simultaneously, there have been numerous organisational changes. Organisation of a production process involves plant layouts, materials management, work allocation, production schedules, quality management, inventory control, and so on. Some of the recent developments in the area of organisation include total quality management (TQM), Just-in-time (JIT), new standards for scrap management, machine reliability, inventory control and so on.[17] Also, increasing consumer preference for variety has changed the ground rules of competition from the mass production of standardised products to flexible specialisation of manufacturing customised products, which in turn altered the ways of organising the production system. For instance, the plant layout is being changed from long narrow assembly lines comprising of specialised machines to a cluster of all-purpose machines arranged like cells in which different families of products are manufactured. This is changing further the work assignment rules and production schedules.[18]

Exchange of information in business has traditionally been carried out through paper documents delivered by messengers or postal services and of late by fax. With the advent of computer and communication technologies, more efficient alternatives are available nowadays. These new technologies not only enable firms to acquire accurate and up-to-date information but also provide it faster. Timely availability of information is very essential in this fast-changing world. Also, new technologies can store, process and retrieve a variety of data forms ranging from simple numbers to video images.[19]

These developments in various dimensions of technology enable industrial units to supply high-quality products at cheaper prices. At the same time, new technologies are making technological upgradation of industrial units imperative by causing the existing technologies unviable. Unless Indian industrial units continuously upgrade their technologies, it is difficult for them to withstand international competition arising from liberalisation and globalisation. This applies more to small units as they lag both in terms of technology and competitiveness.

In sum, the phenomena of liberalisation, globalisation and rapid technological developments are rapidly changing the global business environments. Globalisation and liberalisation policies are making the business environment more competitive, and creating pressures for industrial units to improve themselves. On the other hand, technological developments are enabling the units to deal with the competitive environments by providing efficient alternatives to improve their competitive strength. To what extent an individual enterprise reacts and adapts to these changes in the environment depends on their current status, the immediate environment and the way it is evolved over time. Accordingly, we need to understand the historical background of Indian small industries, their growth and the context of their operations to study technological change in them.

1.3 PROTECTIVE LOCAL BUSINESS ENVIRONMENT

Small-scale industries in India have attracted attention not only for their contribution but also their typical characteristics that have remained more or less traditional, and the special patronage they enjoy from the government.

The general trade and industrial policies that India adopted till the 1990s insulated Indian industry from competition—domestic as well as foreign. Within this generally insulated business environment, small units were further protected from the competition from large-scale units through various policies. Perceiving that small industries are handicapped on various fronts like technology and finance, the Government of India initiated numerous policy measures to remove their handicaps and thereby to impart competitive strength to these industries. These measures include the provision of infrastructure such as developed plots in industrial estates, credit, and critical materials. At the same time, protection has been provided to these units through policy measures such as reservation and fiscal concessions as these units were considered weak and not in a position to face market competition[20] (policies related to small units are discussed in section 2.3.2).

While protective measures led to the proliferation of small units, discretionary promotional measures without much dissemination of information but with cumbersome procedures made policy assistance out of reach for the majority of small units especially smaller ones. Larger units within the sector that have better access to policy assistance developed perverse incentive in remaining small in order to enjoy the protective umbrella. The result was that the small-scale industries (SSI) sector has been growing in terms of number of units, production and employment but with a dual structure where a large number of tiny units operating with obsolete technologies and hence low productivity levels co-exist with a few larger units working at high productivity levels. In other words, the small-scale sector although growing, remained mostly tiny, technologically backward and hence lacked competitive strength.[21] This can be seen from the evidence presented in the subsequent paragraphs.

The small-scale industries (SSI) sector constitutes 95 percent of the manufacturing units, 40 percent of manufacturing output and 35 percent of total exports of India while employing a little more than 19.2 million persons next only to agriculture.[22] This sector, on an average, has been growing at the rate of 6.5 percent per annum during the period of 1990–91 to 1997–98, and around 8.2 percent for the years 1999–2000 and 2000–01.[23]

Notwithstanding the growth of the SSI sector, an overwhelming 83 percent of its units having an original investment in plant and machinery less than or equal to 100 thousand rupees, contribute as little as 28 percent to the small-scale sector's production. As many as 65 percent of units employing four workers or less account for a mere 12 percent of the total output of the small-scale sector. In several small industries, there exists a considerable gap between the domestic small industries technology frontier and the rest of the world. Thus, the small-scale industries sector at large has not yet acquired the desired levels of competitive strength. This is further corroborated by the fact that nearly 35 percent of the small-scale units were closed by 1987–88, of which, 50 percent of the units were closed within five years of their establishment while sick units constitute 37 percent of the working units.[24] Sample survey by the Development Commissioner, Small Scale Industries (DCSSI) for the year 1999–2000 reveals that the situation remained more or less the same in the nineties with 29 percent of the small units closed after an average life of 4 to 5 years either due to marketing or finance problems, or due to severe competition.[25]

Apart from policy protection, it was geographical and product market segmentation that helped small units to survive so far, despite being non-competitive. Underdevelopment of infrastructure like transport created sheltered local markets for small-scale units by raising transport and transaction costs for the large units to reach semi-urban and rural segments. Examples for this are edible oils, biscuits, laundry soaps and so on. Product differentiation in terms of quality with the existing income inequalities segmented the product market into two parts: price-sensitive and quality-insensitive, and price-insensitive and quality-sensitive. Lower income households and government constitute the former while the higher income households constitute the latter market segment. Small-scale industrial units mostly being producers of lower quality but cheaper products cater to the former segment. Product market segmentation exists in India for numerous consumer items like water heaters, pressure cookers, tape recorders, footwear, etc.

Liberalisation and globalisation policies are expected to reduce policy protection and market segmentation and thus expose these units to market competition. Policy protection is reducing with the reduction in duties and the consequent benefits of duty exemptions to small units and the imports of reserved products. Liberalisation and globalisation are reducing the market segmentation and its protection to small units by intensifying the competitive pressures for large-scale units and hence forcing them to enter rural and lower end markets. Ultimately, small-scale units have to sustain themselves on their own competitive strength by successfully facing competition from large-scale units including multinationals in the increasingly dynamic business environment.

1.4 THE RESEARCH QUESTIONS

Even to provide employment (an argument that has been widely articulated in favour of protection to the small-scale industries) in a sustainable way and to pay higher income, (primary objective of employment generation) firms have to be competitive and commercially viable. Commercial viability and competitive strength depends primarily on technology. Thus, the changing business environment makes it imperative for the small units to upgrade their technologies. It is in this background that we are keen to understand the process of technological change and to investigate the factors influencing it in the small-scale industries in India. To be specific, this study focuses on the following research questions:

- How can one characterise the process of technological change in the small units?
- What are the determinants of technological change in the small units?

- Are there differences in these determinants across industries?
- What is the impact of technological change on competitive strength of small units?

The analysis of determinants of technological change enables one to know what is constraining small units to undertake technological change. Inter-industry differences in these determinants indicate which are industry-specific and which are common for all small-scale industries. This knowledge is essential for the government and other agencies involved in promoting technological upgradation in the small units to focus on the relevant factors. Understanding the process of technological change and characterizing it helps the promotional agencies to serve better these units in upgrading their technologies by taking the relevant parameters of the units into account in the implementation of their measures.

These research questions are investigated with reference to three industries in the National Capital Region of Delhi, namely, Auto components, Electronics and Garments. These industries are selected on the basis of their importance in the national as well as regional economy, and for the rate of technological developments in them. The selected region not only gives access to wider set of small-scale units but also provides better business environment (section 5.2 discusses the selected region). Thus, it enables us to examine the environmental factors that are crucial for technological change and highlight constraints if any.

1.5 OVERVIEW OF THE BOOK

Any study on small-scale industries requires understanding of their characteristics, constraints and the immediate business environment, which together form the local context for the study. Accordingly, Chapter 2 focuses on the growth and structure of the Indian small-scale industries sector, and the business environment in which they have been operating. Section 2.2, which deals with the composition of the Village and Small Industries (VSI) sector shows that the sector is dominated by the modern small-scale segment vis-à-vis traditional segment. Small-scale industries (SSI) sector, primary constituent of the modern small-scale segment is further dominated by tiny units. Most of these are non-factory units run by the owner on a proprietary basis. A large number of smaller units operating at lower productivity levels co-exist with a few larger units working at higher productivity levels indicating dual structure of the sector. Inadequate flow of credit, use of obsolete technology, poor quality standards and inadequate infrastructure facilities are considered as the major problems for the small units (section 2.3).

Autarkic, basic and heavy industrial development strategy pursued by independent India through the ideological framework of 'socialist pattern of society', assigned the State direct responsibility for the development of industry. The State's direct involvement resulted in the formation of a dominant public sector and a heavily regulated private sector. The net effect of these policies was the creation of a business environment characterized by infrastructure and key input bottlenecks on the supply side, and protected and segmented markets on the demand side. These policies provided doubly insulated market environment for small-scale units. The only competition that these units faced so far was from the other small units. This had not provided any incentives for the small units to reorganize themselves in terms of technology and product so as to be competitive and grow (section 2.4).

The business environment in India has been undergoing transformation since the nineties owing to policy reforms. These reforms are not only making markets more and more competitive but also changing the nature of competition. Small units now have to compete with large units including multinationals and imports. This requires small units to upgrade themselves in all aspects including technology. However, small units have to struggle to do so within the still persistent infrastructure bottlenecks and input constraints such as inadequate credit (section 2.5).

Chapter 3 explores the theoretical base that can provide a conceptual kit with which an appropriate analytical framework can be developed to understand the process of technological change in the small industrial units and the factors influencing it, the primary objective of the study. As there is no ready-made theoretical framework that suits our purpose, we follow an *eclectic* approach and draws on the relevant concepts from evolutionary economics, literature on technological change, technological capabilities and organization theories. Accordingly, the chapter briefly reviews this literature.

Section 3.2 brings out the basic principles underpinning the evolutionary economics, its characterization of technological change and firm, and its limitations. The present study makes use of the concept of selection mechanism, characterization of the process of technological change and its salient features from the evolutionary economics. The selection mechanism operates through the process of competition. Firms compete with each other by offering different products at different prices to the market. Firms producing more desirable products and more efficiently are selected in the sense that they not only survive but also improve their position in the market. In order to be more competitive, firms focus their innovation activities on the promising lines of development. In the evolutionary economics, innovation is, thus, taken as the result of deliberate human actions and characterized as a process of search for, discovery, experimentation, development and adaptation of new products, production processes and organizational set up. Technological outcomes of these activities are contingent upon the match between the internal capabilities of a firm and its external environment.

Section 3.3 reviews the technological change literature from which we draw the definition and determinants of technological change. This literature defines technological change broadly as to 'encompass improvements in products, production processes, materials and management methods in economic systems' but the empirical works mainly confined to the changes in products, production processes and materials. As regards the factors influencing technological change, this literature considers the market structure, scale of operation, finance, technological capabilities, availability of materials and relative factor prices as the important determinants.

Section 3.4 discusses briefly literature on technological capabilities as it is considered prerequisite for technological change. Firm-level technological capabilities, namely, production capabilities, linkage capabilities, innovation and investment capabilities are essential for the technological change to occur in the firm. These capabilities are determined by the attitudes, education and experience of the concerned individuals.

Since we are dealing with the firm-level technological change, it is important to know the internal structure of a firm. For the purpose of knowing the basic components, functions and structure of economic organization, section 3.5 looks into the literature on organization theories. This literature provides five natural structural configurations of organizations, namely, simple structure, machine bureaucracy, professional bureaucracy, divisionalised form and adhocracy. Many small units remain as simple structures. This organizational structure consists of little more than one-man strategic apex (top management), operating core (workers involved in production operations) and few supporting staff (such as clerical staff). It has a loose division of labour with little formalisation of behaviour. Coordination is attained through direct supervision. Power to make important decisions is centralized in the strategic apex.

Chapter 4 attempts to develop an analytical framework using some of the theoretical concepts discussed in chapter 3, which permits one to describe the firm-level technological change and examine the factors influencing it in the case of Indian small-scale industries. We take firm as the unit of analysis as it is the firm that changes the technologies. Accordingly, the analytical frame starts with the specification of the basic elements of a firm and its business environment in section 4.2.

Firm being a producer of a given set of goods and services, competes with many other firms in the market. Markets, industry (other firms) and other institutions such as policies together form business environment. Business environment keeps changing as all its elements change. Firms strive continuously through different strategies like technological change to maintain and improve their commercial viability in the changing environments.

For the purpose of the study, we focus on three basic elements of the firm, namely, technology (that undergoes change), decision-maker (who undertakes change) and technological capabilities (pre-requisite for change). Technology is taken to include the physical process of transformation of inputs into output, organizational methods that structure these processes and informational flows required to carry out these processes. Thus, the study considers three dimensions of technology namely, transformation, organization and information. Technological changes are referred to the changes in any one or a combination of these three dimensions of technology that are undertaken by the firm to improve its competitive strength. Further, these are regarded as the changes in their existing technologies in the form of either addition of or, replacement by a later vintage technology.

Small industrial units are regarded to have simple organizational structure with one or two owner-managers constituting strategic apex. These owner-managers are the sole decision makers. Thus, decisions regarding technological changes depend on the owner-managers' perception of changes in business environment and their capabilities. Hence, the study provides the definitions of firm-level technological capabilities, i.e., production, linkage and investment capabilities and locates them in the small units. It is the owner-manager who is expected to possess investment capabilities, linkage capabilities and part of production capabilities and hence these can be deduced from the owner-managers' education and experience. The operating core i.e., workforce needs to have the other part of production capabilities that are required to operate and maintain production systems which further depend on their formal education, attitudes and so on (section 4.2).

This chapter also describes firm-level technological change as a deliberately initiated process of search, selection, execution and absorption, and analyses the factors, external as well as internal, influencing each stage of the process. The analysis in the chapter brings out that the product market, owner-managers' perception of market changes, technological capabilities, scale of operation, availability of information, finance, complementary skills and materials, relative factor prices and labour as the possible factors influencing the process of technological change in the small units (section 4.3). In addition, the chapter briefly discusses the empirical approaches to the examination of the issue (section 4.4) and filed of enquiry (section 4.5).

Chapter 5 takes the analysis of technological change and the factors influencing it further keeping the selected characteristics in mind, and deduces the questionnaire. It begins with the selection of the geographical area and industries for the study (section 5.2) and discusses the important characteristics of the selected industries in terms of product composition, nature of the market, industry structure and their likely future with a special emphasis on the position of small-scale units. Of the three selected industries, garments is a small-scale industry in the sense that all its units are small. The auto components and electronics industries have a significant number of small units. While most of the auto component units have direct interaction with their customers, a major proportion of small units in the electronics industry operate in the open market. Market competition has been intense in all the selected industries. The economic policy reforms made it inevitable for these industries to integrate with the global industry where all the selected industries are reorganized as global commodity chains following rapid changes in technology and markets. To get into these chains, Indian small units have to restructure themselves in terms of mechanization, organization and product composition. In this respect, in-house tailoring operations and acquisitions of improved machinery are the basic parameters for the restructuring of garment units. A shift to the sophisticated technology of fully automatic or, numerically controlled machinery and improved organizational methods such as total quality management are the primary factors for the auto component units. Electronics units are required to get into mechanized production, employ high quality testing instruments and to adopt improved organizational methods. In addition, units in all these industries are to connect themselves with the rest through the latest information technologies. Technological changes in this study are taken in terms of the above-mentioned parameters (section 5.3).

We have elaborated the analytical factors influencing the process of technological change (discussed in section 4.3) in section 5.4 in terms of firm-level characteristics and their specific relationship with the technological change. For instance, the kind of product market a unit is serving such as domestic or international market, influences its technological change. Export markets are regarded as more competitive and exporting units are likely to face stricter norms in terms of quality that push these units to improve their technology relative to the units serving the domestic market. The analysis of the section brings down the analytical factors into firm's characteristics, namely, product market served, owner-managers' views about market demand and competitiveness, education and experience of the owner-managers, extent of the use of professional labour, sales turnover, unit's sources of information and finance, owner-managers' opinions about the availability of information, finance, complementary skills and materials, and attitudes and behaviour of labour.

Firm-level characteristics are further specified into field-level parameters so as to frame the questions that are easily identifiable by small units and enable one to collect meaningful information. For instance, transformation technology is specified in terms of mechanization, which further includes four categories keeping the nature of the units in mind. These groups are: only tools and instruments, manually operated machines, semi-automatic machines, and numerically controlled/ computerized machinery. As some of the electronics units are engaged in manual assembling of bought-out components with the help of few tools and instruments, we have included 'only tools and instruments' category.

Many of the parameters are captured using objective criteria as well as through the subjective opinions of the owner-mangers as we believe that the latter plays equally important role in the decision-making. Questions relating to the subjective opinions of owner-manager have a three-point ordinal scale. Ordered as well as unordered categories are used to capture some of the characteristics of the firm. Questionnaire also consists of a good number of categorical questions such as whether the unit has undergone technological change over time. The questionnaire has been structured to have 13 blocks to collect information under different headings such as outputs and inputs, existing technologies, selection of technology, owner-manager profile, market profile, sources of information and finance. Numerical data such as sales turnover, labour and investment pertain to the year 1998–99. The required information has been collected through a field survey of small-scale units pertaining to the selected industries using purposive sampling method (section 5.5).

Chapter 6 deals with the methodology used for the empirical examination of the factors influencing unit-level technological change and the impact of technological change on its competitive strength - primary research questions of the study. In particular, it presents the field impressions about small-scale units in general (section 6.2), qualifies the intensive survey data and results (section 6.3) and discusses the economic as well as econometric methods used for the empirical examination of the basic research questions of the study (sections 6.4 and 6.5).

To understand the causes and consequences of technological change in the small units, author has personally undertaken survey at two levels. First, an extensive interaction took place with the relevant officials from all those institutions, private and public, that are involved in the promotion of small-scale units or selected industries and located in the National Capital Region of Delhi. This was followed by an intensive survey of small industrial units in the selected industries. The extensive interactions with different promotional agencies and the survey units are summarized as field impressions in section 6.2, which is expected to provide a useful background to the survey data and the final results.

Given the nature of research problem which demands close probing of numerous aspects of the units, problem of locating the small units and their poor response rate, intensive survey could cover limited number of units in each of the selected industry. The study also considers numerous characteristics to represent various dimensions of the basic variables like technology, which could not be aggregated into a single index. Consequently, the study has numerous variables in comparison with the number of observations that limited the use of information and econometric methods. This chapter discusses the problems with the survey data and the consequent adjustments in the specification of variables and equations (section 6.3).

The chapter also discusses the technology equations used in the study and their estimation method (section 6.4) and the production function framework that has been used to examine the impact of technology on the competitive strength of the unit (section 6.5).

Chapter 7 examines the empirical evidence with reference to the objectives of the study, namely, factors influencing technological change and consequences of technological change for one of the selected industries, i.e., auto components. It starts with the field impressions of the author about the small units in the industry, which is meant to serve as a background to the sample units (section 7.2). Later, it discusses the technology and non-technology characteristics of the survey units in order to examine their relevance for the empirical analysis of the study (section 7.3). Finally, it analyses the empirical evidence regarding the determinants of technology (section 7.4) and the impact of technology on the competitive strength of units (section 7.5).

Auto component sample shows the presence of different levels of machinery and the changes in machinery, over time, in some of the units. Suppliers of machinery are the primary source of transformation technology (mechanization) and units purchase machinery keeping their scale of operation and product specification in mind. Most of the characteristics of production organization are turned out to be flexible in the sample units. Only work allocation and quality management practices vary across the sample units. The sample has a good number of units with computers and hence started using modern methods of communication and data management.

Original equipment manufacturers dominate the sample. A good number of owner-managers in the sample are mechanical engineers but use of professional labour is limited. Most of the sample units feel intense market competition is threatening their survival. Reasonable number of sample units obtain institutional finance and do not find information a problem. However, labour attitudes are a problem for a number of sample units.

Empirical results reveal that the level of mechanization (transformation technology) is determined by scale of operation, sources of finance and labour meaning that larger units with access to institutional finance are in a better position to go for higher level machinery like numerically controlled machines. Both organisation and information technologies are influenced mainly by scale of operation. Machine embodied technology turns out to be important for the competitiveness of the units.

Chapter 8 deals with the empirical examination of the basic objectives of the study, i.e., causes and consequences of technological change in the case of small units belonging to electronics industry. Before discussing various characteristics of the sample units to establish their empirical relevance (section 8.3), the chapter presents the field impressions of the author about the industry (section 8.2). Later, the chapter analyses the empirical evidence regarding the determinants of technological change (section 8.4) and the consequences of this change (section 8.5).

The majority of the sample electronic units are involved in the assembling of consumer and industrial electronics. A small number of the sample units have numerically controlled machinery and few units have upgraded their machinery over time. Main source of technology for the sample units is the suppliers of machinery. Most of the sample units are owner-managed. But for work allocation practices, production organization methods are quite flexible and do not vary much across the sample units. Reasonable number of sample units has computers and use modern methods of communication and data management.

Few units in the sample serve specific customers and rest caters to the open market. A good number of the sample units have started feeling intense competition primarily due to the entry of multinational corporations, which is threatening their survival. Almost all the owners are highly educated and good number of them is electronic engineers. Professional labour can be seen in some of the units.

Labour problems are experienced by a reasonable number of sample units but information is not a problem for these units. Although a good number of units are availing institutional finance, half of the sample feels finance a problem.

Transformation technology taken in terms of level of mechanization is primarily determined by labour attitudes towards work prompting units to go for fully automatic machinery. Organisation captured through work allocation practices is explained by labour behavioural problems such as absenteeism and turnover. Information technology considered in terms of data management is explained by scale of operation indicating that large-scale operation makes it worth to use computers for data processing. Sales performance used as a proxy for competitive strength, is influenced primarily by materials, labour and information technologies.

Chapter 9 presents the empirical evidence regarding the causes and consequences of technological change in the case of garments industry. As regards the sample characteristics, good presence of foreign machines can be seen in the sample units. Suppliers of the machines are the primary source of technology. A good number of units have computers and hence use electronic methods of communication and data processing. Most of the owner-managers have higher education though not professionals. Exporting units outnumber the units serving domestic market in the sample. Majority of the sample units feel increasing market competition. Information is not regarded as a problem by most of the sample units. Although good number of units are availing institutional finance, most of the sample units feel finance a problem. Labour problems are felt mainly in terms of threat of unionization and indifference of labour to quality and timely delivery (section 9.3).

Empirical results show that the presence of foreign machinery (proxy for transformation technology) is mainly determined by owner-mangers' perception of market demand. Organization taken in terms of the extent of having in-house production facility is influenced by negative attitudes of labour and information technology by the type of product market, scale of operation and experience of owner-managers. Sales performance, indicator of competitive strength, is not influenced by technology but by the traditional variables of labour and materials.

Chapter 10 summarises the research findings of the study in a comparative perspective and brings out their implications for the industry and policy. Results indicate that technological upgradation is imperative in the current context of globalisaiton and liberalization. Small units should be made aware of this fact along with the available alternative technologies. Promotional agencies have an important role to play in this respect. Since higher level of mechanization is necessitating large scale of operation and availability of finance, it requires total revamp of the existing policies regarding the small-scale units as these could not succeed in improving the accessibility of these units to various inputs such as institutional finance but created perverse incentives to remain small through its protection policies. Another important policy implication relates to the amendments to labour laws. Given the existing labour laws, larger scale of operation (especially in labour intensive industries such as garments) creating potential threat from labour. This necessitates labour law reforms.

Endnotes

1. This was noted by Mahalanobis (1963: 73); The Karve Committee (1955); and the *Industrial Policy Resolution 1956*.
2. Small industries have a natural advantage in the production areas which are characterised by scale neutral, high transport costs, high skill requirements, etc. (See Staley and Morse 1965), and are expected to enter those areas in a market economy.
3. Tendulkar and Bhavani (1997); Report of the Abid Hussain Committee 1997; Report of the Working Group on the SSIs for the Ninth Five Year Plan (1999: 73); Kumar (2000:41); and SIDBI (2001:17).
4. 'Unit' (or firm or, enterprise) usually refers to ownership or decision-making unit in the production of goods and services. The term 'industry' is taken to consist of all units in the production of a specified product. Thus, unit is an element of industry. In this book, we use the term 'industry' when we have to refer to general contexts, i.e. all units of all industries or of one industry. If we have to say something specifically relevant at the level of individual industrial units, we use the term unit. We use unit, enterprise and firm synonymously depending on the context. This has been the case all through the book.
5. Biersteker (1995:174)
6. Bhalla (1996: 2)
7. Harris (1993) cited in Bhalla (1996: 2)
8. Kumar (2000: 33- 35)
9. Bhalla (1996: 9- 12); Chandra and Sastry (1998: 26); Mashelkar (1998: 16); Islam (1996: 13); Ahmad (1996: 40); and Sharma (2000: 40- 3)
10. Kumar (2000: 34)
11. Desai (1984: 249)
12. Author came across many garment exporting units that have to fulfil such conditions imposed by their importers.
13. See for details, Gereffi (1995: 113–118)
14. Gereffi (1995: 119–28)

15. See for instance, Chandra and Sastry (1998: 26) argue, based on their survey of Indian corporate firms, that ".. the real challenge therefore is to improve substantially on several dimensions including quality, shop floor practices, process technology, supply chain co-ordination, new product introduction over a short period of time."

16. Mody, *et al*., (1992: 1797)

17. Mody, *et al*., (1992: 1797)

18. Kapilnsky (1994), "Future Factory" in *The Economist*, 1989; and "Meet the Global Factory" in *The Economist,* June 20, 1998

19. Mody and Dahlman (1992: 1703)

20. Tendulkar and Bhavani (1997: 44–46)

21. *Report of the Expert Committee*, (1997:151); Report of the Working Group on the SSIs for the Ninth Five Year Plan (1999: 73); Kumar (2000:41); SIDBI (2001:17).

22. *SIDBI Report on Small Scale Industries (SSI) Sector* (1999: 17) and *Tenth Five Year Plan* (2002: 709). SSI sector includes only modern small-scale industrial units that come under the purview of Small Industries Development Organisation (SIDO). All the figures presented in this section refer to the modern small-scale industrial units as there is no single data source that includes traditional as well as modern small-scale industries. The data relating to the traditional industries is scanty and scattered and thus could not be obtained. These two parts of the small-scale sector are discussed in detail in the Chapter 2.

23. *SIDBI Report on Small Scale Industries (SSI) Sector* for the years 1999 and 2001a.

24. Tendulkar and Bhavani,*(1997:* 51); SIDBI (2001b: 6)

25. *Handbook of Industrial Policy and Statistics* (2002: 176). Both the 1987–88 census and 1999–2000 sample relate to the small units registered with the State Directorates of Industries and hence do not cover the non-registered units. Non-registered small units are expected to be more in number but weaker in other parameters compared to the registered ones and thus expected to represent a worse situation.

Chapter 2 Indian Small-Scale Industries

Stagnant Units in the Dynamic Business Environments?

2.1 INTRODUCTION

Any study of small-scale industries requires understanding of their characteristics, constraints and their historical evolution, which in turn depends on the surrounding business environments. This chapter, hence, focuses on the composition, characteristics and growth of small-scale industries, and the business environment in India.

2.2 VILLAGE AND SMALL-SCALE INDUSTRIES: COMPOSITION AND CHARACTERISTICS

2.2.1 Composition of the VSI Sector

All the small-scale industries in India are covered under the Village and Small-Scale Industries (VSI) sector. The VSI sector is highly heterogeneous encompassing a wide range of activities which vary in many respects such as technology, nature of product, scale of operation and location. For administrative purpose, all the small-scale industries are broadly categorised as 'traditional' and 'modern' small-scale industries.

Traditional industry is characterised by a technology that is craft-based and is passed from one generation to another through on-the-job training. It produces an output, mostly for final consumption that is carried on usually in rural households with very little hired labour.[1] These traditional industries mostly use locally available materials and skills to produce consumer goods for the local market.[2] As a result, these traditional industries are highly scattered, unorganised and hence invisible compared to their modern counterparts. All village and cottage industries including Khadi, Handlooms, Handicrafts, Coir, Silk and Wool[3] are taken to be traditional industries. The Government of India deals separately with the traditional industries through a different set of policies implemented by specialised agencies namely, Khadi and Village Industries Commission (KVIC), Handlooms Board, Handicrafts Board, Silk Board, Coir Board and Wool Board.

Modern small-scale industries occupy an intermediate position between traditional cottage and village industries, and large-scale industries. The modern small-scale industries are nearer to large-scale industries as regards the nature of the product and the use of mechanised and often power-driven technology that is capable of producing standardised output for intermediate or final consumption on a scale larger than that of traditional small-scale industries.[4] But they stand closer to cottage and village industries in terms of organisational features such as having few self-employed persons. The owner-cum-manager has personal and informal links with the hired labour as well as suppliers.[5] Modern small-scale industries include power looms and other small-scale industries.

Power looms come under the jurisdiction of the Textile Commissioner. Other modern small-scale industries come under the purview of the Small Industries Development Organisation (SIDO).[6] SIDO covers all those small-scale industrial units that are defined in terms of the maximum ceiling limit on the original value of investment in plant and machinery. The ceiling limit has been undergoing an upward revision over time.[7] Currently, it is Rs 10 million for a small-scale unit and Rs 2.5 million for a tiny unit.[8] In a way, SIDO covers all those residual units that are not covered by other statutory bodies mentioned above.[9] However, there is an overlap between SIDO and village industrial units that come under KVIC as some of the KVIC units are also registered with the State Directorates of Industries and thus automatically come under SIDO's purview.[10] All those small-scale units that are covered by SIDO are generally referred to as Small Scale Industries (SSI) sector. This sector is estimated to constitute almost 96 percent of production, 43 percent of employment[11] and 83 percent of the exports of the VSI sector during 2000-01.[12]

As mentioned earlier, traditional small-scale industries are mostly, in the unorganised household sector and thus invisible. In addition, there is hardly any single source of data that provides information about all the traditional industries. For this reason and also because the units selected for the study belong to the SSI sector, this section now onwards confines to the SSI sector.

2.2.2 Growth and Structure of the SSI Sector

The SSI sector had been showing high growth rates in important aspects, namely, number of units, production, employment and exports in the 1970s and 1980s although growth rates varied widely across the variables. The number of small units grew at the rate of 6–10 percent per annum barring two years. With the exception of three years, production growth rates were above 15 percent. Annual growth rates of exports for the sector, for the specified period, are highly volatile ranging between –1.66 to 43.98 percent. Growth of employment was the lowest, among the specified variables, with annual growth rates that were less than 9 percent for majority of the years during the 1970s and 80s.[13] Although small units have been showing growth in all respects during the post-reform period of 1990s, growth rates are smaller compared to that of pre-reform period. The growth rates of number of units in the sector during the 1990s have been varying between 3 to 8 percent per annum and the production in the range of 3–11 percent per annum. Annual employment growth rates lie in the interval of 3–5 percent in the 1990s. Though exports from the SSI sector have been growing positively in the post-reform period, annual growth rates are highly fluctuating from 7.6 to 43.7 percent [see Appendix Table A.4].

Growth rates of SSI sector (production) in the nineties are higher compared to that of the Indian industry sector in general, and seem reasonable in comparison with the growth rates of industry sector in most of the Asian economies [see Table A.4 and A.5 in the Appendix].

We have used the *Second All-India Census of Small Scale Industrial Units* as a source of information to study the structure of the SSI sector. The Development Commissioner Small Scale Industries (DCSSI) has so far conducted two Censuses of Small Scale Industrial Units, which provide comprehensive data for the SSI sector. While the first census was conducted in the early seventies with 1973–74 as the reference year, the reference year for the second census data was 1987–88. The third census has been recently conducted for the year 2001–02 but only summary figures are released under 'Quick Results'. Details are yet to be made available. Hence, third census data has been only for the sector aggregates. For detailed structural characteristics of the SSI sector, we have to depend on the second census results. We take this census to represent the sector reasonably even in the 1990s.[14] The average unit of the sector during 2001–02 has 2.25 lakh[15] rupees investment in plant and machinery, employed around four persons and the output produced was worth rupees 15.23 lakhs.[16]

The study considers the structure of SSI sector in terms of its size composition, form of business organisation and location. Whatever be the criterion one uses—employment, production or investment in plant and machinery—one finds that the smaller units dominate the sector bringing down the size of the average unit of the SSI sector over time. In particular, 82.8 percent of the units had an investment in plant and machinery that was less than one lakh rupees accounting for 28.1 percent of total production, 33.2 percent of total fixed investment and 53.9 percent of employment of the sector. Similarly, 64.5 percent of the units of the sector employed four or less workers and contributed only 11.7 percent to the total production, 21.5 percent of fixed investment and 22.4 percent employment of the sector.[17]

Around 93 percent of the units of the SSI sector during 1987–88, were employing, on an average, five persons and thus were not covered under the Factories Act.[18] These non-factory units taken together accounted for 55 percent of the value of output, 70 percent of employment and 67 percent of the fixed investment of the sector.[19]

Proprietary concerns constituted 80.5 percent of the SSI sector during 1987–88. These units, on an average, employed four persons, had a fixed investment of 0.83 lakh rupees and produced output worth 2.62 lakh rupees. Another 16.8 percent of the units of the sector were organised as partnership firms. At an average level, partnership firms employed 13 persons, had 3.42 lakh rupees in fixed investment and produced material worth 20.48 lakhs of rupees. An insignificant proportion (2.1%) of firms were limited companies with an average employment of 36 persons, a fixed investment of rupees 15.16 lakhs and produced goods, at an average, worth rupees 77.67 lakh rupees during 1987–88.[20]

Nearly 42 percent of the SSI sector's units during 1987–88 were located in rural areas and accounted for 33.3 percent of the total employment, 29.4 percent of fixed investment and 26.8 percent of production. Another 48 percent of the units were located in urban areas, which constituted 50.4

percent of employment, 51.9 percent of fixed investment and 50.9 percent of the production of the sector. The remaining 9.8 percent of the units were in metropolitan cities and contributed 16.3 percent, 18.7 percent and 22.3 percent of the sector's total employment, fixed investment and production respectively.[21] Of the total number of units of the SSI sector, 62.2 percent were located in backward regions. These units in the backward regions together accounted for 50.4 percent of total employment, 46.6 percent of fixed investment and 42.2 percent of production of the sector.[22]

Another feature of the sector is that 18.8 percent of its employment constituted self-employed persons.[23] SSI sector units, on an average, have more than one (1.19) self-employed persons implying that the owner is involved in the day-to-day production activities of the unit.

In effect, tiny units dominated the SSI sector. Most of these were non-factory units run by the owner on a proprietary basis. Also, the SSI units were geographically widespread with a good proportion of them in rural areas and in backward regions. In addition, the relative proportion of units and their contribution in production, investment and employment of various groups indicate that the SSI sector was characterised by a dual structure. A large number of smaller units, operating at lower productivity levels, were co-existing with a few larger units working at higher productivity levels.[24] The dual structure of the sector is also apparent in the fact that a good proportion (35.2%) of the units of the sector were closed units and equally large number of working units (37%) were sick. One finds exporting units too in the sector though present in very small numbers.[25] Sick units constitute around 10 percent of the total number of units in the nineties.[26] Inadequate flow of credit, use of obsolete technology, poor quality standards and inadequate infrastructure facilities are considered as the major problems faced by the small units[27] and hence responsible for the above-mentioned structure of the sector.

2.3 BUSINESS ENVIRONMENT IN THE PRE-REFORM INDIA

Business environment in India was mainly set by the state-dominated economic policies pursued by the government till the recent economic policy reforms of 1990s. Hence, in this section, we discuss the economic policies that have been pursued by independent India, general as well as policies relating to small industries, their impact on the business environment, especially the product market that has further influenced the structure and behaviour of the industry.

2.3.1 General Economic Policies

Independent India, since the beginning, aimed at rapid economic growth, i.e. "sizeable increase in national income so as to raise the levels of living in the country."[28] Industrialisation especially the development of basic and heavy industries was considered as the best instrument to attain the basic objective of economic development.[29] The primary objective, however, has been pursued in an ideological framework of 'Socialist Pattern of Society', which sought to stress equitable distribution.[30] In order to ensure equitable distribution, the State, as the principal agency acting on behalf of the society as a whole, assumed direct responsibility for the development of industry. In this respect, the State had not only taken up the task of initiating development wherever the private sector was unable or unwilling to enter but also decided to play a dominant role in shaping the entire pattern of investments in the economy.[31] In order to attain the basic objective of economic growth, the Government of India followed a policy of planned industrial development. The State's direct involvement in the development of industry resulted in the formation of a dominant public sector and a heavily regulated private sector.[32]

To enable the government to control the course of industrial development, public utilities and industries that were essential but required heavy investments, were reserved for the public sector.[33] This does not mean that the public sector was restricted only to the reserved areas. The public sector was free to enter any industrial area, which during the course of time, resulted in an indiscriminate expansion of the public sector.[34] Entrusted with multiple objectives[35] the public sector, however, had been run on anything but commercial lines. A direct consequence of this was the inefficient public sector that could neither generate public savings nor meet the growing infrastructural needs of the economy.[36] Thus the public sector instead of promoting the development of industry in general as well as enabling this in the private sector only acted as a brake on it.[37]

The private sector in India was subjected to controls and regulation through the Industries (Development and Regulation) Act 1951 in order to have it tailored to the programmes formulated in the Five Year Plans and thus make it fit into the wider framework of the social and economic policies of the State.[38] Various policy instruments were used to guide the private sector industry into socially desired patterns namely, industrial licensing, capital issues control, price control and distribution controls.[39] Of these, the basic and the most comprehensive instrument was industrial licensing under which permission was needed to start and expand capacity, to change input or output mixes, or to relocate any industrial unit. In other words, all the key parameters of any investment project, i.e. scale, technology and location were regulated through industrial licensing leaving nothing for the decision of the units.[40] Industrial licensing, during the course of time, had acted as a big barrier to entry and thus had given assured markets to the few existing industrial units.[41]

As regards the external policies, they were guided by the principle of import substitution. The emphasis on import substitution was, to some extent, due to the strategy of self-reliance but to a considerable extent, it was also due to the scarcity of foreign exchange.[42] The continuing and often acute shortage of foreign exchange led to the elaborate system of rationing and allocation of scarce foreign exchange and involved the use of policy instruments like import licensing, quantitative restrictions on imports and high tariff rates.[43] In addition, there were restrictions on direct foreign investment, import of technology and on foreign collaborations of Indian firms. All these policies together provided complete protection to Indian industry by eliminating the scope for foreign competition and thus had an adverse impact on the productive efficiency of industry.[44]

The net effect of the numerous policies, internal as well as external, that were deployed to guide industrial development, was the creation of an economic environment characterised by infrastructure and key input bottlenecks on the supply side and protected markets[45] on the demand side.

2.3.2 Policies Relating to Small-Scale Industries

Since independence, Indian plans and policies have given a special place to the small-scale industries partly due to ideological reasons and partly due to social realities that created political compulsions. Ideological commitment to a 'socialist pattern of society' and the consequential stress on equity required (a) creation of broad-based employment opportunities; and (b) wide dispersal of industrial production. Small-scale industries were taken to be legitimate instruments for generating employment opportunities and enabling the wide dispersal of industrial production.[46] As regards the social realities at the time of independence, Indian industry that mainly consisted of craftsmen and rural artisans suffered a serious setback during the British Colonial Rule.[47] Many of the rural artisans had become agricultural labourers. This increased the pressure on the available cultivable land and intensified rural poverty.[48] Similar apprehensions were anticipated once the large-scale factory industry took off in India.[49] This situation generated the political compulsion to revive village and small industries in order to rehabilitate the displaced artisans and to avoid further technological unemployment.[50]

In view of the perceived handicaps of the small-scale industries in terms of technology and organisation,[51] their immediate need was taken to be protection from competition with their large-scale counterparts. Protection was, however, initially recommended as a temporary measure during the period of transition of these units towards attaining their competitive strength.[52] The long-term objective was to improve the economic viability of small-scale industries and to enable them to compete in the market without handicaps.[53] The lack of competitive strength in the small-scale industries was perceived as due to limited access to the input and output markets. In order to protect the small units from the competition of large-scale units in the short run[54] and to improve their access to the markets and thus their competitive strength in the long run, the government initiated a wide variety of policy measures and programmes. For the implementation of these policies, the government has earmarked huge amounts.[55]

Policy measures regarding small-scale units can be categorised according to the objective they serve namely, promotional and protective. *Promotional* measures are those that seek to impart competitive strength to small units by improving their access to different markets and by providing infrastructure and common industry facilities. Some of the promotional measures that have been in operation are as follows:

- Infrastructure facilities such as developed plots or sheds in the industrial estates;
- Consultancy services relating to the economic, technical and managerial aspects of the industry;
- Training services in the areas of entrepreneurship, management and skill development;

- Industry facilities like tool rooms and quality-testing stations in selected places
- Arrangements for the supply of scarce raw materials, machinery on hire-purchase and credit.

Protective measures seek to protect small units through a preferential treatment of these units vis-à-vis large units. Important protective measures include the reservation of certain products for exclusive production in the small-scale sector, reservation of some products for purchase preference by government agencies, input price concessions like lower interest rates, and numerous fiscal incentives such as excise duty exemptions.

The aforesaid policies designed for the small-scale industries are implemented through a wide network of organisations. At the helm stands the Development Commissioner, Small Scale Industries (DCSSI for short). DCSSI, who comes under the Department of Small Scale Industries and Agro and Rural Industries in the Ministry of Industries, is in charge of the development of small-scale industries.[56] The office of the DCSSI is known as the Small Industries Development Organisation (SIDO). It formulates policies relating to the SSI sector and is involved in their implementation. For the purpose, it co-ordinates the work of the central and state government agencies involved in the development of the small-scale industries and maintains liaison with the concerned organisations like the Reserve Bank of India (RBI), the Planning Commission and financial institutions. In addition, it provides a comprehensive range of services such as consultancy in technical, economic and managerial methods and provides common facilities like tool rooms, quality testing stations, etc. While the consultancy services are mainly provided through 28 Small Industries Service Institutes (SISIs) and 30 branch SISIs, training in technical skill development is provided to technicians and workers at 42 workshops attached to the SISIs. Whereas, training related to entrepreneurship development and management training is provided by National Institute for Entrepreneurship and Small Business Development (NIESBUD) and National Institute of Small Industry Extension and Training (NISIET) along with SISIs. Apart from the SISIs, SIDO provides promotional services through four Regional Testing Centres (RTCs), eight Field Testing Stations (FTS), ten Tool Rooms (TR), two Central Footwear Training Institutes (CFTI), one Production Center and six Product-cum-Process Development Centers (PPDC).

In addition to the SIDO network of organisations, the National Small

Industries Corporation (NSIC) is another institution that is involved in the promotion of small-scale industries at the central level. It is an autonomous public sector organisation that provides services in the areas of supply of machinery, raw materials, finance and marketing through its widely spread branches. To help the small-scale industries to acquire new technology, NSIC has its own Technology Transfer Centre. The Small Industries Development Bank of India (SIDBI) is the principal institution for financing the small-scale industries. SIDBI also co-ordinates the small-scale industries-related activities of other financial institutions including banks.

All the development financial institutions like IDBI, IFCI, and ICICI along with some of the commercial banks, have instituted the Entrepreneurship Development Institute of India (EDII) at Ahmedabad and Technology Consultancy Organisations (TCO) at different places to cater to the needs of the small-scale industries.

At the state level, one finds another set of institutions involved in the promotion of small-scale industries. This set includes the District Industries Centre (DIC), State Financial Corporation (SFC), State Industries Development Corporation (SIDC) and State Small Industries Development Corporation (SSIDC). DICs are set up to help the small-scale industries by providing consultancy services and arranging for machinery, critical raw materials, credit and marketing of the product. SSIDC takes care of the small-scale industries through the construction of industrial estates and other infrastructure facilities, by extending seed capital assistance, supply of machinery on hire-purchase, and by providing management and marketing assistance. SIDC is supposed to take care of the infrastructure facilities and capital requirements whereas the efforts of SFCs are mainly focused on the capital needs of the small-scale industries.

The presence of governmental organisations alone in the development of small-scale industries reflects the dominant role of the government in the industrial development of the country. These policy measures are implemented through the specified organisations with a considerable overlap of functions and without specific responsibility entrusted to each organisation. For instance, technical consultancy is to be provided by SISI, NSIC, DIC and TCO. The absence of inter-institutional co-ordination[57] has led to the ineffectiveness of promotional measures.[58] In addition, the short run objective of protection, in the due course of time, got translated into a virtually perpetual protection of the small-scale industries as a goal in itself.[59] The perpetual protection along with the not-so-effective promotional measures has resulted in the stagnant SSI sector that is still dominated by tiny units operating with obsolete technologies and thus at lower productivity levels.[60] These numerous smaller units, however, could so far survive along with the large-scale factory units due to the geographical and product market segmentation in addition to the policy protection. Product market segmentation has been the result of the existing inequalities while geographical segmentation has been the consequence of the underdevelopment of infrastructure. Thus, the business environment encouraged numerous less efficient small-scale units that were overcrowding the lower end segment of the otherwise protected markets.

In sum, the general trade and industrial policies that India adopted till 1991 insulated the Indian markets from competition, domestic as well as foreign. Within this generally insulated environment, small-scale industries are further protected from the competition of the large-scale factory industry through a set of protection measures. The protection for small-scale industries is being further compounded by the geographical and product market segmentation that gave small-scale units isolated sheltered markets. The *only competition that small-scale units have so far faced is the competition with each other due to overcrowding*.

2.4 POLICY REFORMS OF THE 1990S AND CHANGES IN BUSINESS ENVIRONMENT

A major reform process in the Indian economic policy regime has been underway since July 1991 in response to a serious macro-economic crisis. The new policy regime's aim has been to liberalise the regulations on domestic economic transactions and a much greater integration with the world economy. Hence, the reforms included, on the external front, the devaluation of an over-valued exchange rate, removal of quantitative restrictions on the imports of a majority of the items, reduction in tariff rates, permission to foreign direct investment for entry in every sector of the economy, etc. Domestic policy reforms include the abolition of licensing requirements for investments for majority of industries, opening of hitherto reserved areas of the public sector to the private, removal of restrictions on the operation of large industrial houses, reduction in price controls, reforms in the financial sector and in capital markets.[61] As expected, policy reforms injected a good measure of competitiveness and market orientation in the

Indian industry.[62]

These reforms are yet to touch the policies relating to the small-scale industries. However, the Government of India has realised the need for reforms in the existing policies for the small-scale industries to facilitate the growth of viable and efficient small enterprises in the changing environment. Therefore, the government had constituted an Expert Committee on Small Enterprises under the chairmanship of Dr. Abid Hussain.[63] The expert committee submitted its report in January 1997 and it is still under consideration by the Government of India.

The expert committee recommends that the guiding principle for the promotion of small-scale industries should no more be protection but the objectives of growth and competitiveness in these industries. Accordingly, the committee recommended the abolition of a reservation of products for the exclusive production in the small-scale industries, one of the most controversial protective measures. The expert committee emphasised promotional measures like adequate supply of credit, services, technological assistance and infrastructure facilities. It was recommended that these measures were better served through the development of linkages between the enterprises and their support institutions, partnership between the private sector and the government, and by streamlining the legal and institutional framework. For this purpose, the cluster approach, i.e. the development of the existing clusters of small and medium enterprises, is considered to be the best instrument. The expert committee considers the cluster development as a part of regional development and thus entrusts its responsibility with the state governments. Further, it is suggested that state governments can for the purpose, make use of the District Industry Centres (DIC) with some modifications in their structure. The suggested form of DICs should have an autonomous status and should involve the participation of business associations, banks and other related agencies and would be known as District Enterprise Promotion Agency (DEPA).

Realising that the supply of credit to small-scale enterprises is highly inadequate, the expert committee recommended

- a thorough overhaul of the existing institutional arrangement,
- establishment of local credit rating agencies in the clusters, and
- and tapping of other funds like equity participation by large scale enterprises.

Support institutions for the small-scale industries are, so far, largely government-owned. The expert committee recommended that the government should withdraw as far as possible from direct delivery and it should instead fund the cost of services accessed from efficient sources. Whatever government agencies remain in these services, such agencies should change into a corporate structure and compete in the market.

The expert committee also recommended the widening of the scope of small-scale industries so as to include service units, that the ceiling limit for the definition be raised, and that a basic law relating to small-scale industries be enacted. Apart from the ceiling limit recommended, which has been raised immediately only to bring it down within two years,[64] the rest of the recommendations are yet to be considered by the government. Irrespective of the status of implementation of the measures recommended by the expert committee on the small-scale enterprises, these enterprises have already been affected by the reforms in the general trade and industry policies. For instance, an overall reduction in excise duty and customs duty automatically reduced the benefit given to small-scale industries in terms of the level of concessions. The placement of more items in the open general license (OGL) list to import, and the abolition of industrial licensing for a large number of industries automatically increased the scope for competition. Driven by the competitive pressures in the domestic market, large-scale units are entering the lower end, semi-urban and rural market segments and reducing the protection to small units created by market segmentation and increasing the competition for small units.

On the whole, the policy reforms of the 1990s exposed small units to market competition by reducing protection, and intensified this competition. In these open and increasingly competitive markets, small units are to operate with numerous handicaps such as obsolete technologies, inadequate credit and infrastructure.

2.5 SUMMARY

Small-scale industrial units in India so far operated in a *doubly* protected market environment. The only competition these had in this closed and protected market is from the other small units. This has not provided any incentive to these units to reorganise themselves in terms of technology and product so as to be competitive and to grow. Consequently, the small manufacturing segment is still dominated by tiny, non-factory units run by the owner on a proprietary basis. A large number of these units are operating at a lower productivity level and with under-capacity utilisation constrained by older technologies, inadequate credit and infrastructure. The market environment in India has been undergoing transformation since the nineties due to policy reforms. These reforms are not only making markets more and more competitive but also changing the nature of competition. Small-scale units now have to compete with large-scale units including multinationals, and imports. This requires small units to upgrade themselves in all respects including technology. However, small-scale units have to struggle to do so within the still-persistent infrastructure bottlenecks and input constraints such as inadequate credit.

Endnotes

1. Tendulkar and Bhavani (1997: 41)
2. Staley and Morse (1965: 1–25); and Dhar (1979: 172–5)
3. Wool industry in the unorganised sector was added to this traditional segment later.
4. Tendulkar and Bhavani (1997: 41)
5. Bhavani (1989: 6)
6. SIDO is the office of the Development Commissioner, Small Scale Industries (DCSSI).
7. The only exception is the recent downward revision in 1999 to 10 million rupees from the previous 30 million rupees. Table A.1 in the Appendix A presents the ceiling limits that are in practice at various time periods.
8. *Economic Survey 1999–2000*, p.127
9. *Report of the Working Group on SSIs for the Ninth Five Year Plan*, vol. 2, p.3
10. SIDBI (1999: 27)
11. Employment contribution of the sector might have been an underestimate considering the fact that most of the employment in traditional industries is part-time while that of the SSI sector is full time.
12. Tenth Five-Year Plan, Vol. 2, pp. 595, 716–39. See Tables A.2 and A.2a in Appendix A for the relative position of traditional and modern small-scale industries in the VSI sector over time.
13. See Appendix Table A.3
14. Many government reports such as Abid Hussain Committee Report 1997 show that the SSI sector is still in the same position.
15. 10 lakhs = one million
16. "Quick Results" ,Third *All-India Census of Small Scale Industrial Units, 2001-02, DCSSI, New Delhi*,

17. See Table A.6 in Appendix A.

18. All those units using power and employing equal or more than 10 employees, and units that do not use power but employ equal or more than 20 persons, are supposed to register under the Factories Act 1948. Once a unit is registered as a factory, it is subjected to labour laws and specified working conditions. All those units covered under Factories Act are generally referred to as organised sector while the rest are treated as unorganised segment of the manufacturing.

19. *Report of the Second All-India Census of Small Scale Industrial Units*, pp. 63–64

20. *Report of the Second All-India Census of Small Scale Industrial Units*, pp. 140–41

21. *Report of the Second All-India Census of Small Scale Industrial Units*, p. 38

22. *Report of the Second All-India Census of Small Scale Industrial Units*, p. 38

23. *Report of the Second All-India Census of Small Scale Industrial Units*, pp. 79–80, T-54. Self-employed includes proprietors, partners or members of the family of the proprietors or partners who work in the unit regularly.

24. See columns 6 and 7, Table A.6 in Appendix A.

25. Tendulkar and Bhavani (1997: 5, 62–64)

26. *Handbook of Industrial Policies and Statistics 2000*, p. 374

27. *Ninth Five year Plan 1997- 2002*, Volume II, p. 609; Kumar (2000:41); and SIDBI (2001a:17)

28. *Second Five Year Plan*, p. 24

29. It was considered that "if industrialisation is to be rapid enough, country must aim at developing basic industries and industries which make machines are needed for further development." *Second Five Year Plan*, p. 25.

30. *Second Five Year Plan*, p. 24

31. *Second Five Year Plan*, p. 22

32. Tendulkar (1993:282)

33. *Industrial Policy Resolution* 1956; and Srinivasan (2000:2)

34. It can be seen from Marathe (1989:47) that "Over a period of time, however, the trend was towards the State entering areas not specifically reserved for it, for example, modern bakeries, photo films, cement, paper and fisheries."

35. The numerous objectives of the State's policy can be seen in Marathe (1989: 165–66), which states that "... apart from a widening and deepening of the industrial system and accelerating the pace of industrial development, avoidance of concentration of economic power in the hands of a few and, therefore, measures for restricting the growth of large or interconnected business houses; greater regional dispersal of industry particularly with a view to developing industry in backward areas; encouragement to small scale industry and to the growth of entrepreneurship; moving towards greater self-reliance through an orderly process of import substitution and technological self-reliance; and protection of environment."

36. Srinivasan (2000: 5); Ahluwalia (1988:152); and Bhagawati and Desai (1970: 147-50, 165)

37. Srinivasan (2000: 5)

38. *Industrial Policy Resolution* 1956; and Marathe (1989: 46)

39. Marathe (1989: 36); Srinivasan (2000: 3-4); Bhagawati and Desai, (1970: 120-24); and Lucas (1988: 185)

40. Srinivasan (2000: 3-4); Bhagavati and Desai (1970: 120)

41. Bhagawati and Desai, (1970: 269); Ahluwalia (1988:153); and Tendulkar (1993:287)

42. Bhagawati and Desai (1970: 282-83); and Marathe (1989: 168)

43. Bhagawati and Desai (1970: 283-+95); and Marathe (1989: 168)

44. See, for example, Bhagawati and Desai (1970: 325), "the import allocation system in force had virtually eliminated the possibility of competition system either foreign or domestic." Ahluwalia describes (1988:153) the situation as "indiscriminate and indefinite protection from foreign competition."

45. See, for example, Bhagawati and Desai (1970: 272), "We are thus in an economic situation where the possibility of competition from potential entry by domestic or foreign rivals is minimised." Tendulkar (1993:289) states the same "Insulation from world trade provided protection from international competition and the industrial licensing system blunted internal competition."

46. *Industrial Policy Resolution* 1956.

47. Gadgil (1973: 163)
48. Myrdal (1968: 1208)
49. *Karve Committee Report* (1955: 15)
50. Tendulkar and Bhavani (1997: 42)
51. Mahalanobis (1963: 23); *Karve Committee Report (1955:* 18)
52. Mahalanobis (1963: 23, 71); *Karve Committee Report (1955:* 30)
53. It was stated explicitly in the *Industrial Policy Resolution,* 1956 —"the aim of the state policy will be to ensure that the decentralised sector acquires sufficient vitality to be self-supporting…. The state will therefore concentrate on measures designed to improve the competitive strength of the small scale producer."
54. Though protection was started as a short run policy, it is been continuing till today.
55. See Table A.7 in Appendix A for the plan outlays for the sector.
56. Currently, there is a separate Ministry of small-scale Industries.
57. Vepa (1988: 47); *SIDO: Annual Report 1988-89*, p.30; and Goldar and Gupta (1989)
58. Tendulkar and Bhavani, (1997: 48)
59. Tendulkar and Bhavani, (1997: 48).; *Report of the Expert Committee on Small Enterprises(1997:* s-1)
60. Tendulkar and Bhavani, (1997: 51)
61. Ahluwalia (1996: 18- 29); Ahluwalia (1999) and Srinivasan (2000: 6)
62. Ahluwalia (1996: 18)
63. Government of India Order F. No. 13(24)/ 95-SSI (P) dated December 29, 1995 that constitutes the expert committee on the subject states thus: "Globalisation and change in technology are also emerging as the major forces that will modify and mould the environment for small business and entrepreneurship over the next decade and beyond….It is, thus, necessary to address the need for reforms in the existing policies and design new policies for small and medium enterprises development which will facilitate the growth of viable and efficient enterprises that can adjust to technological change and remain internationally competitive."
64. The enhanced ceiling limit of 30 million rupees was officially announced in December 1997, which has later been reduced to 10 million rupees in 1999 owing to political pressures.

Chapter 3 Firm-Level Technological Change: *What Does Theory Say?*

3.1 INTRODUCTION

Neo-classical economics which is otherwise widely practised, does not provide a theoretical framework to study our objective of understanding the process of technological change and to examine the factors influencing it at the firm level as its main concern is to understand "what makes world coherent and ordered" rather than change and hence emphasise on the "characterisation of states of equilibrium".[1] Also, neo-classical economics treats 'firm' and 'technology', the two basic elements dealt within this book, in a summarised form. Firms are taken as producers and suppliers of goods and services that decide what is to be produced, how much to be produced and how to produce (technology), given the relative factor prices and product prices, with an objective to maximise its profits. Prices are determined by the interaction of supply and demand in the market. Supply equals demand and no loss-making firm exists in the equilibrium state. Neo-classical economics, thus, takes firms as supplying units and concentrates on how market structure (primarily taken in terms of the number of suppliers) determines prices and outputs. It does not, however, consider the internal structure and decision-making process within the firm.

Technology is considered, in neo-classical economics, as *exogenous* to the economic systems especially at a firm level.[2] Neo-classical economics also maintains that all the firms are aware of, and have access to all the existing technologies. Of these, they select a particular technology depending on the existing relative factor prices. Once the selection of a technology is done, its installation is easy and its impact on the factor combination and/or factor productivities is automatic. Hence, neo-classical economics measures the technological change *indirectly* in terms of the changes in factor proportions and/or productivities. As a result, it is not equipped to deal with the actual process of change in technology in a firm. Hence, we cannot consider neo-classical economics as a theoretical base for the present study.

In our attempt to explore the theoretical base that can provide us a conceptual kit with which an appropriate analytical framework can be developed to further the primary objective, the evolutionary theory of economics came as the first choice as the primary concern of this theory is to understand "what makes the world change".[3] It deals with the internal structure and decision-making process of the firm and changes in these as firms continuously interact with their environment.[4] Evolutionary economics takes technological change as *endogenous* to the economic systems both at the macro and micro levels. Evolutionary economics, however, has its own limitations in that it does not provide us conceptual tools that are compatible with each other and can be used for a meaningful empirical analysis (discussed in the next section). In other words, evolutionary economics only broadly satisfies our theoretical requirements by giving certain concepts to characterise our research problem but cannot provide the full analytical frame to study our research objective. We need to supplement these ideas with the concepts from the existing literature on technological change, technological capabilities and organisations. We follow, thus, an *eclectic* approach and draw the relevant concepts from various existing theories and develop our own analytical framework in the following chapter, keeping in mind the typical characteristics of the Indian small-scale industries.

3.2 EVOLUTIONARY ECONOMICS

Evolutionary economics is developed on the basis of different principles that are drawn from various research traditions. Biology, systems theory, non-equilibrium thermodynamics, firm and organisation theories, and evolutionary interpretations in economics (which can be found in the writings of Spencer, Marshall, Veblen, Schumpeter and Hayek), have all exercised a great influence in forming modern evolutionary theories.[5] The important principles underlying evolutionary economics are variety, selection, reproduction and inheritance, irreversibility and path dependency.[6] These principles are briefly discussed below.

3.2.1 Underlying Principles[7]

Based on the theory of biological evolution that says the surviving species have changed over time resulting in the form of new species and extinction of others, the concept of *variety* in evolutionary economics takes that the elements of economic systems like products, processes, organisational forms and markets change over time. They change mainly due to innovations that keep adding new forms, products and processes to the existing ones. New products, processes and forms cause some of the hitherto existing ones to be discarded. In other words, an economic system, at any given time, consists of numerous products, processes and markets that are qualitatively different from each other and these elements of the system keep changing over time. Unlike the Darwinian theory of biological evolution, the generation of variety in economics is taken as deliberate and purposeful. That is, firms deliberately change their products and processes through innovations to

1. differentiate themselves from the other firms so as to establish themselves better in the market or,
2. adapt themselves to the changes in the environment or,
3. prepare themselves to the anticipated changes in the environment.

Thus, innovations are considered as purposely initiated by the firms, and shaped to some extent by the external environment. Notwithstanding these features, random elements present as future cannot be known in detail and this makes the outcomes of the firms' innovation efforts unpredictable. With its focus on search and selection, evolutionary economics seeks to have an explanation of the processes that generate economic variety in terms of product and process specification.

The *selection* mechanism of evolutionary economics is drawn from the biological evolutionary theories, which state that randomly produced variations of biological organisms have a different suitability with respect to the external environment. The variations, which fit better, are more likely to survive and those which do not fit well, are more likely to disappear. In economics, the selection mechanism operates through the process of competition. Firms compete with each other by offering different products at different prices to the market. Firms producing more desirable products and more efficiently are selected in the sense that they not only survive but also improve their positions in the market by growing at a faster rate. In order to be more competitive, firms focus their innovation activities on the promising lines of development where the degree of promise depends on their judgement of the environment. It is this judgement which along with the firms' abilities to create or to operate with superior technologies, determines their competitiveness and hence survival. Thus, the selection mechanism operates at two levels. First, the *ex ante* selection of products or technologies for the development or adoption by the firms based on their cognitive structures, visions and competences. Secondly, *ex post* selection occurs in the market that selects the firms that chose well their products or technologies and eliminates or forces reforms on the other firms.[8]

The concept of *reproduction and inheritance* is also taken from the biology research tradition, which considers that all the biological species reproduce themselves. While reproducing, these species carry certain characteristics over generations, i.e. inheritance. Following it, evolutionary economics takes that economic organisations like firms carry over time certain abilities to perform production transformations that are embodied in their rules and routines. Here, reproduction refers to the maintenance of production abilities over time and it is their rules and routines that are inherited over time. However, owing to the mechanisms of generation of variety and selection, firms keep changing some of these routines to maintain and/or to improve their abilities.

The concept of *irreversibility and path dependency* in evolutionary economics is drawn from the theories related to the chemical and physical systems. Evolutionary economics treats economic organisations as open systems that continuously interact with their environment exchanging information. At one level of interaction, the behaviour of economic organisations changes fundamentally and becomes irreversible. In the neighbourhood of the transition point, i.e. point of fundamental change, the behaviour of the organisations is indeterminate in the sense that one does not know which direction it takes. This is where random factors play an important role in shaping the behaviour of economic organisations. Evolution of economic organisations is thus due to their inherent openness and the inductive nature of the development process. Economic knowledge grows through the experience. It is the mechanism of accumulation of experience, which is local and cumulative, that underpins irreversibility and path dependency in economic evolution.

3.2.2 Technological Change

Technological change in evolutionary economics is mainly referred to as innovation. *Innovation* concerns the search for, discovery, experimentation, development and adaptation of new products, production processes and organisational setup.[9] In the literature, two kinds of innovations namely, radical and incremental, are considered. By taking technology in terms of its technical and service characteristics,[10] Saviotti (1996) defines r*adical* innovations as the ones that lead to a new technology, which has an internal structure, i.e. technical characteristics, that is entirely different from the existing ones. Discovery of the railways and roadways are the examples of radical innovations. Railways have a totally different technology than the then existing animal-driven carts. Similarly, roadways (like passenger cars) have a different technology than the railways. Both of them were innovated to serve the need of transportation. *Incremental* innovation aims at improving the service characteristics of the product by changing the levels of the parameters of a given technology without any change in its internal structure. Attempts at reduction in the fuel-consumption levels of a car engine are an example of incremental innovations. With a new technology that has a totally different internal structure, radical innovations require completely new capabilities, i.e. knowledge and skills. As a result, radical innovations make the existing skills and knowledge obsolete and thus destroy the existing competence. Contrary to this, incremental innovation enhances the existing knowledge.[11]

The difference between radical innovation and incremental innovation creates a trade-off between exploration and exploitation at a firm level.[12] IBM can provide a classic example to explain this trade-off. For over thirty years (i.e.1950–80), IBM dominated the computer industry. The IBM 360 was an extremely successful solution to the problems encountered by the computer industry in the sixties. By the late seventies and early eighties the market had grown considerably and costs had fallen dramatically calling for new solutions like the open modular architectures based around the RISC design.[13] IBM's preference for the exploitation of its profitable mainframes and mini computer systems is one of the important reasons cited for its inability to explore the RISC technology and the loss of leadership in the PC business. Despite being the early discoverer of RISC (Reduced Instruction Set Computing), it did not develop the RISC machine. Any attempts towards it were thwarted by the requirements of 360/370 compatibility.[14] Same is the case with its development of PC (personal computers).[15]

Technologies at the beginning of their evolution are characterised by product innovations with a multiplicity of product designs and flexible process technologies. As technology matures, all the product designs converge on one dominant design and innovation becomes process oriented leading to more specialised processes.[16] For instance, in the early history of automobiles, various engine models like fuel-based internal combustion engines, steam engines and electrical engines were developed and tried. Gradually fuel-based internal combustion engines came to dominate and the other two were abandoned.[17] Once the internal combustion engine was established, the efforts were directed towards improving some of its parameters like speed, fuel consumption and so on. Technological evolution can, thus, be taken as a pattern of a radical innovation followed by relatively long periods of incremental innovations with an established framework. This pattern of evolution of a particular technology is, broadly, referred to as 'technological regimes' by Nelson and Winter (1977), 'technological guide posts' by Sahl (1981), and 'technological paradigms' by Dosi (1982).[18] Technological progress over time is taken to exhibit certain strong irreversibilities. For instance, electronics-based production technologies are unequivocally superior to electro-mechanical production technologies in the sense that had they existed before they would have been adopted even at 'old' relative factor prices.[19]

Evolutionary economics literature views technological changes primarily the result of deliberate human actions.[20] There has been a shift over time in the origin of search activities from individual innovators to formal R&D organisations that are increasingly integrated with the manufacturing firms. Technology has, therefore, been taken as *endogenous* to the economic organisations. Innovation activities are, hence, strongly selective and finalised in rather precise directions.[21]

Garud et al. (1997) and Dosi (1988a, b) attempted to bring out the salient features of innovation processes based on case studies. According to these studies, the technological outcomes of innovation are uncertain and contingent upon the match between the internal capabilities of a firm and its external environment. Technological choices are constrained by the past technological decisions and capabilities of firms. The decision-making in this respect is a complex problem and constrained by bounded rationality and bias in human judgment. We will discuss, briefly, each one of these features below.

Innovations involve uncertainty as what is searched for cannot be known with any precision before the activity. In other words, technological outcomes of innovation activities are not known *ex ante* and thus create uncertainty. Actual outcome depends on the degree of correspondence between firm-level capabilities and external environment. This is because innovation activities involve some perception of yet unexploited technical and economic opportunities. Technological opportunities stem from scientific developments and economic opportunities flow from the needs of its immediate market. The knowledge that the firm possesses in these respects is crucial to perceive these opportunities. In other words, in order to seize the opportunities, a firm is required to have scientific and technical knowledge, and an insight into the needs of its market segment. This knowledge is located in different parts of the firm. For example, it is the marketing department of a firm that knows the requirements of the market in terms of product characteristics. The R&D department possesses the required knowledge to translate the latest scientific developments into technical characteristics and the production department has the knowledge to transform the technical characteristics into the product characteristics. Close correspondence of the knowledge possessed by the different departments of a firm is critical for a firm to succeed in its attempts to innovate.[22] Also, the external environment keeps changing making it more difficult to forecast a technological outcome and judging its success.

Much of the innovation activities originate from learning-by-doing and/ or learning-by-using, by solving a production problem, meeting specific customer requirements. Also, firms seek to improve or diversify their technologies by searching in the neighbourhood zones of the existing technology. Successive investments in these lines result in increasing momentum in a particular direction thereby creating a *trajectory*. The whole process leads to '*path dependency*' wherein what a firm can do technologically in the future is constrained by what it has been doing in the past. Investments on the lines mentioned above are characterised by increasing returns to scale, which makes path dependency particularly strong.

Finally, technological decision-making is a complex process and human judgment is limited and biased. These limits and biases result in a technological choice that can be a foresight or oversight known only by hindsight.

Technologies do not directly compete with each other in the markets for their own sake. "Technologies are incorporated within firms … firms are considered as 'carriers of technology' and the technology they use affects their own survival."[23] So, it is important to know what a firm is. In this context, we discuss how a firm is treated in evolutionary economics.

3.2.3 Firm

Evolutionary theories take firm as a bounded rational entity acting in a complex and changing environment. Firms are characterised in terms of *routines* and *competencies* that are intertwined with *learning*.[24] Learning, which is a cumulative development of skills and knowledge, becomes institutionalised in the form of standard operating rules, i.e. routines.[25] Competencies, being the ways of organising and getting things done,[26] are, mainly, determined by the routines. Thus, learning is at the base of the accumulation of competencies.[27]

Learning relates to the activities aimed at the solution of specific problems. It concerns the development of sets of problem-solving routines in order to cope with an ever-changing environment. Learning involves collection, integration, storage and processing of information coming from various sources and with different objectives. Learning by being *local* and *cumulative* plays an important role in the development of firms. Learning is local as it is highly affected by the cognitive frameworks (of concerned people) and (specific) context. Learning is cumulative in the sense that it builds on what has already been built. Local and cumulative aspects of learning together lead to firm-specific trajectories that are path dependent. Persistent differences across firms in strategies and/or performance are, thus, due to diverse learning practices.[28]

Competencies include the areas of applicability, effectiveness of problem-solving procedures, ability to utilise external knowledge, mastery over technology and production and an understanding of customer needs. Competencies are tacit (i.e. cannot be fully articulated), specific and complex.[29] Competencies of a firm depend upon its processes that are represented by routines, and position in terms of its current technology, customer base and supplier relationship, etc.[30]

Routines are the regular and predictable behaviour of a firm and include pricing rules, procedures for choosing alternative combinations of inputs and output, work allocations and so on.[31] Routines, in particular, can be defined as the application of skills in a particular environment in a repetitive way.[32] In one way, routines embody the knowledge that is accumulated through learning. Applying this knowledge to solve problems, routines lead to further learning. On the other side, routines being rule-guided behaviours in a specific environment serve as mechanisms of control and governance. Routines, thus, have two dimensions namely, cognition and governance.[33] Routines cannot be entirely codified and hence need to be practised constantly to improve performance.[34] Nelson and Winter (1982, pp. 16–18) distinguish between three kinds of routines:

(i) First set of routines is the operating procedures that govern the short-run behaviour of a firm. They determine how much to produce and how to produce given the capital stock and other fixed variables;

(ii) The second group of routines set the investment behaviour of a firm and more generally its growth;

(iii) The final set of routines includes the rules that frame the search processes for better ways of doing things, i.e. routines that govern the first two types of routines.

Operating procedures transform the current internal state of a firm (i.e. plant and machinery and information) into actions (outputs). Current actions of the existing firms in the due course of time, determine the market environment. The interaction of the current firm's state and the changing market environment leads the firm into a new form through the application of investment rules in the medium term and search rules in the long term. Thus, it is the dynamic process through which firms' behaviour and environment conditions are jointly determined over time. It is the application and skilful performance of routines in a specific context that provides a firm with a distinctive competence. For instance, quality performance is driven by specialised routines like routines for gathering and processing information, for linking customer experience with engineer design choice, for co-ordinating factors and competent suppliers.[35]

Changes in the routines of firms occur as the firms interact continuously with their environment. The environment keeps changing and forces firms to adapt themselves to its changes. In particular, firms are treated as motivated by profits and engaged in searching for ways to improve their profits. However, firms' actions are <u>not</u> assumed to be profit maximising over a well-defined and exogenously given set of choices. Market[36] determines during the course of time, which firms are profitable and which are not, and forces the less profitable and loss making firms to adapt so as to be more profitable. Otherwise, the less profitable and loss making firms are driven out of business. This process of profitable firms to grow and unprofitable ones to go out of business is called natural selection.[37]

3.2.4 Limitations

Most of the limitations of evolutionary economics flow from the fact that "evolutionary theories of economic and technical change do not have the formal elegance, the analytical depths or articulation of more orthodox economic theories."[38] These theories cannot provide a conceptual apparatus, which is compatible and implementable empirically. To be specific, evolutionary theories are yet to explore the relationship between the basic units of analysis like technology, and the behaviour of units like firms which embody technologies and on which selection is supposed to operate.[39] In other words, evolutionary theories of economics are yet to establish the units of analysis at different levels of aggregation and bring out their interrelationships.[40] Also, the selection environment is multi-dimensional. For example, it is not only the product market but also the capital and labour markets and policies that determine the commercial viability of firms. The object of selection is not a single elementary trait but numerous traits interlinked in a structure.[41] Evolutionary theories of economics so far have not taken all these details into account and developed concepts that can be meaningfully applied for empirical analysis. As a result, these theories are not in a position to provide us with a readymade theoretical framework that can be used to explain the process of technological change in firms.

To be specific, the description of firm and technology in evolutionary economics is not only too abstract to be applied to real world firms but also it does not specify the placement of technology within the firm. In addition, evolutionary economics does not deal with the factors influencing technological change explicitly. Hence, we could not make use of the evolutionary theory of firm or its concept of technology. What we have considered from evolutionary economics is its selection mechanism, characterisation of innovation process and its salient features. These concepts have been used in our analytical framework with some modifications to suit the selected field of enquiry, i.e., small-scale industries in India.

3.3 ECONOMICS OF TECHNOLOGICAL CHANGE

Given the above-mentioned limitations of the evolutionary economics especially in dealing with the technology and the factors effecting change in it, we review, in this section, the literature on technological change (that comes outside the purview of evolutionary economics) for the same.

In this literature, technology is broadly taken as "to encompass everything pertaining to the transformation of inputs into outputs". Thus, "technological change involves changes, however minor, in the way inputs are transformed into outputs including the quality of output".[42] More specifically, technology is considered "as a collection of physical processes which transforms inputs into outputs together with the social arrangements (i.e. organisational modes and procedural methods) which structure the activities involved in carrying out these transformations".[43] Technological change definition in the literature broadly follows this and "encompass improvements in products, production processes, material and intermediate inputs and management methods in economic systems".[44] The technology and its changes are taken in the form of hardware (like machinery, tools and final products) as well as software (like designs and documents).[45] Studies on technological change, however, mostly cover the changes in physical processes of transformation including output characteristics.[46] Also, in the empirical works, technological changes are typically associated with innovations[47] and studied mostly, in terms of patents, R&D expenditure or personnel.[48, 49] Changes in the organisational methods are studied independently. Another important thing to note is that though technology is partly considered as information,[50] and information is crucial for the decision-making in the economic organisations,[51] it was not treated explicitly till recently. The faster developments, in the recent years, in the information technology that "includes computers and communications technology as well as the associated software,"[52] however, led to growing literature on the subject separately.

A variety of methodological approaches are used in characterising technological change in the literature. The major ones are events approach, process approach and by differentiating between successes and failures. The events approach takes innovations as the result of a number of events such as scientific, technological, etc., and the relative contribution of the relevant events to the innovation is assessed. The process approach considers innovation as a sequence of stages in which each stage would be triggered by the output of the previous stage. There is, however, no general agreement about the nature of process. In the last approach, a comparison of successful and unsuccessful innovations is done in terms of a number of factors judged to be potentially important for innovation.[53]

The dominant approach in economics for long, has taken technological change for granted without bothering to explain it.[54] Schumpeter (1935, 1942) was almost the first one to deal with the innovation while emphasising its importance to economic growth. Entrepreneurs, large and monopoly firms occupy a central position in Schumpeter's analysis. While entrepreneurs discover the untried ideas from the technology basket and introduce them into commercial reality, large and monopoly firms enable them to do so. Since the Schumpeter's entrepreneur spots the ideas from the available technologies, Schumpeter's works are considered as the origin for the 'technology push theory.'[55] In other words, technology push theory maintains that scientific developments giving rise to technological opportunities are responsible for innovations.

In an attempt to correct the imbalance in taking technological opportunities as the sole cause for innovation, Schmookler (1966) ended up in stressing economic factors especially market demand as the determinant of innovation.[56] Thus, Schmookler has become the exponent of the demand-pull theory of innovation. On the basis of their critical analysis of various studies, Mowery and Rosenberg (1979) conclude that both the availability of technologies and market demand are important determinants of success in innovations. But they stress that the ability to link the available technologies with the market demand is more important.[57]

Following Schumpeter's ideas, numerous studies tried to investigate the relationships among firm size, market concentration and innovative efforts.[58] After Schumpeter, it was Galbraith who argued strongly the necessity of large size for innovations.[59] Over the years, several justifications both for and against the positive association between size and innovation have been offered.[60] A survey of empirical works indicates that firm size has been an important factor in explaining innovative activities and these activities rise monotonically with firm size.[61]

As regards the impact of market structure on innovative behaviour, again one finds theoretical arguments both for and against it.[62] The majority of the empirical works, however, show a positive relation between market concentration and innovation.[63] Some of the models that went beyond innovators to include imitators argue that innovators do better when competition is restrained and imitators do better when there is aggressive competition.[64] In fact, Mansfield (1961:310) showed that "the rate of imitation is faster in more competitive industries".

It was a general observation that the empirical works on the relations among innovation, scale and market concentration are plagued by methodological limitations. Hence, a need was felt for a further evaluation of the Schumpeterian hypotheses in a more complete model of technological change. So, later studies went beyond size and market concentration to consider other firm-level characteristics like cash flow, product diversification, R&D capabilities and very recently various organisational and managerial attributes of firms.[65]

Apart from the above-mentioned literature in the Schumpeterian tradition, there were other explanations of innovation in the literature. The induced innovation theory that was due to Hicks (1932),[66] states that it is the change in the relative factor prices that leads to innovation. Rosenberg (1969) by looking at the historical processes of technological changes emphasises that the technological imbalances among the interrelated products and processes,[67] skilled workers' non-compliance and strikes, and shortage of materials due to wars are responsible for innovations. According to Rosenberg, the above-mentioned forces served as an inducement mechanism either in terms of providing scope to make extra-high profits or of creating an unbearable situation of losing a tangible opportunity or a prospect of being put out of business. In addition, the models of diffusion[68] shows that information availability, capital requirements for the change and profitability of the changes are important for a technology to be adopted by firms.[69]

In sum, theoretical as well as empirical literature on technological change is broadly confined to the changes in the physical processes of transformation including material and output characteristics especially at the innovation level. This literature indicates that the market structure, scale of operation, relative factor prices, finances, technological capabilities, managerial attributes and the availability of materials, are important determinants of technological change. And the models of diffusion show that the information availability and capital requirements for the change are significant factors that determine the adoption of a technology by a firm. We make use of the definition of technology given in this literature and keep all the factors discussed above in mind while developing our analytical framework to study the technological change in the Indian small-scale industries in the following chapters.

3.4 TECHNOLOGICAL CAPABILITIES

In this section, we review the literature relating to another relevant concept of the study namely, technological capabilities. Technological capabilities are considered as pre-requisite for the technological change. The importance of technological capabilities for the technological development is well articulated in the literature.[70] In fact, it was the assumption that Third World countries possess extremely weak technological capabilities, which was responsible for the focus, initially, on the issues of international technology transfer. Later it led to the analysis of the process of technological changes in the Third World countries and further on to the issues of the requirements for strengthening technological capabilities in the Third World firms.[71]

Technological capabilities can be, broadly, taken as the "capabilities needed to identify, acquire, assimilate, use, change or create a technology."[72] Capabilities here include all kinds of "information and skills, i.e. technical, managerial and institutional",[73] required for the above purpose. In the literature, four kinds of technological capabilities are distinguished at the firm level. These are production capabilities, linkage capabilities, investment capabilities and innovation capabilities.[74]

Production capabilities range from the basic skills such as operation and maintenance, and quality control to more advanced skills required for adaptation and improvement. They cover both process technologies as well as monitoring and control functions. These capabilities determine how well a given technology is operated and improved and reflect the usage of in-house efforts to absorb technologies bought.

Linkage capabilities are the skills needed to transmit information, skills and technology, to and from component or raw material suppliers, subcontractors, consultants, service firms and technology institutions. These capabilities affect the production efficiency of a firm.[75]

Investment capabilities refer to the skills required to identify, design or obtain a technology, construct and commission a production facility. It covers areas like project management, project engineering and project execution. These capabilities are required to establish a new production facility and/or to expand any existing facilities.

Innovation capabilities are those capabilities that can create and carry out new technological possibilities to economic use. It is reflected in the ability to improve technology or to develop new products or services that better meet the specific needs of people.

Generally, firms start with the production and linkage capabilities and slowly build on the other two capabilities, i.e. investment and innovation capabilities. This is because experience in production is generally needed to know whether to go for expansions or new plants. Together with production experience, investment experience enables a firm to develop an idea about the possible new products and processes.[76] Acquiring this experience is neither automatic nor is it rapid and effortless. It takes conscious effort over a long period of time. To be specific, it requires efforts to monitor what is going on, to keep track of the developments, to try new things and to accumulate skills,[77] which further depends on the attitudes and motivation levels of individuals.

At the national level, technological capabilities include physical investment, human capital and technological effort. All the three are highly interconnected and one without the other two will not develop national technological capabilities adequately. Physical investment refers to plant and machinery. It is the 'basic' without which there is no industry. Human capital covers all the skills developed through formal education and training, on-the-job training and experience, attitudes and abilities that aid industrial development. Technological efforts comprise a broad spectrum of production, design and research work within the firms, technological infrastructure that provides information standards, basic scientific knowledge and various facilities too large to be owned by private firms.[78]

In sum, technological capabilities both at the firm level like production, linkage, investment, and innovation capabilities and at the national level namely, physical investment, human capital and technological efforts, are essential for technological development. These capabilities are partly determined by attitudes, motivations, education, on-the-job training and experience at an individual level, partly by the technological infrastructure, policies and the incentives that these policies create. In our study, we consider all the firm-level technological capabilities excepting innovation capabilities.

3.5 STRUCTURE OF ECONOMIC ORGANISATIONS

Since we are dealing with the technological change at a firm level, it is essential to know the internal structure of the firm. Apart from evolutionary economics, there exist several economic approaches to organisations like behavioural theory, agency theory, and transaction costs theory. Each one of these approaches emphasises one specific aspect of the firm. For instance, behavioural theory takes the firm as a coalition of participants each having its own interests. Agency theory focuses on delegation of decision-making to an agent whose behaviour can be observed only partly by the owners. Transaction costs approach considers transactional costs as one of the important determinants of the organisational form.[79] None of these approaches enable us to explain the process of technological change at a firm level. Consequently, we look into the non-economic literature on organisations for the basic components, structures and functions of organisations so as to develop our own theory of the firm to study technological change. For this purpose, we draw mainly, on Mintzberg (1979) that synthesises the existing literature on organisations to develop the structure of organisations in relation to their functioning, which we find more useful. The five structures that were developed in this book are considered as the basic in the organization theory even today.[80]

Every organised activity involves two fundamental but opposing things namely, the division of labour into different tasks to be performed and the co-ordination of these tasks to accomplish the activity. So, the structure of an organisation can be taken as the sum of the different ways in which it divides its work into distinct tasks and then achieves co-ordination. Groups of people performing distinct tasks are considered as the basic components of an organisation. Five groups are taken as fundamental and cover all types of contemporary organisations. They are operating core, strategic apex, middle management, technostructure and supporting staff.

Operating core consists of all operators involved in the basic work of production like procurement of inputs, transformation of inputs into outputs, distribution of outputs and other supporting activities like maintenance of machines. *Strategic apex* includes the people who are charged with the overall responsibility for the organisation, i.e. chief executive officers. To ensure that the organisation serves its mission in an effective way, the strategic apex is entrusted with three sets of duties. One is direct supervision including the assignment of people and resources to different tasks, issuing of work orders, monitoring and control of the works. Second, management of the organisation's relationship with its environment that involves the role of spokesman, negotiator in the case of any agreements with outside parties and to develop and tap the external contacts. The third set of duties relate to the development of the organisation's strategy that is required to deal with the time to time changes in the environment. The strategic apex is joined to the operating core by the chain of *middle management* that includes floor supervisors to senior managers. *Technostructure* covers those people who are not part of the operating core but affect the work either by designing or planning the work systems or by training them. *Supporting staff* is those people that support the organisation outside the operating workflow like for example, public relations, legal counsel, industrial relations, accounts and mailrooms. Every organisation always has an operating core and a strategic apex. As organisations grow, they extend typically to include middle management, supporting staff and technostructure.

All the basic parts of organisations are joined together by different flows, i.e. flow of authority, of work materials, of information and decision processes. These flows indicate how an organisation functions and allows us to take organisations as a system of formal authority, as a system of regulated flows like operating work flow, information flow and control flow, and as a system of decision processes. Formal authority represents a limited aspect of organisation. Operating workflow involves movements of materials and information in a variety of combinations. For instance, movements of materials along the assembly line backed up by information flows like work documents and time sheets. The control system regulates the vertical flow of information and decision making from the operating core up the chain of authority. Simultaneously, there exist numerous channels of informal communication. All these flows are there to facilitate the two basic processes of organisation namely, making decisions and the production of goods and services. Here, the organisation as a system of decision processes assumes importance.

Decision processes are categorised as operative, administrative and strategic. Operative decisions are taken routinely and executed quickly. For example, a lathe operator makes an operating decision when he starts and stops his machine. Administrative decisions are taken to guide and co-ordinate operating decisions. For instance, planning, production scheduling and budgeting decisions. These too are mostly routine and usually taken by the middle management. Strategic decisions are significant in their impact on the organisation. They are the least routine and are taken by the strategic apex. A strategic decision may be evoked by a change in the environment like the development of new technologies or by an individual initiative like a manager simply decides that it is time for a new product line. The extent to which decision-making power is given to the relevant individuals depends on how the organisation is designed. In other words, whether the organisation is designed to be centralised or decentralised, if decentralised, is it vertical or horizontal? Centralisation refers to an organisation where all the power for decision-making rests at a single point or an individual. On the other hand, an organisation is referred to as decentralised to the extent that the power to make decisions is dispersed among many individuals. The dispersal of formal power down the line of management is called vertical decentralisation. Horizontal decentralisation refers to the extent to which technostructure and supporting staff control decision processes.

As regards co-ordination mechanism, there are five fundamental ways in which organisations co-ordinate their work. They are mutual adjustment, direct supervision, standardisation of work processes, standardisation of work outputs and standardisation of worker skills. Mutual adjustment co-ordinates work through the process of informal communication. Direct supervision ensures co-ordination by entrusting one individual with the responsibility for the work of the others. The selected individual issues instructions to the workforce and monitors their actions. In the standardisation of work processes, the contents of work are specified. In the standardisation of outputs, the results of the work, i.e. dimensions of products or performances are specified. Skills are standardised through the specification of the contents of the training required to perform work. As the organisation becomes more and more complex, the co-ordination mechanism seems to shift from mutual adjustment to direct supervision to standardisation.

Regulated flows of authority, work materials, information and decision processes, and co-ordination mechanisms are related. These two together with other design parameters like centralisation/ decentralisation and behaviour formalisation, lead to five natural structural configurations that can explain all types of existing organisations. They are simple structure, machine bureaucracy, professional bureaucracy, divisionalised form and adhocracy. In a simple structure, the strategic apex is the key part with full control over decision-making through centralisation and it co-ordinates the activities of the people by direct supervision. Technostucture with limited horizontal decentralisation is the critical part in a machine bureaucracy where the standardisation of work processes is the main co-ordination mechanism. In professional bureaucracy, the horizontal and vertical decentralisation makes the operating core as the dominant component and the activities are co-ordinated through standardisation of skills. In the divisionalised form, there is limited vertical decentralisation giving power to middle management and co-ordination is achieved through a standardisation of outputs. In adhocracy, supporting staff although autonomous involved in decision-making owing to their expertise and play an important role. Power is decentralised selectively and people involved in decision-making are free to co-ordinate through mutual adjustment.

Since many small organisations remain as simple structures,[81] we elaborate a little on the simple structure. The simple structure often consists of little more than a one-man strategic apex, operating core and few supporting staff. It does not have middle management and technostructure. It has a loose division of labour with little formalisation of behaviour. It makes minimal use of planning, training and liaison devices. Co-ordination is attained largely through direct supervision. Power to make important decisions tend to be centralised in the hands of the chief executive officer and he takes the sole responsibility for strategy formulation. Hence, strategies also reflect the chief executive's implicit vision of the place of the organisation in its environment. In other words, strategies can be taken as direct extrapolation of the chief executive's personal beliefs and an extension of his own personality.[82] Centralisation enables simple structures to have flexibility and adaptability in strategic response and it is expected to reflect full knowledge of the operating core. However, at times, centralisation may be disadvantageous as it can create imbalances between strategic and operating issues. There is a tendency for the owner to either get carried away totally by operating problems and thus not being able to see beyond or preoccupied with the strategic responses ignoring operating issues.[83] Centralisation also puts simple structures at risk as the entire organisation functions on the health and whims of a single individual.

As we are dealing with the small-scale industrial units, we confine our study to the simple structure of the firm and develop our analytical framework within this structure in the next chapter.

Endnotes

1. Saviotti (1996: 41)
2. Recent endogenous growth models take technology as endogenous at an economy level.
3. Saviotti (1996:41); Dosi and Nelson (1994:154) states the purpose of evolutionary economics is "to explain the movement of something over time...."
4. Many studies long ago recognised the limitations of neo-classical economics and tried to develop alternatives in the concerned areas but in a scattered way. For instance, Coase (1932); Simon (1947, 1957); Cyert and March (1963); Penrose (1980), have attempted to open the black box of firm by developing alternative theoretical frameworks. Evolutionary theory of firm developed by incorporating some of these ideas. See Saviotti (1996:36) for these references.
5. Saviotti and Metcalfe (1991: 1–3)
6. Of these, variety and selection are considered as the basic ones. It can be seen from the following statement that is made in Saviotti and Metcalfe (1991:10) that "Evolutionary explanation of economic change is driven by two distinct but related mechanisms. The first mechanism generates variety and the second selects between those varieties to change their relative importance over time. Selection also influences the generation of variety." Also see Dosi and Nelson (1994:154)
7. This part is mainly drawn from Saviotti and Metcalfe (1991: Ch. 1); Saviotti (1996:Ch. 3); and Dosi and Nelson (1994).
8. Nelson and Winter (1977:58); and Dosi and Orsenigo (1988:13)
9. Dosi (1988b:222)
10. Technical characteristics are those that embody scientific and technical knowledge and form the internal structure of any technology. Service characteristics refer to product characteristics in terms of serving particular needs. See Saviotti (1996)
11. Saviotti (1996:73)
12. Garud *et al.* (1997:x)

13. Langlois (1997: 84–5)
14. It can be seen from Langlois (1997:85) that "Almost all the company's attempts to develop a RISC machine were either scotched or killed by the requirements of 360/ 370 compatibility."
15. It can be seen from the following observations made in the literature. "At the time of the PC's development, IBM had a stable of profitable mainframes and minicomputer systems. Protecting these profitable cash-flows (particularly mini computers) from any encroachment of the PC was a salient concern." Porac (1997:137); ".....the PC development team made conscious decisions (like choosing the 8088 chip over the more powerful 8086) in order not to intrude on turf elsewhere in the company." Chposky and Leonsis (1988:24) cited in Langlois (1997: 87). Parentheses are original. It can also be seen in Fransman (1998:184) "In the end it was the interest of the mainframe division which trumped.....The political interdependence of the divisions under the hegemony of the mainframe division resulted in IBM's failure to take full advantage even of many of the breakthrough products and technologies which it had been first to invent, such as personal computers and RISC (Reduced Instruction Set) microprocessor."
16. Saviotti (1996: 82)
17. Nelson (1995: 73)
18. Saviotti (1996: 82–84)
19. Dosi (1988b: 227)
20. Garud *et al.* (1997:xi)
21. Dosi (1988b:225)
22. Saviotti (1996: 65&66)
23. Dosi and Nelson (1994: 156)
24. Dosi and Malerba (1996:3)
25. Dosi and Malerba (1996: 6)
26. Teece and Pisano (1998:196)
27. Dosi and Malerba (1996: 3)
28. Dosi and Malerba (1996: 4–8)
29. Dosi and Malerba (1996: 4)
30. Teece and Pisano (1998: 197)
31. Nelson and Winter (1982:14 & 15)
32. Teece (1988:265)

33. Dosi and Malerba (1996:3)
34. Teece (1988: 265)
35. Teece (1988: 198)
36. Market constitutes a part of environment.
37. Nelson and Winter (1982:4)
38. Saviotti and Metcalfe (1991:18)
39. Dosi and Nelson (1994:156)
40. Saviotti (1996:92)
41. Dosi and Nelson (1994: 156)
42. Fransman (1984: 9)
43. Dahlman and Westphal (1982)
44. Stoneman (1995:2); and Radosevic (1999:14)
45. This essentially applies to transformation technologies. Organisational methods are in any case considered as soft technologies.
46. Bos and Cole (1994:232). It is despite the fact that the definition includes both physical processes and management methods.
47. Tietel and Westphal (1984:2)
48. Patel and Pavitt (1995)
49. At the level of imitation that involves transfer of technology from the proprietor firm of technology to the other firms, literature is full of studies on the issue of international technology transfer.
50. Radosevic (1999: 14–15)
51. Hayek (1945); and Mintzberg (1979)
52. Mody and Dahlman (1992:1703)
53. Coombs *et al.* (1987: 96–103)
54. Coombs *et al.* (1987: 4)
55. Coombs *et al.* (1987:94)
56. See for instance, Schmookler (1962:117), "the fundamental conclusion of this paper is that technological progress is intimately dependent on economic phenomena .... new goods and new techniques are unlikely to appear, and to enter the life of society without a pre-existing - albeit possibly only latent - demand."
57. Coombs *et al.* (1987: 101)

58. For the latest survey on this see Cohen (1995).

59. It can be seen from the following statements made in Galbraith (1957: 86–87). "Not only is development (technological) now (twentieth century) sophisticated and costly but it must be on a sufficient scale so that successes and failures in some measure average out." "Because development (technological) is costly, it follows that it can be carried on only by a firm that has the resources which are associated with considerable size." (Parentheses added).

60. Some of the important reasons offered for a positive relation between size and innovative activity are, large firms have better access to capital markets, better appropriability and scale economies in R&D function. Some of the important counter arguments rely on propositions like loss of managerial control, lack of incentives for individual scientists with size. See Cohen (1995: 184–185)

61. Cohen (1995: 185–186)

62. Some of the arguments in favour of positive impact of market concentration on innovation highlight factors like the easier appropriability of innovation in concentrated markets. Some others argue that market concentration breeds bureaucratic inertia and discourages innovation. Cohen (1995: 192)

63. Cohen (1995:192)

64. Elster (1983:145)

65. Cohen (1995:197–206)

66. It comes under neoclassical tradition.

67. Rosenberg (1969) provides numerous examples to show this point. For instance, the improved designs of automobile engines have led, through the achievement of higher speeds, to the invention of improved braking system.

68. Diffusion being the process of spread of a new technology (Karshenas and Stoneman, 1995:265), it is also relevant for the technological change in the selected industrial units of the study as they are imitators not innovators of technology.

69. Karshenas and Stoneman (1995: 270–274)

70. See for instance, Dahlman *et al.* (1987:759) that "inventing products and processes is not at the centre of the technological development needed for successful industrialisation. It is at the fringe. What is at the centre is acquiring the capabilities needed for efficient production and investment." At a specific level, Bell and Pavitt (1992: 261) argue "to generate continuing

incremental changes in the existing facilities, the user of the technology must play an active role and must therefore have the relevant technological capabilities."

71. Fransman (1984:4–6)

72. Dahlman *et al.* (1987:762)

73. Biggs *et al.* (1995:16)

74. One finds innovation capabilities in Dahlman, *et al (1987)* and linkage capabilities in Lall (1992). The remaining two namely, production capabilities and investment capabilities are considered by both the works. Discussion about the individual capabilities including their definition is mainly drawn from these two sources.

75. The significance of linkage capabilities in increasing productivity is well recognised in the literature. See for references Cohen and Levin (1989).

76. Dahlman, *et. al* (1987:764)

77. Dahlman, *et. al* (1987: 759, 764)

78. Lall (1992)

79. Douma and Schreuder (1998)

80. Shukla (2002)

81. Mintzberg (1979:310); and Douma and Schreuder, (1998:148)

82. Empirical studies on Indian industrial houses show that even in large-scale units: "Management decisions are based on personal experiences, aims and visions of one person. Usually it is the head of business or chairman of a company" Piramal (1966: x)

83. Our Dutch collaborator in IDPAD project surveyed the semi-rural units found this imbalance in a good number of units.

Chapter 4

An Eclectic Approach to Study Technological Change

4.1. INTRODUCTION

This chapter makes an attempt to develop an analytical framework, using some of the theoretical concepts discussed in the previous chapter, which permits us to describe the firm-level technological change and examine the factors influencing it in the Indian small-scale industries. Following Dosi and Nelson (1994), we take it explicitly that 'technologies' do not change themselves. Technologies are embodied in firms and affect their competitiveness. Hence, it is the firm that changes the technologies it carries to improve its competitive strength.[1] So, we take firm as our unit of analysis. Accordingly, we start the analytical frame with the specification of basic elements of a firm and its business environment. We analyse the process of technological change and deduce factors affecting it using these basic elements of firm. This chapter also deals, briefly, with various empirical approaches to study technological change and the field of enquiry for the sake of completeness. Details of the latter are provided in the next chapter.

4.2. FIRM AND BUSINESS ENVIRONMENT

We take *firm* as an economic organisation that produces a given set of goods and services for a specified market. Following the selection mechanism of evolutionary economics, we take it that our firm competes with many other firms of the industry that are producing similar or substitute products in the market. Market and industry together with various other macroeconomic institutions such as capital market, consultancy organisations and government policies, form the firm's *business environment*. The business environment of a firm changes continuously as all its elements keep changing. Markets change as the incomes, tastes and preferences change, causing shifts in the demand for the specified products. For instance, the recent shift in preferences towards motorbikes reduced the demand for scooters in the two-wheeler industry. The number and nature of firms in the industry including the substitutes they produce change and affect the supply of the given products and their costs. Passenger car industry where the entry of multinationals changed the number of products as well as their prices can provide a good example. Government policies as well as institutions change over time further influencing the demand and supply structures. The demand and supply structures affect the prices of goods and services and thereby the profitability and commercial viability of firms. Firms producing more desirable products more efficiently get selected by the environment in the sense these firms are not only able to survive but are also able to improve their positions in the market. The variations in the environment, however, keep shifting the parameters of selection of the successful firms. Firms have to strive continuously to get selected, i.e., to maintain and to improve its commercial viability through different strategies in the face of changing environment. For instance, it was the strategy of 'diversification' that fetched profits for Indian firms, especially the larger ones, during the regime of regulation with the closed market. It is, however, the strategy of 'focus' that Indian firms are turning to, to improve their competitive strength in the regime of liberalisation and open markets of the nineties. We treat the changes in technology as one such strategy of the firms to operate effectively in the changing environment.

The term 'firm' is too abstract to formulate any strategy. Somebody within the firm does the job of formulating and implementing strategies. We refer to them as 'decision makers'. A change of technology requires knowledge about technology, i.e. technological capabilities. Accordingly, we focus on three basic elements of a firm to study the firm-level technological change. They are *technology* (that undergoes change), *decision-maker* (who undertakes change), and *technological capabilities* (pre-requisite for change). The structure of a firm in relation to its environment is given in figure 4.1.

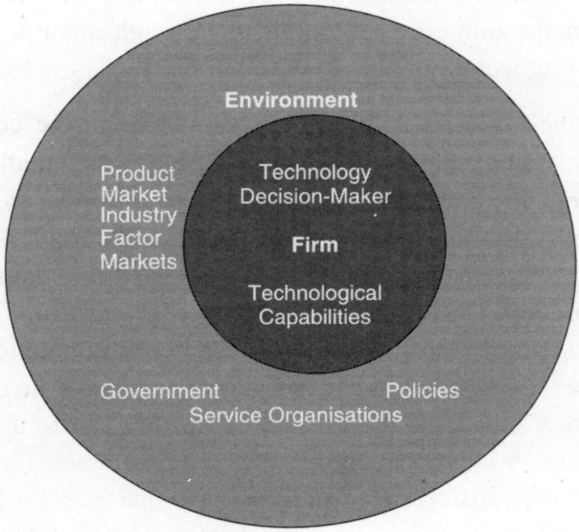

Figure 4.1 Firm and Business Environment

For the purpose of study, *technology is taken to include the physical process of transformation of inputs into output, organisational methods that structure these processes and information flows required to carry out these processes*. Thus, the study considers three dimesions of technology, namely, transformation, organisation and information discussed in the section 3.3.[2] We take the *transformation* aspect of technology to include plant and machinery, components, tools, accessories, materials and products. The *organisation* aspect of technology is considered at two levels namely, structure and operation. At a structural level, it refers to the way firm is organised as a business concern (such as a proprietary concern) and how it is managed (owner-managed or, professionally managed). At an operational level, it refers to the organisation of production process that includes plant layouts, methods of procurement of materials, components and accessories and their inventories, production schedules, work allocations, and quality management. The *information* aspect includes the means of communication with the outside agents like suppliers and customers as well as the ways of storing and processing of information/ data (i.e. data management) within the unit. Of the three, transformation technology is considered as the '*core*' of technology. *Technological changes are the changes in any one of these or a combination of these three dimensions of technology* that are undertaken by the firm to improve its competitive strength either through cost reductions or, through quality, productivity improvements, or a combination of these three.

Further, we take technological changes that can be considered as innovations[3] as an exception rather than a rule in the small-scale units. These units are almost the last set of imitators in the sense of adaptating a technology long after its commercialisation.[4] Accordingly, *technological changes* in our selected industries mostly refer to the *changes in their existing technologies either in the form of addition of, or replacement by a later vintage technology* that has already been in practice elsewhere in the industry.[5] Technological changes of this type in a firm, however, can be *radical* like a shift from the practice of farming out to the fabricators towards in-house production in the garment industry. Radical shifts involve change in both the transformation and organisational aspects of technology. Technological change can be *incremental* like a change of instruments like multimeters in an electronic unit.[6]

In order to locate the decision maker and technological capabilities within a firm, we take small-scale industrial units to have simple organisational structure with a strategic apex and an operating core as it is considered the most appropriate for small units (see section 3.5). The operating core consists of all those workers involved in the basic production process, i.e. the movement of inputs to the machines, machine operation and maintenance, and distribution of output from the plant. Their work is co-ordinated by the strategic apex through direct supervision. In addition, strategic apex in the simple structure, as discussed in section 3.5, deals with the relevant outside agents such as suppliers and customers, and formulates strategies as and when the need arises. The strategic apex in the simple organisational structure has the total decision-making power to make all decisions relating to the organisation. The strategic apex in the small industrial units, often, consists of one or two persons who are the owner-managers. These owner-managers take care of the three basic functions of co-ordination, outside dealings and strategy formulation. As regards decision-making, *owner-managers are the sole decision-makers in the small-scale units* and they take all strategic as well as administrative decisions. Decision-making regarding technological change is taken as 'strategic' and depends on the owner-manager's perception of the business environment and its changes. Equally important are the owner-manager's capabilities to relate the available technologies to the changing markets, to select, adapt, and manage technological change. Here, we turn to the technological capabilities.

As discussed in section 3.4, firm-level technological capabilities encompass production capabilities, linkage capabilities, investment capabilities and innovation capabilities. Of these, we confine only to production, linkage and investment capabilities as we are dealing with the small-scale industrial units where, as mentioned earlier, innovation is taken as an exception. Production capabilities as specified in section 3.4, refer to knowledge and skills required for the operation and maintenance of the production systems as well as control and monitoring of these systems. As regards the skills to operate and maintain production systems, production capabilities are located in the operating core, i.e. the workers (labour force) who do this job. And abilities for the control and monitoring of production system are expected to be with the strategic apex, i.e. owner-manager as they perform these functions in simple structures like that of small units. Linkage capabilities, i.e. abilities required to transmit technology-related information and skills from the concerned outside agents like suppliers and customers are expected to be possessed by the owner-manager in the small industrial units as he/she does all the outside dealings. It is again the owner-manager who is responsible for the expansion of production facilities and hence, expected to represent the investment capabilities, i.e. abilities to search, identify, evaluate, select, negotiate, obtain and commission a new production facility. All these technological capabilities depend, as discussed in section 3.4, on the formal education, training, on-the-job experience, attitudes and conscious efforts to learn, of the concerned individuals. In other words, in the Indian small-scale units, it is *the owner-manager who is expected to possess investment, linkage and part of production capabilities* and these can be deduced from his education, experience and attitudes. *Workforce (labour)* that constitutes the operating core, needs to *have the other part of the production capabilities* that are required to operate and maintain production systems which further depend on their formal education, training, on-the-job experience and their attitudes.

4.3 PROCESS OF TECHNOLOGICAL CHANGE AND FACTORS AFFECTING IT

Following the principle of *ex ante* selection[7] of technologies and products by firms and the salient features of the innovation from the evolutionary economics discussed in section 3.2, we consider technological change at a firm level as a *deliberately initiated process of search, selection, execution and absorption.*[8] To achieve change, concerned individuals have to seek it, *search* for alternatives, i.e. to get to know available alternative technologies in terms of cost, content, sources and modes of acquisition. If alternatives exist, the unit has to *select* among the alternatives, then negotiate and acquire it. Then comes the *execution* which includes modification if need be, and the installation of the machinery or implementation of the acquired technology if it is organisational method like total quality management (TQM). With the execution, *physical change of technology* occurs in the unit. However, installation of a new machine or implementation of a new method does not automatically ensure the purpose of having it. Workers take some time to get to know the machine and to be able to operate it smoothly or, to get used to the new method of organisation. Thus, the actual process of technological change can be taken as completed only when acquired changes are mastered, i.e. *absorbed.* It is the execution followed by absorption that ensures the attainment of the purpose of change, namely, improvements in the competitive strength.

As the process of technological change is treated as a set of distinct, though related, stages, we consider the factors affecting this process stage-wise. Consequently, we analyse the factors initiating search, factors facilitating search, factors influencing selection and factors affecting execution and absorption. Following the salient features of innovation that are brought out by evolutionary economists and discussed in section 3.2, we consider technological change as the result of an interaction of factors that are internal to the firm with the external factors. Hence, we analyse the factors under these two categories. We draw these factors from the literature on technological change discussed in section 3.3.

We take market both in terms of its structure and demand as the main external factor, and perceptions and capabilities of the decision maker as the internal factors that initiate search. Since we are dealing with the imitators especially those that are at the end of the diffusion process, it is the competitiveness of the product market that creates a pressure on firms to improve their technology. The competitiveness of the market can be taken in terms of either increasing number of suppliers, entry of powerful players like multinational corporations, improved performance of the other units of the industry, substitutes, demanding customers, or a combination of these. On the other hand, rising demand for the product[9] may provide an incentive for the firms to go for technological improvements. How far a given unit acts in this direction depends on the decision maker's perception of the demand situation, market competition and its impact on his unit, and his capabilities to foresee the potential benefits of change or potential losses if not going for change. Hence, we consider the *product market, decision maker's perception of market changes* and his technological capabilities especially the *investment capabilities* as the *factors that initiate search* for technological alternatives at the firm level.

The primary factor that facilitates search is the availability of information to the firm. Availability of information depends on the development of informational infrastructure at the national level like documentation centres, trade journals, consultancy organisations and the extent of dissemination of information through trade fairs, seminars, etc. Widespread development of informational infrastructure improves the access of small industrial units to information, and makes it easier for these units to obtain information. Equally important for gathering information is the awareness and resourcefulness of the decision maker, which depends on his/her linkage capabilities. In other words, it is the *firm's access to information sources* together with the *linkage capabilities* of the decision maker that either *facilitates or constrains the search* for available alternative technologies. These factors also determine the *degree of choice* that a unit has in terms of technology.[10]

Once the choice of technology is given, units need to select the technology that suits their requirements. The critical external factors that influence the selection of technology are availability of finances, and complementary factors like materials and skills, and relative factor prices. Availability of finances is one of the basic factors that determine whether a unit can go for change, and if so, what type of change. It further depends on the unit's access to sources of finance and cost of finance. Use of every technology requires specific materials and skills, and their availability in the vicinity thus becomes another important factor in influencing the selection of technology[11] . Availability of complementary materials and skills are important only when a unit is going in for a totally new technology that is not related with the existing technology. Availability of complementary skills depends on the national level (to be taken as the concerned region) technological capabilities. The existing relative factor prices is another factor that the decision maker may keep in mind while selecting a technology so as to choose the one that uses more of a relatively cheaper factor.

As regards the internal factors, investment capabilities that are required to evaluate the available technologies, to select one of them and finally to negotiate, have a direct impact on the selection of technology. In addition, the decision maker may look for such technologies that suit their scale of operation[12] and can be put to use by the existing production capabilities. The importance of the existing production capabilities of the firm is due to the 'path dependency theory' of Dosi, which is discussed in section 3.2.

In effect, *the relative factor prices and availability of finance, skills and raw materials* are important external factors, and *investment and production capabilities, and scale of operation* are the internal factors that *influence the selection of a technology.*

At times, technological changes occur in terms of the production of additional products, i.e. product diversification. Product diversification not only changes the product set but also brings changes in the other parts of technology such as machinery, tools, accessories and materials as well as in organisational methods.

Table 4.1: **Factors Affecting the Process of Firm-Level Technological Change**

Process	Internal Factors	External Factors
Factors Initiating Search	Owner-manager' Perception of Market Changes, Investment Capabilities	Nature of Product Market
Factors Facilitating Search	Linkage Capabilities	Availability of Information
Factors Influencing Selection	Investment Capabilities Production Capabilities, Scale of Operation	Availability of Finance, Complementary Skills and Materials, Relative Factor Prices
Factors Affecting Execution and Absorption	Production Capabilities, Labour	....

Once the new technology is selected, its *execution and absorption depends on the internal production capabilities and labour* (i.e.

workers). Production capabilities are required to unpack, modify if necessary, install and finally operate and maintain the technology. The behaviour and attitudes of labour are as important as their capabilities for absorption of the technology.

In sum, we consider *the product market, decision makers' perception of market changes, technological capabilities, scale of operation, availability of information, finance, complementary skills and materials, relative factor prices and labour as the possible factors influencing the process of technological change in the small-scale units*. All these factors affecting the process of technological change are presented in table 4.1.

It is important to note it is convenient to look for the factors stage-wise and hence the importance of the analytical factors in the context of a specific stage are discussed given their immediate linkage with that stage. However, influence of some of these factors goes beyond the specified stage. For instance, scale of operation may influence all the stages. Availability of finance may initiate the process of technological change at times. Similarly, labour, given the existing Indian labour laws, may be one of the factors that initiate technological change at a firm level.

Equally worth noting is that the above-discussed analytical factors which are taken to influence the process of technological change primarily apply to the transformation (mechanisation) part of the technology. Organisation and information technologies are determined by a subset of these analytical factors. For instance, the form of business organization and type of management are supposed to be determined by owners' preferences and convenience as well as scale of operation. Similarly, changes in communication technologies such as switch over to electronic media depend mainly on the technological capabilities of the owner-manager, type of product market and scale of operation. For instance, in the case of auto components industry, the likelihood of larger units supplying original equipment to big vehicle manufacturers for adapting the latest information technologies using electronic media is greater as their customers are expected to possess these facilities compared to smaller units catering to the replacement market. The same reasoning applies to quality management systems. Work allocation system depends mainly on the technological capabilities of owner-manager, labour and nature of production process.

These factors are further elaborated in terms of the unit-level characteristics and their specific relationship with the technological change in the next chapter after taking the industry-specific characteristics into account.

4.4. EMPIRICAL APPROACHES TO STUDY FIRM-LEVEL TECHNOLOGICAL CHANGE

Methodologically, one can examine the factors affecting technological change at a firm level in two ways. First, it can be studied through a case study method. Case study involves the study of minute details relating to technological change and factors responsible for it in a few industrial units through a series of interviews with all those concerned individuals. Second, one can examine the changes in technologies and its possible determinants in a sample of units through the survey method. The case study method requires more time for each unit and thus can limit the coverage of units given the time constraint. Yet, it may be useful for the larger units where the process of technological change is complex involving many individuals from different departments and hence may not be meaningfully captured in a structured questionnaire. In the case of small units, however, we do not expect many individuals to involve in this process excepting owner-manager and few workers at a later stage. We also take the process to be comparatively simple and hence can be covered by the survey method using carefully structured questionnaire. In the survey method, one can examine the technological changes in two ways: (a) One is the analysis of the differences in the units that have undertaken change and units without any such changes; (b) Alternatively, one can analyse the differences in the levels of technologies of different industrial units. Technological changes can further be taken as the changes undertaken in the technologies of unit over time, or within a specified time interval or changes undertaken after a benchmark year. Benchmark year refers to a watershed year for a specified phenomenon like for example, 1991 in the Indian context. Since the technological changes mostly refer to improvements in technology, we can analyse them in terms of differences in the levels of technologies. These levels of technologies can be specified against a benchmark technology or any other indicator. For example, mechanical, electromechanical and electronic devices can be treated as three different levels of technologies with mechanical devices falling in the lower end of the scale and electronic devices positioned at the upper end and electromechanical lying in the middle.

These indicators of levels of technology differ from industry to industry depending on their nature and the level of development. Establishment of industry-wise benchmark technology is difficult and in itself needs a separate study. Changes after a benchmark year are not useful if a good number of units have started after the benchmark year. An analysis of differences across firms in terms of change cannot be done if the entire set of sample units has undergone some change or the other. Keeping these limitations as well as the industry characteristics in mind, one can select an approach that suits their requirements.

Information relating to technological change and factors influencing it can be collected through a set of direct and indirect questions framed in a questionnaire. For instance, information about technological change can be collected through a set of direct questions such as whether there has been any change in the various parts of technology like machinery, plant layout, etc. The technological capabilities can be proxied through the education, training and experience of the owner-managers as well as of workers. Both the subjective opinions of the owner-manger and objective criteria can be used to obtain information. For instance, the competitiveness of the market can be deduced through the subjective opinion of the owner-manager as well as an objective criterion like the actual market served by the unit. Subjective opinions are equally important as they reflect the perception of owner-manager, which influences their actions more than the reality.[13] Some questions may be categorical like 'yes/no' type and others may have an ordinal scale depending on the nature of the variable. Numerical data may be obtained for output and inputs. Details of the actual questionnaire used for the study is discussed in the next chapter.

4.5 FIELD OF ENQUIRY

For the purpose of study, three industries, namely, Auto Components, Electronics and Garments located in the National Capital Region (NCR) of Delhi, which includes Delhi, Faridabad and Gurgaon of Haryana, and Noida of Uttar Pradesh are selected. Of these, Faridabad and Gurgaon have an Auto Component industry cluster, Noida has an Electronics industry cluster and Delhi has a readymade Garments industry cluster of small and medium enterprises.[14] Thus, the NCR of Delhi provided us with three small and medium industry clusters namely, Auto Components, Electronics and Ready-made Garments.

The selected industries also assume significance for a variety of reasons. For example, the importance of auto components and electronics industries stems from the fact that these industries are experiencing rapid changes in product composition, physical technologies and organisation at global level. These changes are expected to create pressure as well as provide incentives to go for the technological changes at a firm level. Also, the two industries have substantial spread effects on the other sectors of the economy. Garments has been the reserved item for the exclusive production by the small-scale sector and has been the major earner of foreign exchange for the country. Almost all the selected industries contribute substantially to the employment generation.

The NCR clusters are not closed with the homogeneous units producing similar products. These clusters are more widespread geographically forcing us to confine to a sample of units. Given the problem of locating the firms in the selected industries, the nature of the research problem together with the importance of non-sampling errors like non-response and non-reliable information, the purposive sampling method is used. These are elaborated in the next chapter after noting the salient features of the selected industries.

Endnotes

1. This is the widely recognised purpose for which firms undertake changes in technology. However, there can be other reasons that prompt firms to go for change like the non-availability of materials.

2. We have added information aspect to the definition of technology given in Dahlman and Westphal (1982). Our description of technology is also comparable with the Piek (1997) description of the various dimensions of technology namely, technoware, orgaware, infoware and humanware. The three dimensions of technology that our study considers, i.e., transformation, organisation and information corresponds with Pick's concepts of technoware, orgaware and infoware in that order. However, the humanware dimension of technology in Pick's study matches with the technological capabilities concept of our study.

3. In the literature, innovation is defined as the first commercial introduction of a product or process in the international economy (Cooper, 1994:13).

4. After the innovator, other larger units followed by the smaller units of industry in the developed nations where most of the innovations originate, may adopt a technology that is successful. Then larger units of the developing nations may follow suit. At the end of the diffusion process of a given technology comes small-scale industries in the developing nations like India.

5. Here, industry refers to the units producing similar products not only in India but also in other countries.

6. The importance of minor improvements is well recognised in the literature. See for example, Lall (1987:1). Japan's technological development is considered primarily due to the continuous minor improvements on the shop floor. See Hodgson (1982); Bos and Cole (1994).

7. The selection of successful firms by the market/ environment is referred as *ex post* selection in the evolutionary economics. See section 3.2.

8. This is a modified version of Dosi's characterisation of the innovation process that is discussed in section 3.2 of Chapter 3. We have modified it to suit the context of imitation as we are dealing with the imitator firms.

9. Demand for a product refers to the total market demand for product X but

not the demand for product X produced by a given unit.

10. This has significant theoretical as well as empirical implications. Its theoretical significance stems from the fact that the neoclassical economics, the most widely practised theoretical framework maintains that firms have easy access to all the available technologies and thus have a choice of technology.

11. The importance of availability of complementary skills can be seen from the following example. Ramming process is one of the many processes of metal castings. It can be done manually or by machine. In the Howrah region, the traditional region for the metal castings, the availability of skilled mold makers who are capable of achieving greater uniformity of compactness by the hand ramming method is the major reason for the limited introduction of machine ramming techniques. In other regions of India where these skills are not available locally, machine ramming is in use. Little et al (1987:140–41)

12. The importance of scale of operation in the selection of technology can be seen in the steam generation process of the garment industry. Steam is used for pressing the garments and it can be generated through either diesel-operated boiler or electricity-operated boilers. Electricity-operated boiler is inferior to diesel-operated in terms of the quality (i.e. uniformity) of steam it generates. However, many people use electricity-operated boilers, as diesel-operated ones require a certain minimum scale. This example is taken from the field notes of the author prepared during the survey.

13. Author encountered, during her field visit, some owner-managers saying that competition is not new to them as it is always been there. Hence, they neither undertook nor planning to undertake any changes in their technologies. Actually, what these owner-managers were referring to is the competition from the other small units (mentioned in Chapter 2) and they could not see the changes in the nature of competition. The reality is that the nature of the competition changed significantly as now it originates from large-scale units including multinationals.

14. Gulati (1997: 36–40)

Chapter 5

Selected Industries, Questionaire and Sample

5.1 INTRODUCTION

The literature discussed in section 3.2.2 and the analytical framework specified in 4.3 indicate that the firm-level technological change is an outcome of the interaction of factors internal to the firm with the external factors that are due to the business environment. These factors vary across firms as well as industries depending on their nature. Hence, this chapter first attempts to bring out the basic characteristics of the selected industries. Later, it elaborates on the analysis of technological change in these industries and the factors affecting it keeping their characteristics in mind.

5.2 THE SELECTED REGION

For the purpose of examining the factors affecting technological change, National Capital Territory of Delhi (hereafter referred as Delhi) and its surrounding areas has been selected as the geographical area of research. Surrounding areas include Faridabad and Gurgaon of Haryana and Noida of Uttar Pradesh. The selected areas are part of the National Capital Region that has Delhi as its centre.[1] The selected region hosts numerous small-scale industrial units. In fact, all the selected places are known clusters of small and medium enterprises for three industries. While Delhi is known for its cluster of garment industry, Gurgaon and Faridabad are recognised clusters of the auto component industry, and Noida for the electronics industry.[2] As a result, the selected region gives us access to a wider set of small-scale industrial units.

Faridabad, Gurgaon and Noida, being border towns, share the general business environment of Delhi.[3] Hence, we take the business environment of Delhi can be taken as the representative environment for the selected region. Delhi, being the national capital and one of the four metropolitan centres of India, is considered to be relatively better off in terms of infrastructure, institutional support, availability of raw materials and skills, and market links.[4] For instance, Delhi has many consultancy organisations for the small-scale industries like Technology Bureau for Small Enterprises (TBSE), National Small Industries Corporation (NSIC), Small Industries Service Institute (SISI) and a Regional Testing Centre (RTC)—all central government organisations. In addition, Delhi has state-level agencies like Delhi State Industrial Development Corporation (DSIDC) to provide infrastructure facilities like developed plot or shed, and financial assistance. Delhi also has numerous financial institutions including specialised banks like the Small Industry Development Bank of India (SIDBI) and private banks.[5] Trade fairs, both national and international, are held regularly in many business areas in Delhi which being the capital of the nation attracts people too.[6] In addition to having access to Delhi's environment, other selected areas, being industrial towns,[7] have their own facilities. Thus, the selected region is expected to give small-scale industrial units better access to information, input and output markets and can be placed at the upper end of the scale in terms of business environment.[8] This enables one to examine the environmental factors that are crucial for technological change in the small-scale units and to highlight the constraints that are posed by the environment if any.

As regards the selection of industries, namely, auto components, electronics and garments industries, it is a natural outcome of the fact that the selected region has small and medium enterprise clusters of these industries. Apart from this practical reasoning, the three industries are important for several economic reasons:

1. Garments is one of the important exporting items of the country;
2. Both garments and electronics industries in India are labour-intensive and thus generate good employment opportunities;
3. Garments has been reserved for the exclusive production in the small-scale sector till recently and thus dominated by small-scale units. The other two industries also have a good number of reserved products and production by small-scale units;[9]

4. Auto components and electronics industries are highly dynamic sectors in the sense of experiencing rapid technological changes, and in having substantial spread effects.

For both auto component and electronics industries, there have been sweeping changes in physical technologies, organisation and product composition at the global level. In addition, technological advancements in the electronics industry are expected to influence the technological changes in other industries. The auto components industry has good backward and forward linkages with various other industries and services in the economy.[10] To study the technological change in these industries is, therefore, not only interesting but also important.

5.3 THE SELECTED INDUSTRIES

In this section, the important characteristics of the selected industries in terms of product composition, nature of the market, location, industry and production structure and their likely future with a special emphasis on the position of small-scale units are discussed.

5.3.1 Automotive Components

Automotive components refer to all those parts and components that are used in making automobiles except the chassis and body. An automobile consists of more than 20,000 components each performing a different function.[11] These components differ not only functionally but also in terms of the materials that they are made of such as plastic components, rubber parts and metal components. The constituents of each of these groups further vary. For instance, metal components are differentiated depending on the type of metal used (e.g. sheet metal components and tubular parts) or the basic production process involved (like die castings and forgings). Thus the automotive components industry is highly heterogeneous and aptly referred to as 'agglomeration of industries.'[12] This makes it difficult to study the technological change in this industry, which can be observed from the scanty information about the technology employed in the industry.

The Automotive Components Manufacturers Association (ACMA) of India classifies these components into six categories depending on the broad type of function they serve in an automobile. They are engine parts, electrical parts, drive transmission and steering parts, suspension and braking parts, equipment and others. Engine parts include pistons, piston rings, engine valves, fuel delivery system components, etc. Electrical parts cover starter motors, generators, spark plug, distributors, etc. Some examples of the drive transmission and steering parts are gears, wheels, steering systems, axles and clutches. Leaf springs, brake assemblies, brake linings and shock absorbers come under suspension and braking parts. Headlights, wiper blades, wiper motors, electric horns and dash-board instruments are some of the items that come in the category of 'equipment'. Others include all those components that do not fall in any one of the five categories mentioned above because of functional disparities. Major components in this segment are sheet metal parts, pressure die-castings, plastic moulded components and hydraulic pneumatic equipment. Of these, sheet metal parts account for a significant proportion (14%) of the group's production.[13]

Some of the automotive components are vehicle-specific while others are standard. The design of vehicle-specific components depends crucially on the design of the vehicle. Pistons and carburettors are examples of vehicle-specific components. Standard components are those that are same for all types of vehicles. The standard components have scope for mass production and economies of scale.[14]

The automotive components industry in India produces the entire range of parts required by the domestic automobile industry. It caters to nearly 82 percent of the domestic market demand while the remaining 18 percent is served by imports.[15] Production of the automotive components industry for the year 1997–98 was 120.318 million rupees, of which the organised sector produced 92.552 million rupees, i.e. 77 percent. In the organised sector's production, engine parts, electrical parts, drive transmission and steering parts, suspension and braking parts, equipment, and other components constitute 34.2, 7, 20.3, 7.3, 6.3 and 14.9 percents, respectively.[16]

As regards the market for automotive components, a major proportion (nearly 55 percent) of it comes from the vehicle industry for the original equipment. Replacement demand constitutes 35 percent of the domestic production. Exports account for the remaining 10 percent.[17] The original equipment manufacturers (OEMs) market has been growing since the 1980s owing to a rapid growth in the passenger car and two-wheeler segments.[18] Replacement market demand has also been growing with an ever-increasing vehicle population, deteriorating driving conditions that are due to stop-and-go-traffic and poor road conditions.[19] Some of the components that have high replacement demand are fuel injection equipment, filters (air/oil/fuel), piston components, gaskets, gears, alternators, brake lining, rear view mirror, clutches, head lights. Engine, and drive transmission and steering parts constitute a good proportion of exports and they cater mostly the replacement abroad.[20]

The Indian automotive components industry is a low volume and fragmented industry. In terms of turnover, it is only about one-tenth the size the world's largest automotive company namely, Delphi Automotive Systems Corporation of the United States.[21] It has nearly 400 firms in the organised sector and more than 5000 firms in the unorganised small-scale sector.[22] Industry structure of the Indian automotive components industry can be taken as a minor variant of 'dominant firm with a competitive fringe'. This industry structure theoretically refers to an industry that has a single firm with a dominant share of the market and many fringe or small firms each with a trivial share of the market. A firm is dominant either because of a superior product or lower costs or both. Costs of a firm could be lower due to economies of scale, experience including early entry, better technology and management.[23]

In the automotive components industry of India, it is not a single firm but a few firms together control dominant share of the market leaving a tiny share to numerous small firms. Three to five firms corner more than 75 percent of the market for most of the automotive components.[24] For example, three players, namely, Escorts Mahle, India Pistons and Shriram Pistons and Rings, dominate the piston segment by contributing more than 70 percent of turnover of this segment. Jay Bharat Maruti and Mark Auto are the leaders in the production of sheet metal parts with around 70 percent of total turnover of these parts.[25] These firms play a dominant role mainly due to continuing technological upgradation and indigenous product designs.[26] However, quality levels of the Indian component manufacturers, at large, are low in terms of customer rejection rates compared to their international counterparts.[27]

Chennai and Pune are the traditional locations of the industry. Delhi and its surrounding areas have been the new location that came into existence mainly because of Maruti.[28]

The unorganised small-scale sector is estimated to contribute nearly 23 percent to the industry's total production.[29] A majority of these small-scale units are located in the states of Delhi and Haryana. They produce low technology products that require simple production set-ups like gaskets, engine valves and sheet metal components and components for which excise duty is high.[30] Given the excise duty exemptions, small units supply these components at cheaper rates. Most of these units employ older technologies including second-hand machines[31] and cater to the replacement demand with a few exceptions like sheet metal components. The production of sheet metal parts is primarily to satisfy the vehicle manufacturers' demand for original equipment and there is no replacement demand for these parts. Currently, most of the new car manufacturers in the country import their sheet metal components.[32]

The development and structure of the automotive components industry is closely connected with that of the vehicle industry. In India, the vehicle industry till the eighties was characterised by an oligopoly structure, small-scale operations, high cost of production, technological obsolescence and numerous government regulations. In this period, there was a tendency for the vehicle manufacturers to produce parts and components in-house and component manufacturers started mainly to serve the replacement demand.[33] In the eighties, the entry of Maruti Udyog Limited in the passenger car segment and many more entries in the light commercial vehicle segment such as Allwyn and DCM, all with foreign collaborations changed the dynamism of the industry. Relaxation of the government regulations especially on foreign collaborations along with the programme of phased localisation brought a surge in the components industry. Foreign collaborations, technological upgradation and closer relations with the buyers marked the automotive components industry in this time period.[34]

The new economic policy of liberalisation and globalisation of the 1990s changed the rules of the game for this industry once again. Following its endorsement of WTO agreement, India has already opened its economy to transnational corporations which resulted in the entry of many international players like General Motors, Ford, Honda, Peugout, Volvo, Mitsubishi, Hyundai and Daewoo in the vehicle industry and Delphi and Visteon,[35] both United States corporations in the components industry. It is not far away before the Indian automobile industry gets fully integrated with the global industry. The immediate consequence of this is the increasing competitive pressures in the domestic market. In the long run, it is expected that the Indian automobile industry including the components segment will take shape along the lines of global automobile industry.[36]

The global automobile industry is currently undergoing a structural change. Faced with severe competition that is forcing cost reductions, the vehicle industry is going in for consolidation at the manufacturing level and tierisation of the component supply chains.[37] International vehicle manufacturers are consolidating their positions through acquisitions and mergers so as to produce many models economically.[38] These manufacturers are also trying to reduce their costs through the rationalisation of their supply chains. Instead of buying individual components from the numerous component manufacturers and assembling them in their own premises, vehicle manufacturers have started purchasing the systems like the entire engine. In this way, these producers are reducing several of their costs namely, overhead costs, transaction costs, and research and development costs. Vehicle manufacturers are also asking component suppliers to share warranty costs. The system suppliers form tier one in the supply chain and are expected to play a significant role in the development and production of the vehicle. System suppliers further procure sub-systems or components from the other suppliers. These other suppliers form either tier two or three in the supply chain. To become a tier one company, component suppliers have to be really large and technology leaders. Consequently, the component industry is expected to witness a spate of mergers, acquisitions and alliances. So, the future of component suppliers lies in getting into the supply chains, which further depends on their ability to operate globally, integrate systems, raise quality and manage warranty costs.[39]

In sum, the Indian automotive components industry was so far organised on the lines of a 'dominant firm with a competitive fringe' where, the competitive fringe comprises numerous small-scale units producing simple components or components that have high excise duty with older machinery. The new economic policy reforms of the nineties have changed the situation drastically by reducing the importance of fiscal concessions on the one side and by raising the market competition on the other. Industry is now facing direct competition from the international players. In order to deal with the situation, Indian component manufacturers including the dominant players have to improve their technology as also quality and have to get into the global supply chains of the vehicle manufacturers[40] or into the dealer network for the replacement market. In particular, small-scale units have to phase out their older and manual machinery by new and automatic machinery, and to adopt new organisational methods like total quality management systems so as to supply consistent quality products in time.

5.3.2 Electronics

Indian electronics industry[41] comprises six categories namely, consumer electronics, instrumentation and industrial electronics, data processing systems and other office equipment, communication and broadcasting equipment, strategic electronics and electronic components. The consumer electronics segment includes products like TVs, radio receivers, tape recorders, VCR and VCPs, electronic watches and clocks, etc. Instrumentation and the industrial electronics segment covers special application instruments, process control equipment and power electronics equipment for industrial use, and medical equipment such as CT scanners, ultra sound scanners and blood glucose analysers. Data processing systems and office equipment refers to computers, CRT terminals, printers, electronic typewriters, electronic intercoms, paper copiers, etc. Communication and broadcasting equipment includes products like telephone instruments, teleprinters, facsimile, electronic switching equipment, electronic telex exchanges, two-way radio communication equipment and so on. Strategic electronics segment produces all those electronic products used in the areas of aerospace and defence. The electronic components sector produces both general-purpose components like capacitors, resistors, connectors, printed circuit boards (PCB), transformers, transistors that are used in all electronic equipment, and special purpose components like TV components.[42]

The electronics industry constitutes 7–8 percent of the manufacturing value added.[43] It is one of the labour-intensive industries in India though there has been a decline over time in its labour intensity and hence its employment generating capacity.[44] The total direct employment in the industry increased from 130,000 persons in 1981 to 345,000 persons in 1997.[45] It is also one of the fast growing industries of India. This can be seen from the growth of production of the industry from 150 million rupees in 1960 to 1,730 million rupees in 1971; 8,885 million rupees in 1980; 102,000 million rupees in 1991–92, and to 221,000 million rupees in 1997–98.[46] This growth of the industry is primarily due to the phenomenal growth of consumer electronics segment especially TV and audio systems (over 35 percent per annum during the 1980s).[47] The growth of these two subsectors not only led to the growth of the industry directly but also indirectly via growth in the components segment. It is because 70 percent of the production of the components segment goes to consumer electronics (60% to TV production and 10% to the production of audio systems) and only 30 percent to the other segments of the industry.[48]

Of all the segments, consumer electronics contributed a major proportion (34.4%) of the industry's production in 1997–98 followed by the components segment (19.9%). Instrumentation and industrial electronics, and communication and broadcasting equipment accounted for about 14 percent each in the total production of the industry. Data processing and office equipment constituted another 13 percent of the industry's production. The remaining 4 percent of the industry's production came from the strategic electronics segment.[49] The contribution of different segments for various time points is given in Table A.8 in Appendix A.

At the industry level, around 13 percent of the domestic production has been exported during 1997. At the segment level, data processing system stands first with exports amounting to almost 45 percent of its production. Electronic components occupy the second place with 19 percent of its production going in for exports. Exports from the other segments are much lower in percentage terms.[50]

Bangalore, Bombay, Pune, and Delhi have been the traditional centres of the industry. Bangalore has the major public sector corporations, Bombay and Pune have large-scale private units, and Delhi has been hosting a large number of small-scale private units.[51]

As regards the industry structure, there were 3500 units engaged in electronics production during 1997, of which 71 are public sector units, 625 units are in the organised private sector and more than 2800 are registered small-scale units. In addition, there were numerous unregistered smaller units engaged in the assembly of consumer electronics, instruments and electronic components. The top 200 units including 50 small-scale units account for nearly 73 percent of the industry's production.[52] Thus, the industry can be taken to have a competitive market structure.

Small-scale sector accounts for nearly 35 percent of production and 48 percent of employment of the electronics industry.[53] Majority of these units are located in the Delhi region and involved mostly in the production of consumer electronics, computers and components.[54] Some of the consumer electronics products that have been produced by the small-scale sector are TVs, tape recorders, calculators, etc. The manufacturing process in a majority of the cases consisted of manual assembly of mainly imported components.[55] But for a few of the traditional consumer goods like black and white TV and radio receivers whose inputs are produced mostly locally, imports constitute at least half of the required materials and components.[56] Hence, materials and labour are the significant constituents of the cost of production. Most of these units produce low-quality products at lower prices for the lower end segment of the local markets. Even in the components segment, small-scale units are confined to simple assembly-oriented components that require lower investments in plant and machinery. Most of these components are used in consumer products. Some of the components that are typically produced in the small-scale sector are mechanical TV tuners, audio tape deck mechanism, DC micro-motors, magnetic heads, loud speakers and its parts, transformers, foils, printed circuit boards (PCB).[57] Some of the small-scale units also do job work for one or two large-scale units as the latter want to reduce labour costs and avoid unionised workforce.[58]

Currently, the Indian electronics industry is undergoing transformation due to the new economic policy of the 1990s and the rapid technological developments in the electronics area. As a part of its new economic policy, the Indian government has liberalised the wide spectrum of investment, trade and fiscal policies relating to the electronics industry. With the de-licensing of the entire consumer electronics industry and the removal of the restrictions on foreign investments, almost all the important global players like Thomson, Sony, National, LG, and Samsung have entered the Indian industry either directly or through collaborations with the local companies. These multinational companies brought in the renowned global brands and offering consumers wider choice in terms of product features, quality and competitive prices.[59] In addition, all the components, raw materials and capital goods relating to the industry have been made free to import and duties on these imports are reduced.[60] Import duties are rationalised by fixing the duties on raw materials broadly at 35 percent, for processed parts at 50 percent, for components and peripherals at 80 percent and for final products in the range of 90 to 150 percent.[61] All these changes have not only intensified the competition in the domestic market but are also expected to transform the domestic industry on the pattern of international electronics industry.

The international electronics industry has been experiencing faster technological developments. Rapid technological changes are not only affecting the product composition but are also transforming the manufacturing configurations of the industry. Technological progress in the industry is mainly taking place along the lines of integration, miniaturisation, digitalisation and laser-based technology. Integration of image, sound and data from different sources brought together the functions of video products, audio systems and computers under the common platform of multimedia. Multimedia enables consumer electronic products to be integrated with the computers and telecommunications.[62] Miniaturised non-lead components known as surface mount devices (SMD), are replacing the conventional lead components of PCBs. The SMDs, which are also known as 'chip' components offer smaller size, high performance, improved reliability and lower cost for electronic assemblies.[63] Consumer electronics products are increasingly based on digital systems rather than analogue signals. A digital device switches signals rather than smoothly amplifying a signal. It turns the flow of current on or off in response to a signal. Because of this all-or-nothing, in other words one or zero quality, digital devices perform logical operations.[64] Laser technology is increasingly used in the compact disc systems. Digital electronics combined with the optical or laser-based methods of mass storage is minimising undesirable noise.[65] Rapidity of the technological change can be seen in the increasingly short life of some of the basic technology products. For example the life of an application-specific integrated circuit (ASIC) is just over one year.[66]

The aforesaid technological developments, on the one hand, are creating a new set of products that are fast replacing the old ones. For instance, in consumer electronics new products such as high definition, large screen colour TV, CD systems both in audio and video lines are replacing old products like black and white TVs, audio systems, and audio and video cassettes. This can be seen from the short product life cycle, i.e., time period from the commercialisation of a product to the decline of a market for it, for many electronic products. For instance, product life cycle is currently only three years for instrumentation, one and half years for computer products and one year for consumer electronics.[67]

On the other hand, new technologies led to automation in manufacturing[68] as semiconductor technology is more amenable than vacuum tubes to automation of assembly.[69] The new technological developments necessitate the use of costly and complex automated manufacturing and testing facilities and highly skilled personnel.[70] Labour is becoming less important, and capital and technology are increasingly becoming more important factors of production in the electronics industry.[71]

Technological innovations have also offered potential for lower costs at higher volumes[72] and hence making scale important. As a result, large firms dominate the markets although small-scale firms have a scope in niche markets. For example, large firms dominated the established markets in the computer industry where small firms are present in new markets and products.[73]

Technological changes have also made various parts of the industry interdependent and have transformed electronics as a global industry.[74] In the past, functions of research and development, design, manufacturing, sourcing, distribution and end-user application have been carried out in sequence and independently from one another. However, now the trend has changed into the integration and interdependence of all these functions.[75] Materials, parts and subsystems for the manufacture of electronic equipment are sourced worldwide.[76] This trend is forcing firms across the world to go for strategic alliances, joint ventures, equity participation and marketing arrangements.[77]

Another emerging feature of the electronics industry is that the difference in the sophistication and quality between consumer electronics and other sub-sectors like industrial electronics has been vanishing. Similarly, the quality requirements of high-end and low-end products are converging. Slowly, trade-offs among different parameters like quality and cost are disappearing.[78] All these features of the electronics industry indicate that a firm's competitiveness can largely be built through latest technology and supplier and customer networks.[79]

To sum up, the electronics industry in India has so far been dominated by small and medium enterprises that are mostly involved in the manual assembly of low-end consumer electronics with the help of few tools and instruments. However, the entry of global players in the wake of globalisation and liberalisation along with rapid technological developments in electronics is changing the product composition as well as the structure of the industry. The entry of global players has not only intensified competition in this already competitive industry but is likely to transform the Indian electronics industry along the lines of the global structure. These changes are making the manual assembly of lower end products by the small-scale units no longer feasible. The survival of the Indian electronic firms in future depends critically on developing or acquiring and adapting the latest technologies. Given the high costs of technological development and short-product cycles, it is required that the Indian firms to go in for collaboration with other firms both for acquiring technology and for marketing their products. All these demand that the Indian small-scale units effect not a marginal change but a total transformation such as a shift away from manual assembly to automation.

5.3.3 Garments

The garment industry is one of the dynamic sectors of the Indian economy which has grown at a rate of 20 percent per annum during the past two decades.[80] It is also one of the major earners of foreign exchange for the country. The exports of garments were worth US $ 2.58 billion in 1990–91 and has risen to US $ 4.91 billion by 1997–98.[81] These exports accounted for about 9 percent of total Indian exports in 1981–82. The share has almost doubled to 17 percent by 1994–95.[82] The average annual growth rate of garment exports for the period of 1985–86 to 1989–90 has been as high as 32 percent.[83] Nearly 33 percent of the domestic production of hosiery and garments by small-scale industrial units was exported in 1987–88.[84] Garments is also one of the highly labour-intensive and hence employment-generating industries. Direct employment of the sector was about 0.6 million persons in 1980 and has gone up to around 2.0 million persons in 1992.[85]

A description of the garment production process enables us to understand the industry structure better. Production of garments involves a sequence of designing, pattern making, fabric processing and testing, cutting, stitching, zipping/ button work and finishing. Design is a highly creative and skilled activity. Pattern making is a process in which design is translated into a pattern on a cardboard or a particular paper for different sizes and shapes. It is again a highly skilled job. Fabric is cut according to the given specifications by placing it on the relevant pattern marker. Before it is cut, grey fabric is processed for colour, prints, etc. and tested for things like texture and inflammability. The cut pieces are stitched together as per the specifications. Then comes zipping, button working, etc. Once the garment is tailored, it is trimmed, checked for dimensions and then sent for finishing. Finishing involves, washing, spot removing, ironing and packing. Value added activities like embroidery or sequin work are done either before or after the stitching. Of all these, stitching is the major operation both in terms of time involved and costs. Sewing machines constitute around 87 percent of the total machinery and tailors account for 80 percent of the employment of the industry.[86]

All the stages of production are separable allowing an industrial unit to make or subcontract any number of operations. Stitching, the major production operation can be organised in two different ways. The whole garment is stitched either by a single operator or on an assembly line where several operators do a specific stitching each. In addition, all the production operations can be done manually or by manually operated machines or by power operated machines. The industry, hence, permits numerous configurations both in terms of physical technologies and the organisation.

The Indian garment industry began in an unorganised way in the sense that scattered, small players entered the business to avail immediate gains rather than to develop a proper industrial unit. This character was further enhanced by the reservation of garments for exclusive production in the small-scale sector.[87] As a result, the garment industry in India is highly disintegrated and consists of disparate groups of small-scale units which are confined to a particular small acitivity.[88] According to the Textile Committee Report 1991, 80 percent of the units in the industry are very small and tiny units. In a majority of the cases, pattern making, cutting and finishing jobs are done in-house. Tailoring, the basic production operation has, generally, been subcontracted to numerous fabricators located in residential, commercial and industrial areas of metropolitan cities.[89] Fabricators are none other than a group of tailors operating independently with their own sewing machines. Even within the unit, majority of the employees including tailors are hired on contract and paid on a piece rate basis. Significant activities like processing of fabrics and value-added activities like embroidery, applique and sequin work are carried out in several non-descript and tiny units.[90, 91] As regards the physical technologies, industry, at large, employs older technologies. Pattern making and finishing operations are done, mostly, manually. Though cutting machines are present, a good number of units cut the fabric using hand shears and treadle machines. Manually operated sewing machines account for 83 percent of the sewing machines.[92] As the industry consists of a very large number of small-scale units and there are no entry or exit barriers excepting reservation, the industry structure comes nearer to perfect competition.

As regards the market, the Indian garment industry serves both the international and domestic market. However, the two segments of the market are independent of each other in terms of the units serving and the nature of product. This Industry in a way had started in response to the demand in the West, i.e. the export market.[93] The exports of textiles have been subjected to quantitative restrictions in the importing developed countries under the Multi-Fibre Arrangement (MFA) since 1974 which was replaced by the Agreement on Textiles and Clothing (ATC) in 1995. Under MFA/ ATC, quotas are fixed for each exporting country in terms of volumes of exports for different textile products including garments through bilateral negotiations. A major proportion of the Indian garment exports has so far been to quota countries like USA, UK and Germany though the percentage share of these countries in the Indian garment exports has been declining over time.[94] Also, the Indian garment exports are confined to few product categories like men's shirts and women's tops.[95] Further, cotton-based apparel dominate the Indian garment exports and most of the fabric is obtained from the power loom sector.[96] The Indian garment exports are of relatively low value added, non-branded simple products and low fashion garments in the low and medium range prices.[97] Hence, cost competitiveness is more important than product differentiation. Fashion garments are highly seasonal with shorter lifespan on the shelf and thus demanding shorter lead times.[98]

The exports segment of the garment industry has been located in and around three metropolitan centres viz., Delhi, Mumbai and Chennai. These centres accounted for 84 per cent of quantity and 89 per cent of value of Indian garment exports in 1987.[99] Delhi has specialised in fashion garments while Chennai has been in basic garments and Mumbai has both types. Consequently, Delhi's garment units are, at large, smaller than that of Mumbai and Chennai but their exports fetch higher unit value realisation.[100]

A majority of the Indian garment export firms deal indirectly with the marketing and manufacturing of their products. This can be seen from the dominant presence of merchant-exporters and fabricators in the industry. Of the 30,844 garment exporters registered with the Apparel Export Promotion Council (AEPC) by 1994, 9.97 percent were manufacturer-exporters and 90.03 percent were merchant-exporters.[101] At the production level, as mentioned earlier, core tailoring operations are mostly subcontracted to fabricators. The significance of the fabricators can be seen from the fact that they have 71 percent of the total machinery and contribute an equal percentage to the total employment of the industry. It indicates less control over quality, time, costs and the ability to satisfy the customers.[102]

With respect to the domestic market, traditionally, Indians wear custom-tailored clothing made in small tailoring shops that are spread in every nook and corner of the country. It was only in the 1960s that factory-made ready-to-wear clothing known as readymade garments came into practice in large metropolitan cities. Still, a majority of the population even in urban areas go for made-to-measure clothing.[103] Notwithstanding, the domestic market for garments has been growing at a rate of 25 percent per annum and was estimated as worth US $ 5 billion rupees in 1994.[104] Domestic demand is mainly for children's clothing. The domestic market, though large, is less visible as are the units serving it. The garment units serving the domestic market are conconcentrated in three metropolitan cities namely, Delhi, Calcutta and Mumbai.[105] They are highly unorganised and widely scattered in comparison with the exporting units. Further, this domestic market is dominated by wholesale dealers who get the garments made by tiny fabricators after supplying them the sample piece and fabric.

Changes in the rules of international trade in textiles as well as the on-going domestic policy reforms are expected to aggravate the market competition for Indian garment units. As mentioned earlier, international trade in textiles has been regulated by the ATC. As per the ATC, quota restrictions on different textile products by the importing developed countries will be eliminated by the end of 2004. Consequently, international trade in textile products will directly come under the jurisdiction of the World Trade Organisation (WTO). With the elimination of quotas, there would be a free-for-all situation in which a large number of exporting countries have to compete with each other.[106] With the entrance of other low-wage countries like Bangladesh and Vietnam, there would be severe competition for Indian garment units even in the low-end market segment. Integration of the textile trade with the WTO would add to the situation the rigours of some of the new clauses of trade relating to the environment and labour.[107] On the other side, India has already opened its domestic market to textile imports from the United States and European Union as per its bilateral agreements. Import restrictions were to be phased out for several more products by the year 2003.[108] In addition, liberalisation of investment policies is bringing in multinational companies to the domestic market. The net result would be severe competition for Indian garment units in the domestic as well as the export markets.

On the demand side, there has been a shift from the mass produced, standard products to a demand for differentiated ones. This has further transformed the production structures and marketing strategies.[109] The textile industry is transforming into a global industry with different operations of its production located in different countries. This has added several layers to marketing and distribution.[110] Micro-electronics-based technologies like computer-aided design and pattern marking and numerically controlled cutting machines have also come into existence.[111]

In order to effect the above-discussed changes, the Indian garment industry has to undergo a total metamorphosis. First, this would require dealing with the manufacturing and marketing of the products directly. Direct dealing with the manufacturing demands in-housing of tailoring operations immediately and vertical integration of as many operations as possible in the long run. Vertical integration is expected to bring the requisite scale besides control over technology, quality and delivery. In addition, a shift from low quality manually-operated machinery to power-driven machinery is essential to ensure speed and quality. Marketing through direct channels like manufacturer-importers and developing strategic alliances with these help Indian units to get to know the markets as well as technological changes, and equips them better to deal with the rapid market changes.

Of the three selected industries, namely, auto components, electronics and garments, the garments industry is a small-scale industry in that all its units are small-scale. The auto components and electronics industries also have a significant number of small-scale units. While the auto component and garment units have low-key interface customers, a major proportion of small-scale units in the electronics industry deal directly with the consumer market. Market competition has already been severe for the units in all the three selected industries. The new ecomomic policy reforms of India made it inevitable for these industries to integrate with the global industry. At a global level, all the three selected industries are restructured as global commodity chains[112] following the rapid changes in technology as well as markets. Auto components and electronics industries are organised as producer-driven commodity chains and garments as a buyer-driven commodity chain.[113] It is essential for the Indian units to get into these global commodity chains for their future survival for which they have to restructure themselves in terms of physical technology employed, organisation and the products. In this context, in-housing of tailoring operations and acquisition of improved machinery are the basic parameters for the restructuring of garment units. A shift to the sophisticated technology of fully automatic or numerically controlled machinery and to improved organisational methods such as quality management systems, is the primary factor in the case of auto component units. Electronic units are required to get into mechanised production (which is becoming increasingly automated), employ high quality testing instruments and adopt improved organisational methods. In addition, units in all these industries are to integrate themselves with the rest of them through the latest information technologies.

5.4 FACTORS INFLUENCING TECHNOLOGICAL CHANGE

Analysis of section 4.3 brings out that product market, decision makers' perception of market changes, technological capabilities, scale of operation, availability of information, finance, complementary skills and materials, relative factor prices and labour are the possible factors influencing the process of technological change in the small-scale units. In this section, these factors in terms of firm-level attributes and their specific relationship with the technological change are elaborately dealt with.

The first of these is the product market. The kind of product market a unit is serving namely international or domestic market, influences its technological change. For instance, export markets are more competitive, and exporting units are likely to face stricter norms in terms of quality that push these units to improve their technology relative to the units serving the domestic market. Similarly, we expect the units catering to the national market, which is wider as compared to local markets, to have more incentives as well as pressures to go in for technological upgradation due to greater demand and more competition. Original equipment manufacturers for specific customers usually feel more pressures to go for improvements in machinery, quality management systems and other organisational methods compared to units catering to the replacement market.

Owner-manager's perception of product market changes is taken in terms of their views on demand for the product, market competition and the likely impact on the concerned unit.[114] If owner-managers view that demand is a problem in the sense that it is stagnant or falling, they do not have an incentive to make improvements in the technologies of their plants.[115] On the other hand, rising demand for the product induces units to go for technological upgradation. If the markets are becoming increasingly competitive in the owner-managers' view, they consider upgradation of technology so as to improve their units' competitive strength and to maintain commercial viability. Finally, if owner-managers consider the market changes as opportunities of growth for their units, they go ahead with the technological change.

Technological capabilities of the units are deduced from the formal education of owner-managers, their experience in the relevant area and the extent of the use of professional labour. It is argued that the higher the education and experience of the owner-managers, greater is the unit's capabilities to undertake and manage technological change, as educated and experienced owners understand technologies and markets better and can relate them easily. The larger the proportion of professional labour, the easier it is for the units to master new technologies and in less time.

Scale of operation is taken in terms of annual sales turnover because it is how much the unit sells that matters in deciding whether or not to go for changes in technology as well as the type of technology that the unit should adapt. Larger firms vis-à-vis smaller firms are usually in a better position to undertake changes in terms of resources and market to absorb the consequent rise in production.

It is easier for the unit to search for and select new technologies if it has better access to information, which in turn depends on the sources of information. Access to information can be taken as better if the unit makes use of multiple sources of information rather than relying on one or two sources of information. Alternatively, inaccessibility to information can be deduced from the concerned unit's difficulties in obtaining information.

With respect to the access to finance, the greater the access, the easier it is for the firms to go for technological changes. Better access to finance also widens the units' choice. Access to finance can be considered better if the unit has easy access to financial institutions including commercial banks rather than relying solely on the personal finances of the owner-manager. Alternatively, the unit's access to finance can be deduced from its problem in obtaining finance.

Availability of skills and materials play a role in the selection of new technology only when the unit is looking for a technology that is radically different from the existing ones. Another factor that influences the selection of technology is relative factor prices. If labour is cheaper compared to capital, units are expected to select labour-intensive technology that reduces their cost of production.

As regards the role of labour, the behaviour and attitudes of the workforce not only affect the absorption of technological changes but can also induce these changes. The existing labour laws in India make labour as fixed instead of a variable factor. It not only hikes the price of labour but also affects adversely the work culture and attitudes of labour. Although most of the small-scale units being non-factory units come out of the rigours of labour laws, labour legislation can still cause the growing units to go for higher levels of mechanisation as it requires less labour to operate. Once a unit undertakes changes in its technology, the attitudes and behaviour of the existing labour play an important role in the absorption of these changes. Attitudes of labour are taken in terms of their willingness to work and learn, i.e. whether labour gives its best even when the owner-manager is away and is willing to work on new machinery.[116] If the labour attitudes are positive (negative) and hence (not) giving their best when owner-manager is away or (un) willing to work on a new machine, it is (difficult) easier for the units to master the technologies and get maximum benefits.

The behaviour of labour is considered in terms of absenteeism, unionisation and turnover of the workforce. While absenteeism and unionisation problems are mostly associated with the regular workers, turnover generally presents among the casual workforce. Even if labour laws do not apply to non-factory small-scale units, regularisation of at least a part of the labour is common due to the fact that the operation and maintenance of production operations require special (process and machine-specific) skills in a majority of the industries including the auto components and electronics. These skills are to be imparted within the unit, as they are not easily available. Once the trained worker leaves a unit, it not only suffers an immediate loss of production but also has to train new persons again. It becomes a big problem if there is high rate of turnover. To avoid this situation, units in these industries employ part of their labour on a regular basis. Notwithstanding the presence of a regular workforce, problems of unionisation and absenteeism are lesser given the small number of employees per unit and informal and personal relations between the workers and owner-manager. Labour problems in the small-scale units are mostly due to the attitudes and turnover of the labour.[117] However, this is not the case with the industries like garments where labour is hired on contract and paid on a piece rate basis (see section 5.3). This kind of arrangement is possible as the skills required for tailoring and many other jobs of garment production are easily available. Also, majority of the labour in the garment industry such as tailors, work independently outside the factory premises. Consequently, most of the labour attitudes and problems in this industry are related to maintaining quality and delivery timings of the product.

All these analytical factors including technology, and the firm-level characteristics representing these factors are given in Appendix B. The importance of these factors varies not only across firms but also across industries and regions. For example, competitiveness of the market, demand for the product, availability of skills and materials, all vary across industries.[118] So, it has been decided to study whether there have been any variations in the factors influencing firm-level technological change across the industries.

In addition, the study examines the impact of technological change on the competitive strength of the units. Competitive strength of a firm can be defined as its ability to do better than comparable firms in sales or, market shares or, profitability.[119] Technological change is taken as the primary determinant of the improvements in competitive strength that comes through cost reductions or through quality or productivity improvements or a combination of these. Consequently, this study seeks to investigate the impact of technological change on competitive strength of small units taken in terms of sales performance and factor productivities. Sales performance is expected to reflect all the components of the competitive strength mentioned above.

5.5 THE QUESTIONNAIRE AND THE SAMPLE

5.5.1 Questionnaire

Information relating to all the above-mentioned characteristics of the units is collected through a field survey of industrial units using a structured questionnaire. The questionnaire includes questions about the numerous variables and characteristics relating to the above-mentioned factors. To frame questions that are easily understandable to small units so as to capture reality better, firm-level characteristics are further deduced into field-level parameters. Majority of the characteristics are captured through objective criterion as well as subjective opinions of owner-manager as we believe the latter plays an equally important role in the decision-making.

Both the current levels as well as the changes over time are considered for all the three aspects of technology, viz. transformation, organisation and information. The levels and changes in any technological aspect should not be treated as totally different characteristic but are to be taken as different ways of looking at the same characteristic. Transformation technology in our selected industries mainly refers to mechanisation as it reflects the changes in the other components such as product composition. Technological changes in this respect are, thus, the changes in machinery and tools including the shift from manual operation to mechanisation. It is important to note here if a newly acquired machine is the same as that of the existing ones we consider it as capacity expansion in the case of additional machinery, and maintenance of capacity in the case of replacement of machinery but not as technological change. If the newly acquired machine is different from the existing ones in terms of its ability to improve the quality of the product or to speed up the production operation or due to the introduction of a new product, it is treated as a part of technological change. [see Block V in the questionnaire for changes in the existing technology].

As regards the level of mechanisation, we have considered four levels keeping the characteristics of selected industries in mind. They are: only tools and instruments, manually operated machines, semi-automatic machines and numerically controlled/ computerised machines [Block IV (A-D)]. As discussed in section 5.2, some of the electronic units are engaged in the manual assembly of bought-out components of simple products. These units employ tools like soldering iron to assemble the components and a few instruments like multimeters to test the product at various stages. Similarly, garment units that farm out a 100 percent of their tailoring operations have only cutting and ironing machines in their plants which are nearer to tools than to machines. So, we have decided to include the category of 'only tools and instruments'.

Organisation at a structural level is taken in terms of three forms of business organisation and two kinds of management. The three forms of business organisation that have been considered in the study are—proprietorship, partnership and limited company[120] [See II (E)]. Management is primarily considered in terms of owner-management as it is the most widely practised among the small-scale units. In the case of non-owner management, we have taken into account two kinds, viz., general and specialised. Specialised management refers to management by function-specific managers who have acquired specialised skills in specific areas like finance, production and marketing. On the other hand, general management refers to management by one or two general purpose managers supervising all aspects of manufacturing [II (H)]. At an operational level, the organisation includes plant layout, material management, quality management, production schedules and work allocation. Under the materials management, suppliers of materials, methods of procuring materials and inventories of materials are covered [IV (F)]. Questions about quality management are posed in terms of recognised standards of quality of the product like that of the Bureau of Standards or systems like ISO 9000 series or physical check up of product by the unit before it is packed and sent out [IV (G)]. Physical check up of every single piece produced is in practice in garment units and in some of the electronic units. Work allocation refers to the ways of assignment of jobs to workers—whether jobs are fixed or rotating, and whether a worker is given a single or multiple jobs at a time. The latter concept applies more to the auto component or electronics industry where semi-automatic machines are present. These machines enable a worker to operate 2 or 3 machines at a time [IV (E)].

Information technology is taken in terms of the ways of communication with the outside agents and the kinds of storing and processing of data within the unit. Three ways of communication viz., person/post/ phone, fax, and electronic mail and two ways of storing and processing of data (data management) namely, paper files and computers, are considered for the purpose of the study [IV (H-K)].

Owner-managers' perception of product market changes are considered in terms of whether they consider demand a constraint, markets competitive and the changes in the market as opportunities of growth for their units. Questions related to the reasons for increasing market competition, ways of dealing with the changing markets and collection of market information are also included. About the kind of product market that is being served by the units, we have taken into account the export market, domestic market (national as well as local), specific customers and after market. After-market or the replacement market is relevant in the case of the auto components industry. In addition, there are questions about the payment period and problems, distribution channels and brand names. The brand name applies more to electronic units that are engaged in the production of consumer electronics. [All these questions are covered in block VII (A-L).] Technological capabilities of the units are captured through the various attributes of owner-managers including their education and experience in the relevant area [block VI (A-G)]. In addition, we have a provision in the questionnaire to collect information about the level of education possessed by workers [III (C)].

Units' sources of information regarding technologies as well as their difficulties in getting it are captured through a set of questions given in block VIII in the questionnaire. We have tried to capture all the possible sources of information namely, trade fairs, trade journals, consultancy organisations, suppliers of machinery, internet, seminars and conferences, business associates, industry associations and customers.

The sources of finance for the units and their problems in obtaining finance are covered through the questions presented in block X in the questionnaire. In this case, the option of personal/relatives/friends has been included as it is the most important source of finance for the small-scale units. In addition, financial institutions like commercial banks, chit funds/credit co-operatives, equity finance by larger firms have also been considered.

Information about the role of availability of skills and materials and the existing relative factor prices in the technological change, is collected through a direct question related to the reasons for the selection of technology [block XI]. Information about the behaviour and attitudes of labour is captured through a set of questions related to turnover, absenteeism, unionisation and training of workers, and willingness of workers to work on new machine. These questions are presented in block XIII in the questionnaire.

Numerical information relating to sales turnover and the values of inputs like plant and machinery, materials and labour have also been collected [block III].

In addition, numerous other areas such as sources of technology including the use of first/second-hand machinery and Indian/imported machinery [block IX], ways of technology acquisition [block XII], general information like year of establishments and factory status have been covered [block II]. Along with the sales turnover, a provision for the percentage of in-house production in the case of garment units in view of the existing practice of subcontracting in the industry has been given. Finally, given the policy protection afforded to the small scale sector and the fact that the business environment so far is controlled by the government policies, questions relating to government assistance to these units and the owner-managers' opinion about government policie have been included [block XIV].

Questions relating to the subjective opinions of owner-manager, mostly, have a three-point ordinal scale with 0, 1 and 2. Zero indicates the absence, one means presence and two means presence with a high degree of a given problem like market demand, information and finance availability or a given situation like competitiveness of market. Education of the owner-managers is again considered in three ordered categories such as schooling and less (1), more than schooling but non-professional (2) and professional (3). Professionals include engineers, MBAs, CAs and lawyers. In the case of sources of information and finance, types of markets, reasons for market competition, views about government policies, etc. there are unordered categories. In addition, a good number of catergorical questions like whether the unit has undergone technological change, whether the unit availed of any assistance from the government and so on are included.

The questionnaire has been structured to have 13 blocks to collect the information under different headings like general information, outputs and inputs, existing technologies, changes in the technologies over time, owner-manager's profile, market profile, sources of information about technology, sources of finance, sources of technology, selection of technology, ways of technology acquisition, labour or technical personnel, government policies. Numerical data such as sales turnover, labour and investment pertain to the year 1998–99. The questionnaire is presented in the Appendix B.

5.5.2 The Sample

Using the above-discussed questionnaire, information has been collected to examine the factors determining technological change in the small-scale units through a field survey of these units in the selected industries. For the purpose of the survey, the official definition of small-scale industrial units has been followed. Small-scale industrial units are defined in terms of a maximum ceiling limit on the original value of investment in plant and machinery, which was 30 million rupees during the period of field survey.[121] It has been confirmed during the field visits whether the unit is a registered small-scale unit, if not whether its original investment in plant and machinery is less than or equal to the official limit. Within this broadly defined set, the sample has been selected using purposive sampling. The purposive sampling method has been preferred instead of random sampling for reasons of non-availability of the complete list of small-scale units and the nature of study.

Random sampling requires a list of all the existing small-scale industrial units in the specified region. The only list that may be available in this respect is that of small-scale industrial units that are registered with the state Directorates of Industries. The selected region of the study necessitates obtaining the required list from three state Directorates of Industries, namely, Delhi, Haryana and Uttar Pradesh. Given the time frame and the number of personnel of the project, this is difficult. Difficulties are further compounded in terms of time and personnel if one wants the list to be industry- and city- specific. The list of small-scale industrial units registered with the state Directorates of Industries, even if available, does not cover the entire set of the existing small-scale industrial units as the registration is voluntary.[122] Estimates reveal that at least one-fifth of the total small-scale industrial units are not registered with the Directorates of Industries.[123]

The ultimate purpose of selecting a sample is to make judgments about the population in terms of the specified characteristics on the basis of the sample characteristics. An efficient sampling design like the random sampling is expected to eliminate the sampling errors, i.e. the difference between the value of the estimator and true value of the population parameter to be estimated.[124] However, random sampling or for that matter any other sampling design cannot take care of non-sampling errors relating to non-response, incorrect response and others which are often far more important than the sampling errors.[125] Non-sampling errors are particularly high in the context of small-scale industrial units. Small-scale industrial units especially the smaller ones are known for their poor response to surveys. Even when they respond, most of the smaller units are not in a position to provide reliable information as they hardly maintain records.[126]

In addition, if the research objective is to study any economic phenomenon closely, the sample has to be smaller in size and richer in information relating to the phenomenon and respondents have to be highly co-operative—conditions that a random sample can hardly satisfy. In such a situation, the researcher may have to select his sample in such a way that it satisfies these conditions.[127] In the current study, the objective is to examine the factors influencing the process of technological change that requires a close probing of industrial units. So the sample needs to be selected in such a way that the selected units are willing to respond, provide reliable information, and there is a high likelihood that at least some of the selected units have undergone technological change. Such a sample may not allow us to obtain quantitative estimates to approximate population parameters, but yields qualitative information that is relevant beyond the sample, to some extent to the entire population.[128]

Keeping the above-mentioned conditions in mind, purposive sampling has been opted for and the desirable sample has been obtained by approaching the relevant government agencies and industry associations. The concerned government agencies that have been approached are Small Industries Development Bank of India (SIDBI), National Small Industries Corporation of India (NSIC) and the relevant offices of Delhi Administration. SIDBI and NSIC could get us very few units in the selected region and industries, as their coverage is much wider. As regards the business associations, in the beginning, industry-specific associations like Automotive Components Manufacturers Association (ACMA), Electronics Components Industries Association (ELCINA), Apparel Exporters and Manufacturers Association (AEMA) and Garment Exporters Association (GEA) were approached. Since the coverage of these associations is wider in terms of location and size, to get a readily available list of specified units found to be difficult. Thereafter, the local industry associations such as Okhla Industries Association, Faridabad Small Industries Association, Noida Small and Tiny Industries Association were contacted. These associations again could locate the names of a few more units but were not able to provide a readily available list of units, as their members are not organised on the basis of industry. In addition, the informal networks of the industrial units were made use to get the required sample within time limits.

The questionnaire was filled by a direct interview with the owner-managers of the sample units. Along with the collection of information through the filling of the questionnaire, the factory premises of the each selected unit were visited to confirm the same. Thus collected information have been processed and analysed to examine the evidence for the research objectives of the study in the next few chapters.

Endnotes

1. National Capital Region includes, apart from our selected areas, Sonipat, Panipat, Rohtak and Rewari districts of Haryana, Ghaziabad, Bullandshahr, Meerut districts of Uttar Pradesh and Alwar district of Rajasthan. National Capital Region Planning Board (hereafter referred as NCRPB) (2000:11)
2. Gulati (1997:36–40)
3. The only exception being state government policies and administration as the selected areas belong to different states.
4. In this respect, NCRPB (2000:22) states: "… better social and physical infrastructure in Delhi have greatly influenced in past the decision making regarding location of industry and trade." "…it (Delhi) gradually emerged as a big distribution centre and almost every wholesale trade generated from North India found its base in Delhi. The area of procurement and distribution cover a wider field and extends not only over to North India but for some commodities even the whole of India." (p. 25) Parentheses added.
5. NCRPB (2000:22) states that "it (Delhi) has also developed as a centre of international commerce, banking and insurance institutions and provides ample opportunities to the people for international commercial dealings." Parentheses added.
6. NCRPB (2000:22)
7. Faridabad is an old industrial town and both Gurgaon and Noida are upcoming industrial towns developed by the respective state governments.
8. It does not mean that all is well and there is no problem at all in the NCR of Delhi. But definitely, this region is a better place compared to many other places in India.
9. See Appendix B for the list of reserved items in the selected industries.
10. ICRA (1999:36–37)
11. ICRA (1999: 31)
12. ICRA (1999: 3)
13. ICRA (1999:104)

14. Narayana (1989:43); NCAER (1999:25)
15. These percentages refer to the year 1996- 97. Domestic market demand is calculated as the sum of domestic production and imports minus exports. The contribution of the domestic industry is taken as the percentage share of domestic production minus exports in the domestic market demand. Domestic production, exports and imports of the automotive components are given in ACMA (1997–98:35,82&89)
16. ACMA (1997–98:35). Group-level contribution is not available for the unorganised sector.
17. ICRA (1999: xi)
18. ICRA (1999:110)
19. ICRA (1999:33–4)
20. NCAER (1999:2.15)
21. ICRA (1999: 36)
22. ICRA (1999: 38); These figures seem to be likely guesstimates as they differ from study to study. For instance, NCAER (1999:2) reports that "the auto component industry comprises 600 units in the organised sector and there are approximately 6000 units engaged in fabrication of automotive components in the small scale sector."
23. Carlton and Perloff (1990:180–85)
24. ICRA (1999: 32, 40); Narayana (1989:39–40); and Gumaste (1988:70)
25. ICRA (1999:55,104); ICRA study discusses the industry leaders of many automotive components.
26. Narayana(1989:49)
27. ICRA (1999: 41)
28. ICRA (1999: 37)
29. ACMA (1997–98:35)
30. ICRA (1999: 38); NCAER (1999:2.11)
31. ICRA (1999: 38)
32. ICRA (1999: 104)
33. Narayana (1989:10–12)
34. ICRA (1999: 30); Narayana (1989: 44–46); Varadharajan and Kannan (1998:299)
35. Delphi and Visteon are controlled by General Motors and Ford respectively. These two companies manufacture almost all the automotive

components with a few exceptions. *Business India*, April 19 - May 2, 1999, pp. 113–116

36. This has already been perceived by some of the Indian companies. See for instance, Suresh Krishna, Chairman and Managing Director, Sundaram Fasteners Ltd. says, "I don't think India will be able to bypass the global trend of mergers and acquisitions. There will be contraction of players in India." *Business India*, April 19 - May 2, 1999, p. 113
37. ICRA (1999:20–23)
38. See "Whose Car Is It Anyway?" in *Business Standard*, Weekend, July 15/16, 2000, p. viii for the picture of consolidation of major international players like General Motors, Ford, Daimler Chrysler, Volkswagen and Fiat.
39. ICRA (1999:7)
40. ICRA (1999:105 &111)
41. The present study considers only hardware not software.
42. Guide to Electronics Industry (hereafter GEI) (1999:1.4–1.11)
43. Gowen and Hefler (1993:209)
44. Gowen and Hefler (1993:120); Bagchi (1995:16); Joseph (1995:132)
45. GEI (1999:120)
46. GEI (1999:1.4)
47. GEI (1999:120); Gowen and Hefler (1993:209)
48. GEI (1999:1.9)
49. GEI (1999:1.4)
50. GEI (1999:7.1)
51. GEI (1999:1.16)
52. GEI (1999:1.13)
53. See Table A.9 in the Appendix A.
54. GEI (1999:1.16 & 1.18); Also see Table A.10 in Appendix A for the segment-wise share of small-scale units.
55. Chhachhi (1999:9); Joseph (1995:129); Khan (1997:15); and Papola (1989:75)
56. Gowen and Hefler (1993:209)
57. GEI (1999:1.10&1.16)
58. Chhachhi (1999:11&12); Papola (1989:75); Chatterjee (1998:141)
59. GEI (1999:1.2)

60. GEI (1999:1.3); and *The Hindu Survey of Indian Industry*, p.121
61. Gowen and Hefler (1993:212); Chhachhi (1999:12)
62. Ex-Im Bank (hereafter referred as EIB) (1996:51&53)
63. EIB (1996: 83)
64. Langlois *et al* (1988:9)
65. Langlois *et al* (1988:9:50&51)
66. Miller (1993:19)
67. Miller (1993:19)
68. Wellenius (1993:5); Miller (1993:18)
69. Hart (1993:63)
70. Wellenius (1993:7); Joseph (1995:136); Sakuma (1995:177)
71. Wellenius (1993:6); Kimmel (1993:158- 59); Gowen and Hefler (1993:214)
72. Wellenius (1993:5)
73. Flamm (1993:49)
74. Langlois *et al* (1988: 5- 7)
75. Thomson (1993:96); Miller (1993:19)
76. Kimmel (1993:156–58); Miller (1993); Wellenius (1993)
77. Thomson (1993:96–98)
78. Miller (1993:18–21)
79. Wellenius (1993:6); Ernst and O'Connor (1992:9)
80. NIFT (1998:2)
81. NIFT (1998:2)
82. See Table A.11 in the Appendix A
83. Chatterjee and Mohan (1993)
84. *Report on the Second All-India Census of Small Scale Industrial Units,* p.119
85. Koshy (1997:72)
86. Textile Committee Report 1991 cited in Berry (1997:3&7)
87. The production of garments has been reserved for small-scale units officially defined in terms of ceiling limit on the original value of investment in plant and machinery. This industry was opened for large-scale units in July 1993 subject to an export obligation and a limit on the investment in plant and machinery. Recently, Government of India has de-reserved the

garments industry unconditionally. *Economic Survey* 2000- 2001, p. 145

88. Koshy (1997:1); Khanna (1991:77)
89. Khanna (1991:114)
90. Koshy (1997:1)
91. Data relating to the various aspects of the industry are almost non-existent even with the government as it is highly unorganised. Whatever little information is available pertains to the export sector (Khanna 1991: 47–48). Most of the details are collected through primary surveys conducted by individuals. Accordingly, details presented in this section, mostly, relate to the export segment. Limited qualitative information presented about the domestic market is collected through the author's interaction with the industry associations and individual entrepreneurs.
92. Koshy (1997:72–73); Khanna (1991:127)
93. Khanna (1991:104)
94. Bhavani and Tendulkar (2000:4)
95. These two items together constitute 40.25 percent in quantity and 43.48 percent in value of total garment exports in the year 1994. See Koshy (1997:16); Khanna (1991:77–78); Ramaswamy and Gereffi (1998:125)
96. 81.44 percent of the exports in 1994 were of cotton garments. See Koshy (1997: 83); Khanna (1991:41 & 78)
97. For cotton woven garments, unit value realisation (UVR) of India is much lower than Malaysia, Hong Kong and China. See Koshy (1997:83); Khanna (1991: 41&78); Meyanathan and Ahmed (1994:15)
98. Koshy (1997:43)
99. Khanna (1991:104)
100. Koshy (1997:52&82); Khanna (1991:116)
101. Koshy (1997:68)
102. Textile Committee Report 1991 cited in Berry (1997:4&6)
103. Khanna (1991:104)
104. Koshy (1997:12)
105. Textile Committee Report 1991 cited in Berry (1997: 3)
106. Quota regime led to the entrance of several countries in to the textile exports than otherwise. See Raffaelli (1994:67)
107. Some of the companies surveyed by the author reported that they had to satisfy environmental and labour standards to procure export orders.

108. WTO (1998:146)

109. Meyanathan and Ahmed (1994:10)

110. Pepper and Bhattacharya (1994:5, 55)

111. Meyanathan and Ahmed (1994: 2)

112. Gereffi (1995)

113. Gereffi (1995:113- 16); Ramaswamy and Gereffi, (1998:123)

114. Perceptions are important, as people act not the basis of reality but on their perception of reality. Refer to footnote 13 in chapter 4.

115. It is quite possible that units may go for technological change through product diversification if the demand for their product is falling.

116. This is relevant in the case of small units where owner-managers deal with the outside agents along with the direct supervision of production activities, are away from the units for quite some time in a day. Also, workers try the new machine mostly under the supervision of owner-managers.

117. Empirical evidence points that there is a problem of turnover in small-scale units. See Patvardhan (1985) and Ramesh (1991).

118. As mentioned in the earlier chapter, literature has ample evidence on the inter-industry variations. See Cohen (1995).

119. Lal (2000:4)

120. These are the common forms among Indian small-scale units. See section 2.2.

121. In December 1999, the ceiling limit has been reduced to 10 million rupees. See Appendix A, Table A.1.

122. Registration is necessary only when a unit wants to avail any policy assistance such as finance.

123. *Handbook of Industrial Policies and Statistics 1998*, Ministry of Industry, Government of India, New Delhi

124. Kmenta (1971:8)

125. Vaidyanathan (1989:18)

126. Sample survey registered SSI units conducted by DCSSI for the year 1999- 2000 shows that only 15 percent of these units maintain records. *Handbook of Industrial Policies and Statistics 2002*, p.176

127. Rudra ((1989:218)

128. Rudra ((1989:218)

Chapter 6

Empirical Analysis: *Methodology*

6.1 INTRODUCTION

This chapter deals with the methodology used for the empirical examination of the primary objectives of study, namely, factors influencing unit-level technological change and the impact of technological change on the unit's competitive strength.

We have conceptualised firm-level technological change, identified the possible factors influencing it, and deduced these factors further into firm-level characteristics in chapters 4 and 5. Our analysis concentrates on three dimensions of technology, namely, transformation, organisation and information, and relates them to different characteristics of the firm. The firm-level characteristics that are taken to represent the three dimensions of technology are: mechanisation, form of business organisation, type of management, plant layout, materials management, production schedules, work allocations, quality management, means of communication and information/ data management. Analysis of the study indicates that product market, owner-manager's perception of this market, technological capabilities, scale of operation, availability of information, finance, materials and skills, relative factor prices and labour are important factors in determining firm-level technological change. These factors are further taken in terms of the product market served, owner-manager's perception of market demand and its competitiveness, education and experience of owner-manager, usage of professional labour, sales turnover, firm's sources of information and finance, owner-manager's opinion about the availability of information, finance, materials, skills, attitudes and behaviour of labour, and relative factor prices. We have considered the consequences of technological change in terms of its impact on competitive strength of the concerned units, which is proxied by sales performance.

To understand the causes and consequences of technological change in the small-scale units, the primary objectives of our study, the author has personally undertaken survey at two levels. First, an *extensive* interaction took place with all those institutions, private as well as public, that are involved in the promotion of small-scale units or the selected industries and located in the National Capital Region of Delhi. This was followed by an *intensive* survey of industrial units in the selected industries. Information relating to all the required characteristics and variables is collected through an intensive survey of industrial units belonging to the three selected industries.

6.2 FIELD IMPRESSIONS REGARDING SMALL UNITS

The author interacted with wide-ranging agencies, from policy-making body like the Development Commissioner, Small Scale Industries (DCSSI) to field level agencies like the Small Industries Service Institute (SISI); from specialised agencies like the Technology Bureau for Small Enterprises (TBSE) to multipurpose bodies like the National Small Industries Corporation (NSIC); from national industry associations like the Confederation of Indian Industry (CII) to the local industries' associations such as the Okhla Industries Association (OIA); from large-scale industries' associations like the PHD Chamber of Commerce to small-scale industries associations like the Faridabad Small Industries Association; from industry-specific associations like the Automotive Components Manufacturers Association (ACMA) to general purpose associations like the Federation of Associations of Small Industries of India (FASII).[1] As it is not a formal survey with a structured questionnaire, free and frank discussions were held in an informal atmosphere with the concerned officials of the relevant organisations with regard to the status of the small-scale units in India especially with respect to technology, possible reasons for their current technological status and its expected consequences in the on-going process of liberalisation and globalisation. These discussions gave the following impressions about the small-scale units in general.

Large majority of the Indian small-scale units are still operating with obsolete technologies, which need to be replaced with more modern technologies. Otherwise, these units may not be able to survive in the era of globalisation and liberalisation. Continuous use of older technologies is due partly to the characteristics of the small-scale units and partly due to policy measures. A majority of these units are owned and managed by people who have limited education and hence lack understanding of newer technology and the wider market that can be accessed. Their problems are compounded by limited information, finance and their smallness. Policy measures could not help small units much in terms of easing the access to essential inputs like finance and information, and in improving the basic infrastructure facilities like roads and electricity. Instead, policy measures provided strong incentives for these units to remain small, the basic reason for most of their problems.

The important observation is about the outlook of small producers who do not visualise their units as industrial units aspiring to grow and establish themselves in the concerned area of production over time. Rather these units are taken as a means of earning. This attitude stems from their background. Most of the small producers are small business people (or self-employed) involved in production activities sensing the opportunities created by supply-demand gaps and policies that can earn them good profits (earnings). This sector has a good presence of traders. These producers shift from sunset activities to sunrise activities, which is made possible by their smaller investments, taking different names for their units. As a result, most of these units never focused on technology upgradation unless it is expected to raise their profits (earnings) substantially.

The most important observation made by all the three parties concerned, namely, government agencies, industry associations and small units, is that small units do not trust either their own associations or government agencies, and hence prefer to go on their own way. This shows the state of affairs of developmental agencies in India without which it is difficult for the small units to grow. It is high time that these organisations instilled trust and confidence in small units so as to make them work collectively to grow. Small units' mistrust was seen in their cold response when the author initially approached the units for the purpose of survey, through associations or government organisations. In fact, author could not continue the survey for this reason.[2]

6.3 REMARKS ON EMPIRICAL ANALYSIS

As regards the presentation of intensive survey information, we first describe the general economic features of our sample units in terms of output, inputs and their ratios like capital and labour productivities. Later, we discuss the evidence regarding sample units' characteristics representing technology (we refer them as *technology characteristics*) and other characteristics (we refer them as *non-technology characteristics*) so as to deduce their relevance for the empirical analysis. Finally, we focus on the relationships among the specified variables.

We have collected information for all the technology and non-technology characteristics specified earlier. Information regarding technology characteristics covers both the current levels/forms as well as changes in these characteristics over time period. We treat a given characteristic as relevant for the empirical analysis if it shows a reasonable variation across the sample units. For instance, type of management is relevant if more than one form is present in the sample. On the other hand, if almost all the sample units are having the same type of management, say, owner-managed, we do not consider the type of management for the further empirical analysis. Similarly, if a particular characteristic, say, production schedules, is too flexible to take care of the day-to-day needs of the units, we do not consider it for the empirical analysis.

Although information about the changes in various technology characteristics along with their levels/forms was collected, information relating to the levels/forms has only been used as far as possible in the econometric estimation since it is a cross-section analysis. Since technological changes refer to improvements in technology, we can analyse the changes in terms of differences in the levels of technologies.

Similarly, although we have taken the form of business organisation like proprietorship as one of the representative characteristics of the organization technology and collected information about it, we have not used it in the econometric estimations. This is because owners decide about business organisation much before the operation of production unit and it reflects owner' preference than any other current characteristics of the units.

As mentioned in section 5.5, the nature of our research problem demands close probing of numerous aspects of firms. Consequently, we could cover only limited number of units for each selected industry although we have collected detailed information for each one of the sample units in our survey. We have taken numerous characteristics to represent the basic variables of study. For instance, we have covered three dimensions of technology i.e., transformation, organisation and information which in turn are represented by many (ten) characteristics of the unit. These technology characteristics could not be aggregated into a meaningful single index. So is the case with the non-technology variables. For example, technological capabilities are represented by three attributes, namely, education and experience of owner-manager, and extent of the use of professional labour. It is difficult to make an aggregate index of these attributes. Hence, we have numerous characteristics in comparison with the number of observations, which limited the use of information and econometric methods.

We could not make use of full information because of limited number of observations. We have three categories for majority of the characteristics but could not make use of them. We have to reclassify them into two categories for the econometric estimation. For instance, we have information about three levels of mechansation for the auto component units i.e., manual, semi-automatic and fully automatic machinery but reclassified the units into having and not having fully automatic machinery. Similarly, we have three levels of education, schooling/more than schooling but non-professional/professional, but has re-ordered these into professional and non-professional.

For the same reason, we could not use all the non-technology characteristics at a time in the equations to examine their importance, as there is a scope for the problem of degrees of freedom. Consequently, we have tried out different combinations of non-technology characteristics to explain technology levels. We can expect other econometric problems like simultaneity, multicollinearity and heteroscedasticity depending on the specification of equations.

In particular, simultaneity problem can arise when we use sales turnover as proxy for scale of operation and thus an independent variable in the technology functions but as a dependent variable in the production function, which has technology variables as explanatory variables. In reality, technology decisions are taken keeping in mind not only the current scale but also the expected sales of future time points. Once technologies are upgraded, it is expected to influence sales. This interdependence of technology and sales turnover give rise to simultaneity problem. We do not, however, expect this problem to be serious as our technology equation is estimated by maximum likelihood method[3], and sales turnover is taken in logarithmic values in the production function.

Nonetheless, we have attempted to establish causal relationships among the specified variables using econometric methods. To be specific, we have used Probit model to explain the technology changes/ levels as it is a binary variable. This technology equation is estimated with the alternative combinations of non-technology characteristics that are taken as independent variables, by Maximum Likelihood method. Impact of technology on the competitive strength of the unit is examined in the production function framework using Cobb–Douglas function and estimated through Ordinary Least Squares method. We elaborate on these in the subsequent sections.

Given the above-discussed problems and the fact that we have used purposive sampling, our estimated coefficients are *not* to be taken as population parameter estimates in a *strict sense*. As mentioned in section 5.5, these coefficients can safely be taken as broad indicators of the specified relationships and their relative significance. Despite these econometric/ sampling problems, we consider it as a useful exercise given the importance of our research problem, i.e. explaining technological change in small units.

6.4. SPECIFICATION & ESTIMATION OF TECHNOLOGY FUNCTIONS

As mentioned earlier, the three dimensions of technology that we have considered for the study, namely, transformation, organisation and information technologies differ from each other. Of these, transformation technology is taken as 'core' technology and analytical factors identified to influence technology primarily apply to this aspect. Organisation and information technologies are to be influenced by a subset of the determinants of transformation technology. Hence, we have specified different equations for the three dimensions of technology in terms of the relevant factors. We start with the transformation technology, which is specified as follows:

TRANS = F (SCA, MKT, OMPM, TC, INF, FIN, OMRFP, OMPMS, LAB) (6.1)

where, TRANS = Transformation technology

SCA = Scale of operation

MKT	=	Kind of product market served
OMPM	=	Owner-managers' perception of market
TC	=	Technological capabilities
INF	=	Availability of information
FIN	=	Availability of finance
OMRFP	=	Owner-managers' views about relative factor prices
OMPMS	=	Owner-managers' views about the availability of materials and skills
LAB	=	Labour problems

Transformation technology is represented by the levels of mechanisation defined differently for the three industries depending on the nature of industry. Further, we have regrouped, as mentioned in the earlier section, all the variables including technology variables into two categories for the estimation purposes keeping the relatively smaller number of observations in mind. For instance, we have three levels of mechanisation (LOM), namely, manual, semi-automatic and numerically controlled (NC) machines in the case of auto component industry. However, we take it as a binary variable with the values of zero and one. For the units having NC machines, LOM is given the value of one and for the remaining units it is taken as zero. By doing so, we are not able to use full information in the econometric estimation but it is justified on the basis of economic reasoning. NC machines are substantially different from others (manual and semi-automatic machinery) in their level of sophistication and treated as distinguishably higher technology. It also requires higher amounts of investment to purchase, and higher levels of skills to operate. In other words, the difference between fully automatic machinery and the other two types is wider than the difference between the other two types of machinery, namely, manual and semi-automatic.

All the variables for which information is obtained through the subjective opinion of the owner-manager, are also brought down to two point scale, i.e., zero and one. In specific, owner-managers' opinion about market demand, labour, and availability of information and finance is taken as zero if they feel it as a problem and as one if they do not treat it as a problem. Similarly, usage of professional labour is taken in terms of its presence or absence, as all the enterprises are not using professional labour. It is denoted by one and zero respectively.

Education of owner-manager, which is considered in three ordered categories, is re-categorised into professional and non-professional, and denoted by one and zero respectively. We have numerous sources of information (unordered), which are regrouped into two, namely, units using single source of information (0) and units using multiple source of information (1). As regards the sources of finance, we have units relying solely on personal/relatives/friends finance (0) and units availing institutional credit (1).

With regard to the estimation of the equation, we have used Probit model as our dependent variable is binary. Since, we have many explanatory variables, most of these having more than one proxy, for the estimation convenience, the equation has been estimated with several alternative combinations of explanatory variables and their proxies. Of the alternatives tried out, we have selected the one which has yielded better results in our opinion.

The organisation aspect of technology is taken in terms of the empirically relevant proxy for it, which may differ from industry to industry. For example, quality management specified as having a total quality system called ISO 9000 tuned out to be empirically relevant proxy for the organisation technology in the case of auto component industry. As discussed earlier, it is taken as a function of a subset of variables that are considered for the transformation technology. These are: scale of operation, kind of market and education of the owner-manager. Accordingly, we write our organisation function as

$$ORG = F(SCA, MKT, EDU/ OE) \tag{6.2}$$

where, ORG = Organisation technology
EDU = Education of owner-manager
OE = Owner's experience

SCA, MKT are as defined for equation (6.1)

So is the case with the information technology. For the purpose of estimation, information technology function is specified as

$$INFT = F(SCA, MKT, EDU) \tag{6.3}$$

where, INFT = Information technology

SCA, MKT, EDU are as defined for equation (6.1) and (6.2)

The exact specification of the functions differs across the selected industries depending on the empirical relevance of the concerned variables.

6.5 ESTIMATION OF THE IMPACT OF TECHNOLOGICAL CHANGE

Firms undertake changes in their technologies, as specified in chapters 4 and 5, to improve their competitiveness. Competitiveness of a firm can be taken as its ability to do better than comparable firms in sales, market shares or profitability.[4] In a highly competitive market environment, relative performance of firm in sales (or market shares or profitability) depends primarily on technology. Technology makes higher sales possible in many ways: through the introduction of a new and superior product; by improving the quality of the existing products, through the efficient utilisation of resources (productivity improvements) resulting in cost reductions, by improving access to customers, or through a combination of these. In other words, technology enables firms to raise their sales by making it possible for them to supply increasing quantities of quality goods at cheaper prices.

Neoclassical economics, as discussed in chapter 4, considers technology as exogenous and given to the economic systems especially at the firm level. It measures, hence, the impact of technology *indirectly* in terms of the changes in factor productivities especially through total factor productivity. Total factor productivity growth (TFPG) was initially identified with the technical change (progress). But, later studies considered technology as one of the primary determinants of TFPG.[5]

In this study, we are trying to measure the impact of technology *directly* by considering it explicitly in the production analysis. To be specific, we introduce technology as one of the inputs along with the conventional inputs like capital, labour and materials in the production function.[6] Further, we take sales turnover as a dependent variable instead of conventionally used production because sales turnover represents the actual size of the market the unit is catering to and hence its competitiveness.[7] Accordingly, our production function is written as

$$Y = A(T)\, f(K, L, M) \tag{6.4}$$

Y = Sales turnover

K = Capital—original investment in plant and machinery

L = Labour—number of employees
M = Materials—value of materials consumed during the year
T = Technology

Since our study covers three dimensions of technology namely transformation, organisation and information, we rewrite the production function given in (6.1) by taking simple Cobb–Douglas form and the three technology variables

$$Y = A K^{\alpha} L^{\beta} M^{\gamma} \quad (6.5)$$

where, $A = e^{\theta_1 T + \theta_2 O + \theta_3 I}$

In the log-linear form, it is written as

$$\ln Y = C + \alpha \ln K + \beta \ln L + \gamma \ln M + \theta_1 T + \theta_2 O + \theta_3 I + \mu \quad (6.6)$$

Y, K, L and M are as defined earlier in (6.4)

T = Transformation technology
O = Organization technology
I = Information technology
μ = Random error term.

We determine the unit-level characteristics representing the transformation, organisation and information technologies from the industry background and the survey data, and specify the exact function in the industry chapters. The specified functions are estimated through Ordinary Least Squares Method. We have used SPSS and LIMDEP software packages for data processing and estimation purposes.

Endnotes

1. The list of organisations visited is given in the Appendix (B4)
2. One of the associations' official suggested the author to approach the units through fellow business associates who have friendly relations and himself sent the author to his friends in the area. This approach helped the author to complete the intensive survey of industrial units.
3. Maximum likelihood estimated are not supposed to get affected by simultaneity like ordinary least squares estimates.
4. Lall (2001: 4)
5. See for example, Ahluwalia (1991); Griliches (1996); Link (1987); and McGuicken, Streitwieser and Doms (1996).
6. Few studies have used this approach earlier. For instance, Griliches (1995) and Stiroh (2001)
7. Although market shares are better proxy for the competitiveness of firms, it is not possible to obtain these as most of the small units operate on the fringe. Hence, we confined to the differences in sales turnover.

Chapter 7 Empirical Analysis of Technological Change: *Auto Components*

7.1 INTRODUCTION

In this chapter, we examine the empirical evidence with reference to the objectives of our study, namely, factors influencing technological change and consequences of technological change for one of the selected industries i.e., auto components.

As mentioned in the previous chapter, we, first, present the economic features of our sample units in terms of output, inputs and some of the structural ratios based on output and inputs. Later, we discuss the evidence regarding technology and non-technology characteristics and their relevance for the empirical analysis of the concerned industry. Finally, using the selected econometric methods, we attempt to measure the relation between technology and non-technology characteristics.

7.2 FIELD IMPRESSIONS

Initially, small-scale auto component units in the vicinity of Delhi were started to cater to the needs of replacement market. The entry of Maruti Udyog Limited and others in the vehicle manufacturing in the eighties opened the market for original equipment. Some of the relatively bigger units hitherto catering to the replacement market diversified into original equipment manufacturing. In addition, many new small-scale units started at this time to supply original equipment to the vehicle industry. These units were mostly setup by professionals such as engineers who had work experience in one of the vehicle manufacturing units and had started their units perceiving the potential gains in the original equipment manufacturing. A few of them do not have any work experience but have good contacts with the management of the vehicles manufacturing units (who may have been relatives or family friends). During the course of time, some of these units have been able to procure bigger orders and have grown up. In the process of growth, these units have accumulated semi-automatic or fully automatic machines depending on the size of their orders and the availability of finances. Some others have added new products to the list of their existing products and hence new machinery.

Globalisation and liberalisation of the nineties had its impact on the original equipment manufacturing segment of the industry. The original equipment manufacturers were pressurised by their customers to improve their quality, efficiency and reduce costs further. A few of the original equipment manufacturers have gone or, trying to go in for total quality management systems like ISO 9000 to improve their prospects in view of the entry of multinational companies. But for the pressures by the parent company to improve their performance, small-scale original equipment manufacturers in the auto components industry do not feel any serious threat to their future. They feel secure as long as their parent companies are safe as they have developed good relations with them and most of them feel strongly that their parent companies have a secure foothold. In fact, some of the Maruti vendor companies have informed the author that Maruti cannot be affected by competition in the near future no matter whichever multinational company enters the market. Some of the units that are not sure of their future growth in auto components have contingent plans to diversify into the other related products.

Original equipment manufacturers are, however, smaller in number compared to the units that serve replacement market in the small manufacturing segment of the auto components industry. Initially, manufacturing segment that serves replacement market has mainly small independent producers. But, over time, wholesale traders of the auto components entered into production of these components. Majority of these units use manual machinery. Use of semi-automatic and numerically controlled machinery is negligible. Small-scale auto component units that are serving replacement market do not feel any pressure or threats. Whatever be the degree of competition in the market, these units feel that it has been there from the beginning and there is nothing new about it.

7.3 BASIC FEATURES OF THE SURVEY UNITS

For the purpose of study, we have surveyed 31 small-scale industrial units producing automotive components. But for two, all the surveyed units are involved in the production of metal products such as sheet metal products, turned components and tubular parts. Production operations of these components are mostly involved pressing, forging and machining. All these operations are possible at different levels of mechanisation in the sense that they can be produced either by manual, semi-automatic, or numerically controlled machines.

7.3.1 General Economic Characteristics

Of the 31 auto component units that have been surveyed, 21 units are registered factories and the remaining 10 units are not registered under the Factories Act. Thirteen units have dispersed their production operations over more than one plant either because of the space constraint or for tax reasons. All the sample units excepting two were started by the current owners themselves and not inherited. Only six of the total 31 units have obtained any government assistance. As regards the opinion about government policies, majority of the sample units (18) have shown indifference. The remaining 13 units felt that government should focus on improving infrastructure, amending labour laws and eliminating inspector raj. It would be of interest to know that not a single sample unit has stated that there should be protection for the small-scale units.

As regards the annual sales turnover of the sample units, it ranges between 15 and 2000 lakhs of rupees with a mean value of 222 lakhs.[1] The sample varies widely (167% as given by the coefficient of variation) around the mean. The annual sales turnover of the 12 sample units is less than 50 lakhs of rupees in the reference year. The sales turnover of six sample units lies in between 50 and 100 lakhs of rupees. The sales turnover of nine sample units comes in the range of 100 to 300 lakhs of rupees. The remaining four units have sales turnover that is greater than 300 lakhs of rupees. Descriptive statistics for the sales turnover are presented along with that of other continuous variables in Table 7.1. Percentage distribution of sample

Table 7.1: **Descriptive Statistics for Output, Inputs and Their Ratios—Auto Components Industry**

Variable	Mean	Minimum	Maximum	Coefficient of Variation	No. of Observations
Sales Turnover (lakhs)	222.19	15.00	2000.00	1.67	31
Plant and Machinery (lakhs)	48.95	0.80	300.00	1.34	31
Total Employment (no.)	45.46	3.00	375.00	1.49	31
Owner Experience (years)	20.81	2.00	40.00	0.54	31
Share of Wage Bill	0.11	0.00	0.25	0.62	31
Share of Material Cost	0.55	0.00	0.76	0.38	31
Capital-Labour Ratio	1.43	0.13	11.11	1.37	31
Capital Productivity	8.85	0.40	48.00	1.19	31
Labour Productivity	5.08	0.17	33.33	1.13	31

Source: Field survey

units across the size classes is given in bar figure 7.1.

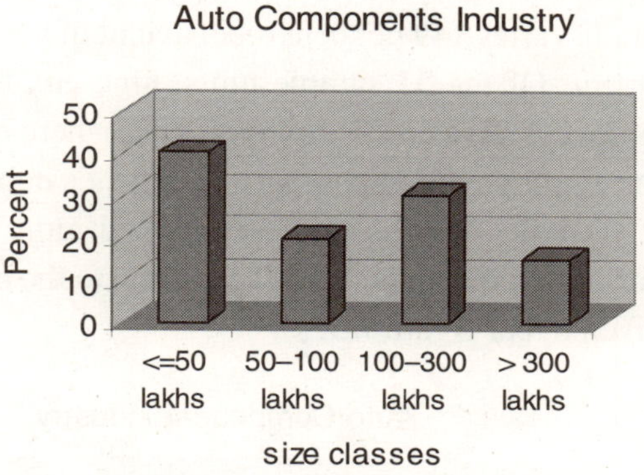

Figure 7.1 Size Groups of Sales

The original investment in plant and machinery in the surveyed units ranges between the minimum of 0.80 and the maximum of 300.00 lakhs of rupees. The mean value of the sample is rupees 48.9532 lakhs. The plant and machinery value of the sample units varies 134 per cent (see the coefficient of variation in Table 7.1) around the mean. Twelve of the 31units have an investment in plant and machinery less than or equal to 15 lakhs. Five units of the sample have invested somewhere between 15 and 25 lakhs in their plant and machinery, and another six units have an investment in between 25 and 50 lakhs. The remaining eight units have invested more than 50 lakhs in their plants. The percentage distribution of sample units in terms of their original investment in plant and machinery can be seen in bar figure 7.2.

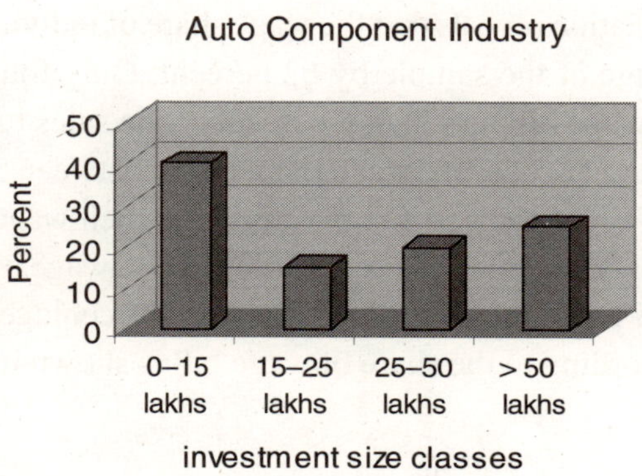

Figure 7.2 Investment Size Classes

As regards employment in the sample units, it varies from 3 to 375 employees. The mean employment of the sample is almost 46. Employment in the sample units varies 149 per cent (coefficient of variation) around the mean employment. Of the 31 sample units, nine employed less than or equal to 10 employees, five units employed somewhere between 10 and 20 employees. The employment of another 11 units lies in between 20 and 50 persons. Only six units of the sample employed more than 50 persons. Percentage distribution of sample units according to the number of persons employed is given in bar figure 7.3.

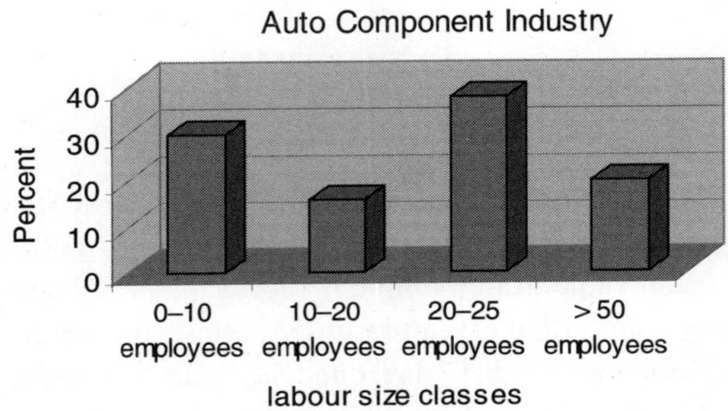

Figure 7.3 Employment Size Classes

We have also collected the share of wage bill and materials in sales turnover for the sample units. Wage bill for our sample of the auto components units constitutes somewhere between 0 and 25 percent. [2] The average share of wage bill for the sample is around 11 percent. The coefficient of variation reveals that the wage share of individual units varies around the average of the sample by 62 percent. Only four of the sample units have their wage bill less than 5 percent of the sales turnover. For the maximum number (12) of units, wage share lies in between 5 and 10 percent of sales turnover. Eight of the 31 sample units have their wage bill in between 10 and 15 percent. The remaining seven units have a wage bill that accounts for more than 15 percent of the sales turnover. Percentage distribution of sample units according to the share of wage bill is shown in bar figure 7.4.

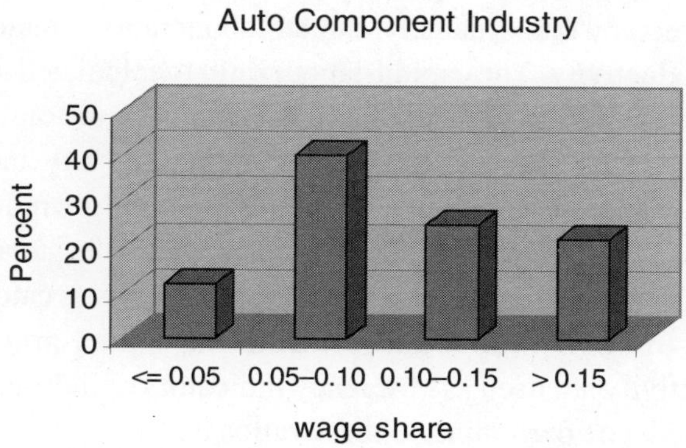

Figure 7.4 Size Distribution of Wage Share

The share of materials in sales turnover varies between 0 and 76 percent in our sample of auto component units. Zero appears in one unit which is doing job work. Otherwise, minimum material share is 18 percent. Mean share of materials in sales turnover for the sample is 55 percent. Coefficient of variation shows that the material share of the individual units varies around the sample average by 38 percent. For 11 units, the share of materials is less than or equal to 50 percent. Six units have their material costs constituting in between 50 and 69 percent of their sales turnover. The maximum number (14) of units has their material costs equal to or more than 70 percent of sales turnover. Percentage distribution of units of the auto component sample in terms of their material share is given in figure 7.5.

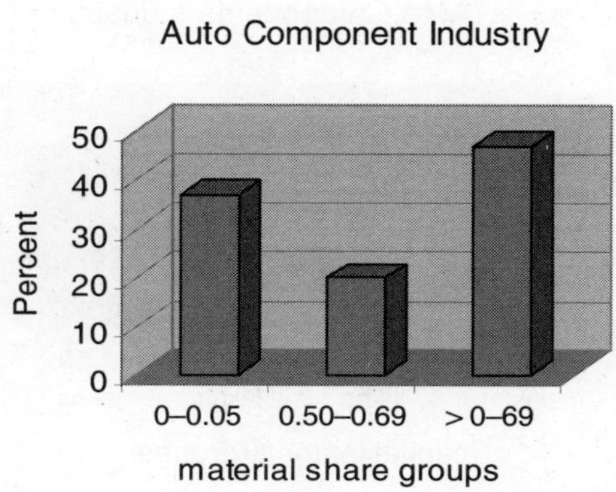

Figure 7.5 Size Groups of Material Share

Based on the data relating to output and inputs, we have measured some of the structural ratios, namely, capital-labour ratio, capital productivity and labour productivity. The capital-labour ratio is calculated as the ratio of original value of investment in plant and machinery to total labour. The inverse of this ratio is taken as an index of labour intensity and used in the comparisons of the employment-generating potential of industries/units. Capital productivity is measured as the ratio of sales turnover to the investment in plant and machinery. Labour productivity is calculated as the ratio of sales turnover to total labour. Both the capital productivity and labour productivity are used as efficiency indicators of industrial units. We discuss the evidence pertaining to these ratios below.

As regards capital-labour ratio of the sample units, it varies between 0.13 and 11.11 with a mean value of 1.43. The variation of individual values around the sample mean is 137 per cent. This means the sample auto component units have, on an average, machinery worth rupees 1.43 lakhs per employee. Of the total 31 units that have been surveyed, for nine units the capital-labour ratio is less than or equal to 0.50. Eight units show a capital-labour ratio that falls between 0.50 and 1.00. For another seven sample units, the capital-labour ratio lies between 1.00 and 1.50. The remaining seven units of the sample have a capital-labour ratio of more than 1.50. It must be noted here that higher the capital-labour ratio of a unit, lower the labour-intensity and the unit' employment generation. Percentage distribution of sample units in terms of the capital-labour ratio is given in bar figure 7.6.

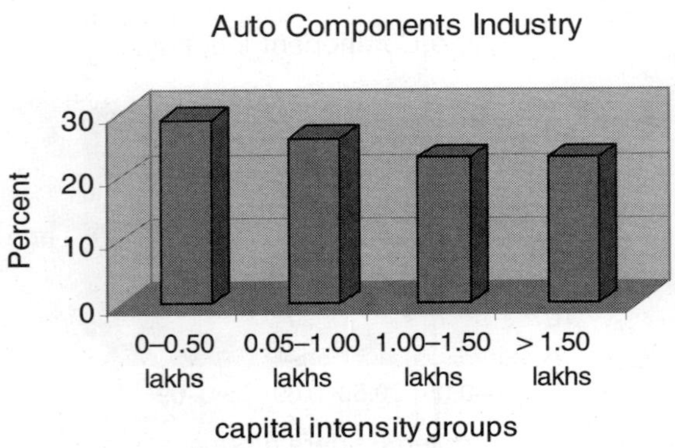

Figure 7.6 Range of Capital Intensity

Our sample of auto component units has shown, on an average, 5.08 lakhs of rupees of sales per employee. This labour productivity ranges between the minimum of 0.17 and the maximum of 33.33 lakhs of rupees. The variation in the labour productivity of individual units around the sample mean is 113 per cent (given by the coefficient of variation). Six sample units have yielded labour productivity that is less than or equal to Rs. 2.00 lakhs and another four units have given a labour productivity that is more than Rs. 6.00 lakhs. The maximum number (21) of the sample has revealed a labour productivity that is in between 2.00 and 6.00 lakhs of rupees. It can be seen from bar figure 7.7, which presents the percentage distribution of units in the specified labour productivity groups.

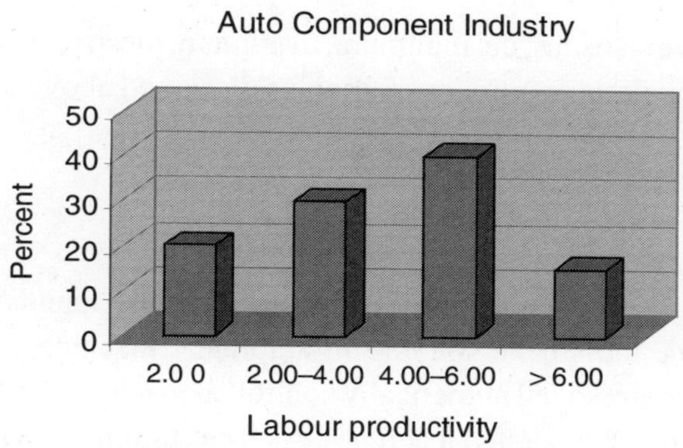

Figure 7.7 Size Groups-Labour Productivity

As regards capital productivity, our sample units have yielded, on an average, 8.850 with a minimum of 0.40 and a maximum of 48.00. Around the mean value of 8.85, individual values of the sample vary by 119 percent as given by the coefficient of variation. Nine of the 31 sample units have shown a capital productivity that is less than or equal to 2.5. Seven units have yielded capital productivity that is more than 10.00. The remaining 15 units could obtain capital productivity that varies between 2.5 and 10.00. Percentage distribution of the sample in terms of capital productivity is presented in bar figure 7.8.

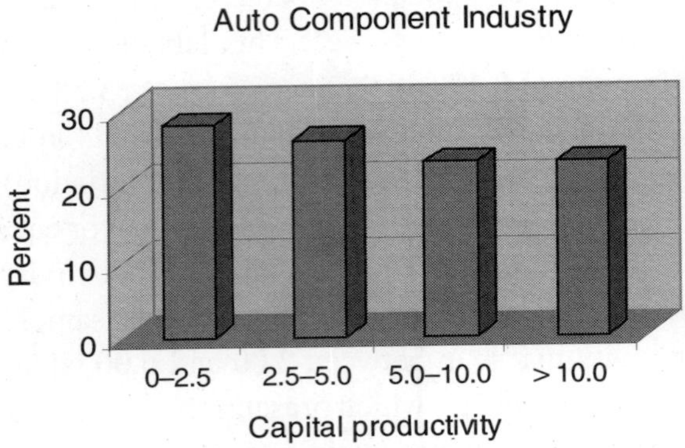

Figure 7.8 Size Groups-Capital Productivity

Descriptive statistics, i.e. minimum, maximum, mean and the coefficient of variation for all the continuous variables discussed above are presented in Table 7.1.

7.3.2 Technology Characteristics

Of the 31 auto component units, 14 units have only manually operated machines. Nine units have some semi-automatic machines, and another eight units have employed numerically controlled machines in their plants in addition to manually operated machines. As far as the changes in machinery are concerned, only ten units have added new machinery over time that is superior to the existing machinery either to speed up the production process or to improve the quality of the product or both. The remaining 21 units either had not changed their machinery at all or, simply added the same type of machinery as that of the existing ones. In other words, these units have not changed the level of mechanisation in their plants, if at all, only increased their capacity. The evidence pertaining to mechanisation is presented in terms of percentage distribution of the sample units in pie figures 7.9 and 7.10.

Suppliers of machinery are the primary source of technology for the sample units of auto component industry. But for 2 units, all the sample units have purchased first-hand machinery. Almost all the units have bought Indian machinery. The presence of foreign machinery is negligible and mostly it is second-hand machinery.

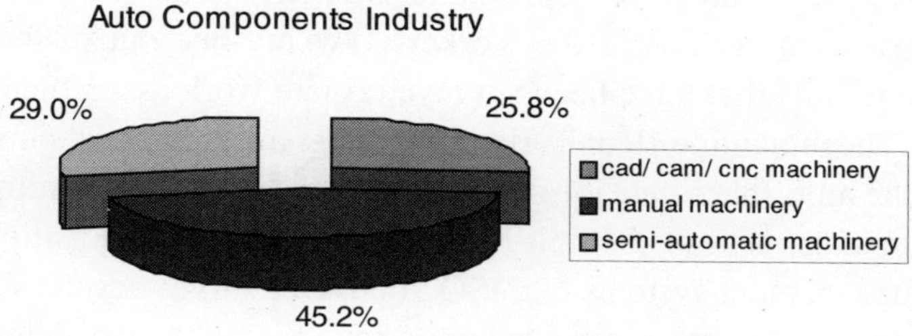

Figure 7.9 Level of Mechanisation

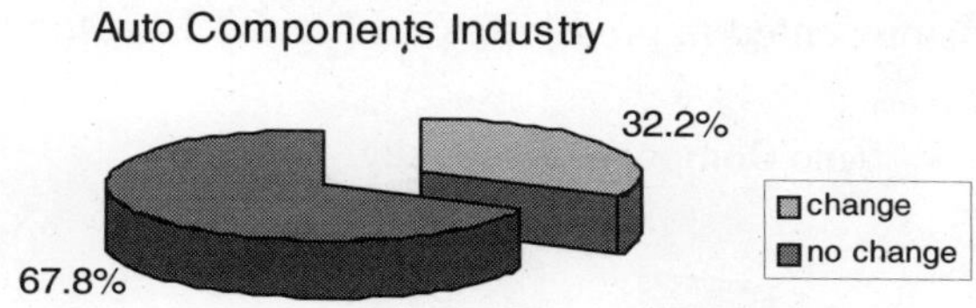

Figure 7.10 Changes in Machinery

An important result of the survey is that only a small number (7) of owners are aware of alternative technologies especially in machinery. A major proportion (i.e. 24/31) of the sample units are not sure of their alternatives. However, when asked about the selection criteria, almost all the sample units have reported that the technologies are selected on the basis of either scale of operation or product requirement. Availability of complementary skills and materials and the relative factor prices are just not taken into account in the selection of technologies by the sample units. In view of the lack of a full awareness of technologies, we explain the selection criteria as the parameters that are placed by the units before the suppliers of machinery, the primary source of technology, to provide appropriate machinery.

Most of the characteristics of the production organisation, i.e. plant layout, production schedules and materials management, turned out to be quite flexible in the sense they can be easily adjusted as per the need of the hour. Accordingly, units buy materials depending on their need, availability, costs and the space available for their storage. Production schedules are extended towards late evenings without much difficulty if the orders need to be sent immediately. Hence, these characteristics are not considered in the empirical analysis. Only work allocation and quality management varied across the surveyed units. Work allocation is taken in terms of the assignment of fixed or rotating jobs to the workers. Twenty-one out of the 31auto component units that have been surveyed rotate work assignments to the workers. The remaining 10 units fixed job assignments for all their workers. Most of the units that rotate jobs to workers also assign them multiple jobs. Quality management of the unit is studied in terms of acquisition of the quality management systems like ISO 9000. Our survey results show that only nine of the 31 auto component units have ISO 9000 certification. The remaining 22 units have not adopted any such quality system. Percentage distribution of sample units in terms of work allocation and quality management is presented in pie figures 7.11 and 7.12 respectively.

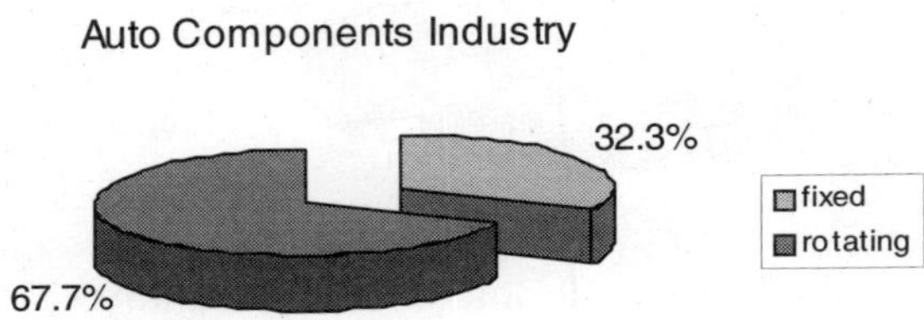

Figure 7.11 Work Allocation

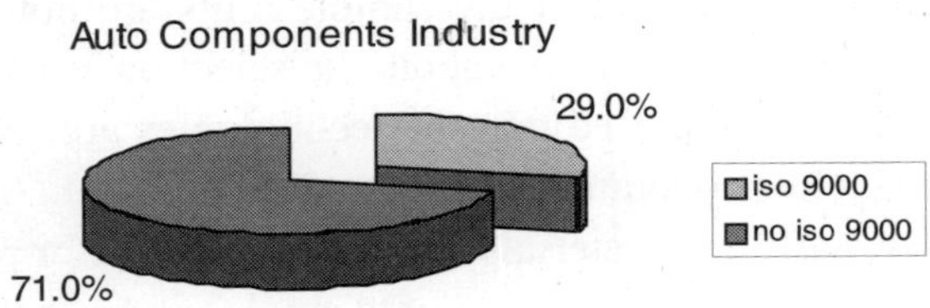

Figure 7.12 ISO 9000

As regards the form of business organisation, our survey data reveal that 11 of the 31auto component units covered are proprietary concerns and another 12 units are partnership firms. Only 8 units have organised themselves as limited companies. The percentage distribution of the sample in terms of the form of business organisation is presented in pie figure 7.13. In the case of management, all the sample units, excepting two, are owner-managed. The non-owner management is again of a general nature not function-specific.

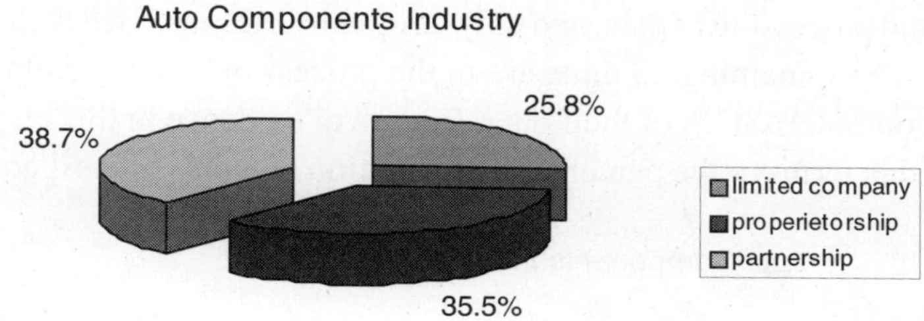

Figure 7.13 Business Organisation

As far as information technology is concerned, we have covered the means of communication with the outside agents like customers and suppliers, and data management, i.e., record keeping for the purpose of storing and processing of data. On the communication front, 16 of the 31 sample units use traditional methods like personal visits or phone. Two units have a fax facility and the remaining 13 units have started using email in addition to the traditional ways of communication. As far as the changes in these technologies are concerned, 13 units have changed their way of communication over a time period and the remaining 18 units have not made any such changes. Percentage distribution of sample units according to the means of communication and changes in these means is presented in pie figures 7.14 and 7.15.

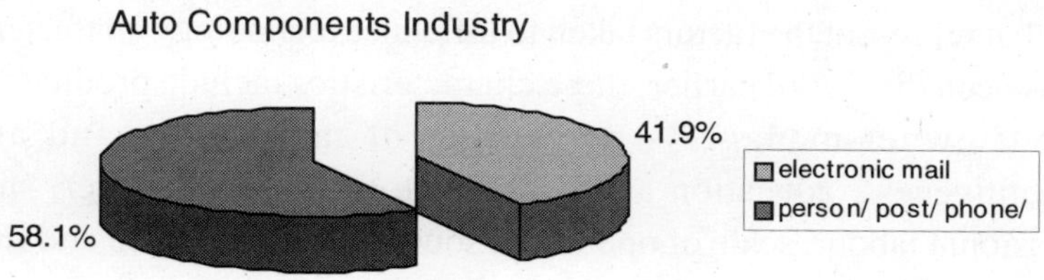

Figure 7.14 Means of Communication

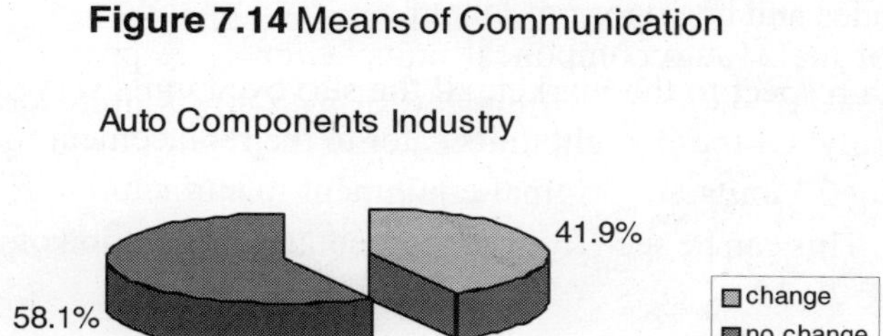

Figure 7.15 Changes in Communication

Fifteen units of the sample still rely on paper files for the purpose of storing and processing of data, and only three units computerised their books entirely. The remaining 13 units are in the process of shifting from paper files to computerisation of their data. Empirical evidence in this respect is presented in terms of the percentage distribution of units in pie figure 7.16.

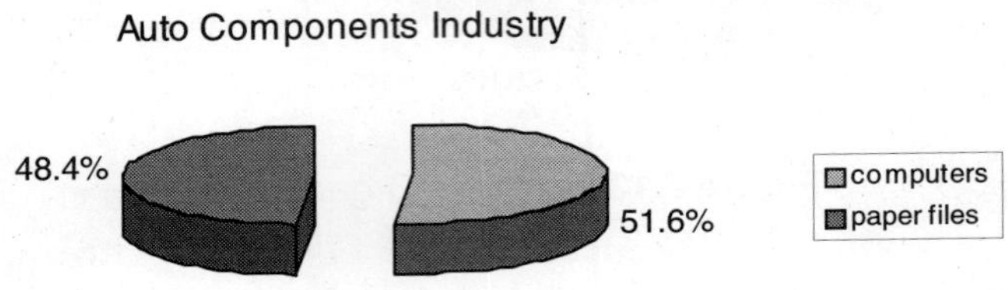

Figure 7.16 Record Keeping

On the whole, all the characteristics representing technology excepting some of the organisation characteristics, namely, plant layout, materials management, production schedules and type of management, show reasonable variation across the sample units and thus found to be relevant for our empirical analysis of the Auto Component industry.

7.3.3 Non-Technology Characteristics

We now examine the evidence for non-technology characteristics of the units that represent the factors taken to influence technology characteristics. As has been discussed earlier, these characteristics include product market served, owner-manager's perception of market demand and its competitiveness, education and experience of owner-manager, share of professional labour, scale of operation, sources of information and finance, owner-managers' opinion about the availability of information, finance, and the attitudes and behaviour of labour.

With respect to the market, all the surveyed units serve the domestic market only. Of these, eight units cater to the replacement market and the remaining 23 units are original equipment manufacturers for the vehicle industry. This can be seen from the percentage distribution of units given in pie figure 7.17.

Survey data also indicate that 5 units do not perceive any competition while 26 units have started feeling market competition. Of the 26 units that could sense market competition, 15 units consider it as severe. In this industry,

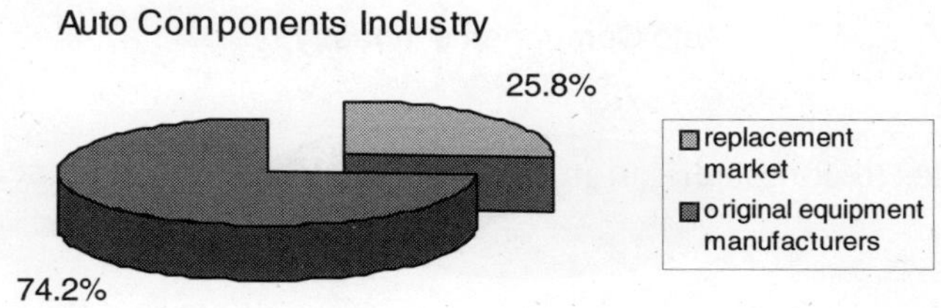

Figure 7.17 Product Market

market competition is mainly expressed in terms of customers demanding better quality at a lower price. The empirical evidence further reveals that 19 units consider the market changes as threatening while the remaining 12 units view these changes as opportunities to grow. In addition, the survey data show that 19 units do not think demand a problem. The remaining 12 units feel overall demand a constraint. Empirical evidence in respect of owner-manager's perception of market is summed up in pie figures 7.18, 7.19 and 7.20. Distribution of the product in the replacement market is done through the wholesale dealers. Eleven sample units have complained of payment problems.

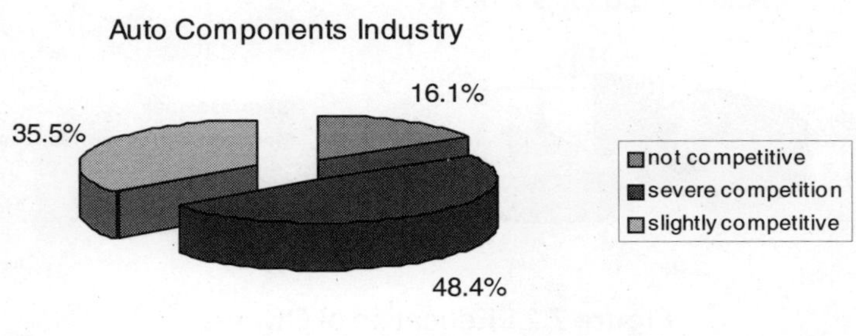

Figure 7.18 Market Competition

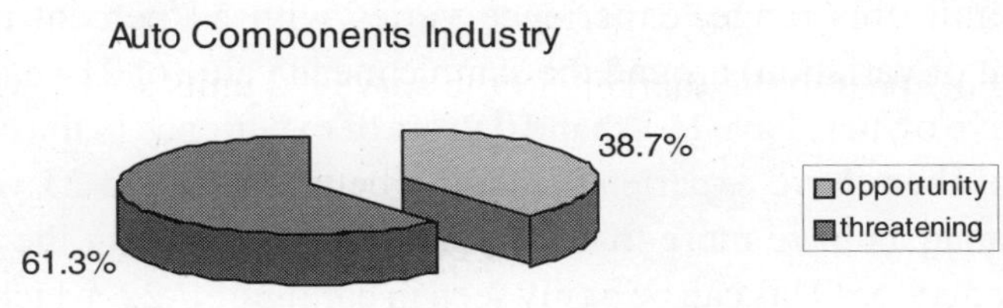

Figure 7.19 Impact of Market Competition

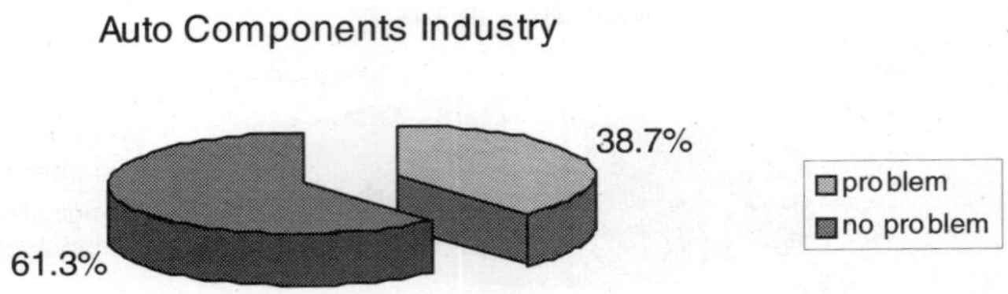

Figure 7.20 Demand Problem

As discussed in the earlier chapters, technological capabilities are taken in terms of the education and experience of owner-managers, and share of professional labour in the total labour. In this respect, empirical evidence reveals that owners in 18 of the 31 auto component units are professionals. Almost all of them are mechanical engineers. Two units however, are owned and managed by people who completed only their schooling. Owner-managers in the remaining 11 units studied beyond schooling though not professional courses. This can be seen from the percentage distribution of survey units given in pie figure 7.21.

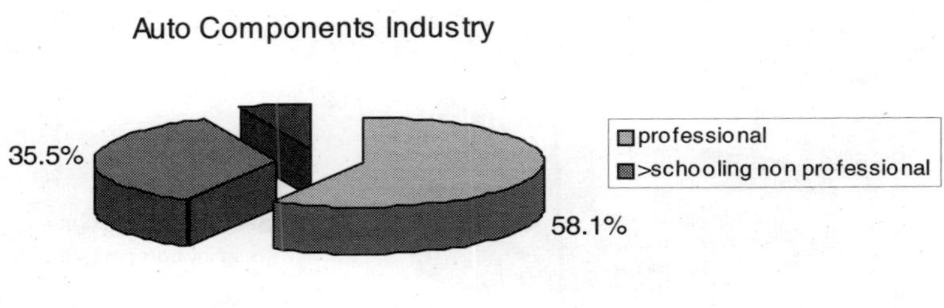

Figure 7.21 Education of Owners

The experience of owner-managers of the sample ranges from 2 to 40 years. Within this range, experience varies with 54 percent (given by coefficient of variation) around the sample mean value of 21 years. Of the total 31, five owners have less than 10 years of experience in the concerned area, 16 of them have experience ranging between 10 and 25 years. Ten owner-managers have more than 25 years of experience in the specified area of production. This can be easily seen in bar figure 7.22, which presents the percentage distribution of units in terms of owners' experience.

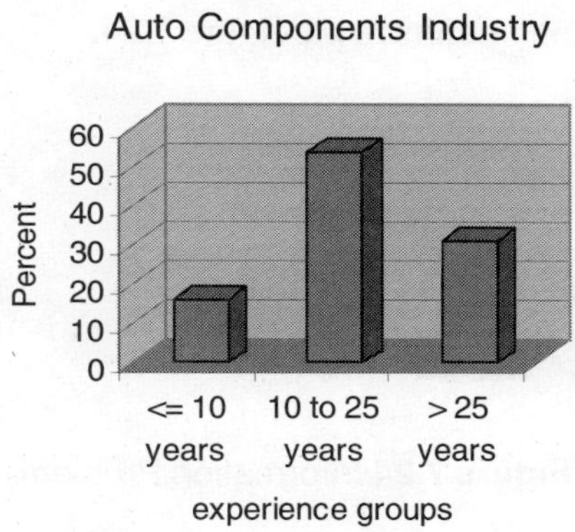

Figure 7.22 Experience of Owners

As regards professional labour, 15 units of the sample have not employed anyone with a formal degree such as a diploma or degree in engineering or any training. The remaining 16 units employed professional people with a maximum of 33 percent of the total labour. Evidence in respect of the presence of professional labour is presented in pie figure 7.23.

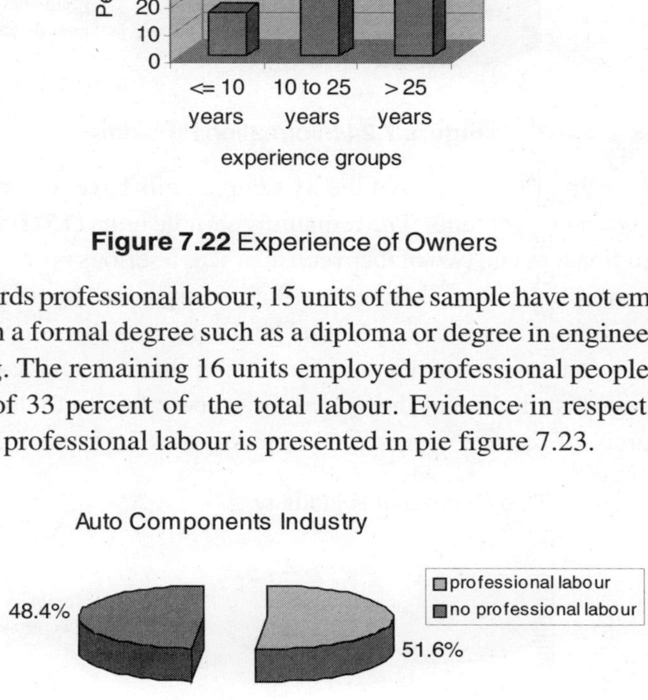

Figure 7.23 Use of Professional Labour

Scale of operation, one of the important characteristics determining firm-level technological change is represented by sales turnover. Survey data regarding sales turnover has already been discussed in section 7.3.1 under the general economic characteristics.

As regards information about technology, 17 of the 31 auto component units surveyed, do not think that access to information is a problem for them. The remaining 14 units find it difficult to obtain information and one of them considers it as a serious problem. Some of the major sources of information that have been reported are personal experience (6), trade fairs (3), customers (2) and a combination of these three (19). The survey data in respect of information problems are summarised in terms of the percentage distribution of units in pie figure 7.24.

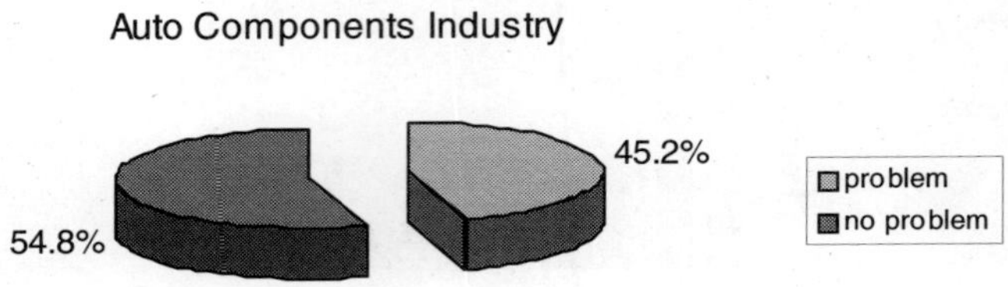

Figure 7.24 Information Problem

Regarding finances, 16 of the 31 sample units have reported that they do not have any problems. The remaining sample units (15) find it difficult to obtain finances and two of them consider it as a serious problem. Nineteen of the sample units have obtained credit from organised institutions such as financial institutions and commercial banks. Rest of the sample (12) units had to rely on the personal sources including internal sources of the unit. Percentage distribution of the survey units according to finance problems and sources of finance is presented in pie figures 7.25 and 7.26.

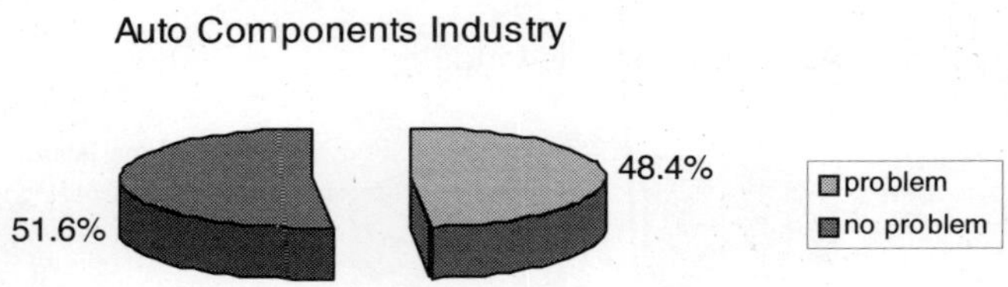

Figure 7.25 Finance Problem

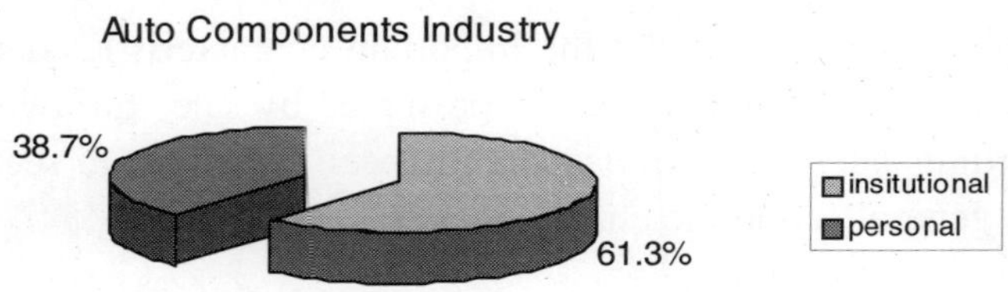

Figure 7.26 Sources of Finance

With respect to the behaviour of labour, 20 units have reported that they do not have any problems like absenteeism, turnover or unionisation with their labour. Eleven units of the sample have complained some of these labour problems. However, the numbers reverse when it comes to the attitudes of labour towards work. Twenty of the 31 sample units have felt that the attitudes of labour are not positive in the sense of not giving their best when owner-manager is away or reluctant to work on the new machinery unless pressurised to do so. Only 11 units of the sample have reported positive attitudes of their labour in these respects. Percentage distribution of survey units in terms of the attitudes and behaviour of labour is presented in pie figures 7.27 and 7.28.

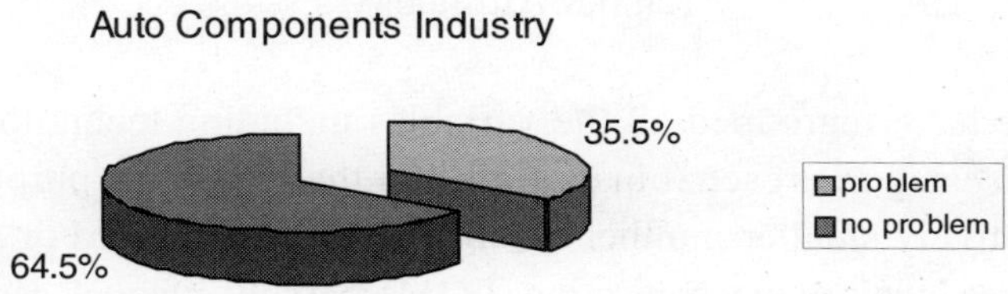

Figure 7.27 Labour Behaviour

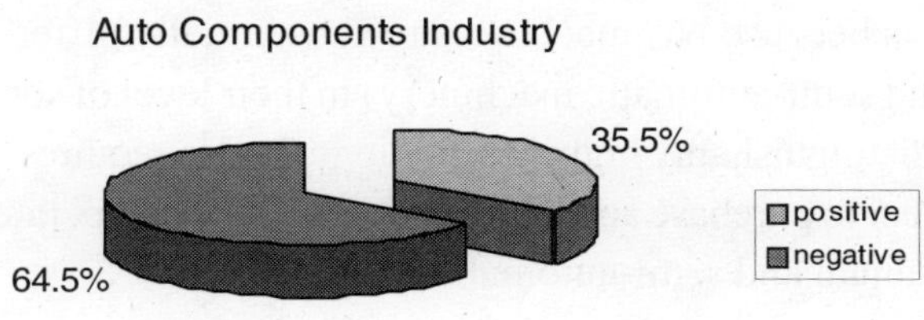

Figure 7.28 Labour Attitudes

In effect, but for the availability of complementary skills and materials, and relative factor prices, all the characteristics considered to influence technologies are empirically relevant in the auto components industry.

7.4. DETERMINANTS OF TECHNOLOGICAL CHANGE: EMPIRICAL EVIDENCE

In this section, we estimate the three technology functions specified in chapter 6 and analyse their results. We start with the transformation technology. As mentioned in the earlier chapter, we have tried alternative specifications of the function with two technology characteristics, namely, changes in mechanisation and level of mechanisation as dependent variable, and various combinations of non-technology characteristics. We have selected the equation, of the alternatives tried out, which has yielded better results in our opinion. Selected equation is presented below.

	LOM	=	F (SCA, INF, FIN, LAB)	(7.1)
where,	LOM	=	Level of mechanization	
	SCA	=	Scale of operation	
	INF	=	Information Problem	
	FIN	=	Sources of Finance	
	LAB	=	Labour Attitudes	

We have regrouped all the variables including technology variables into two categories each (binary form) for the estimation purposes keeping the relatively smaller number of observations in mind. For instance, we have three levels of mechanisation (LOM), namely, manual, semi-automatic and numerically controlled (NC) machines. However, we take it as a binary variable with the values of zero and one. For the units having NC machines, LOM is given the value of one, and for the remaining units it is taken as zero. This is because NC machines are substantially different from others (manual and semi-automatic machinery) in their level of sophistication and treated as distinguishably higher technology. It also requires higher amounts of investment to purchase and higher levels of skills to operate in comparison with the manual and semi-automatic machinery.

Availability of information is taken as zero if the units feel it as a problem and as one if they do not treat it as a problem. So is the case with the labour problem. It is given 0 if units feel labour attitudes are negative and hence a problem, and one if units find labour attitudes positive and thus not a problem. As regards the sources of finance, we have units relying solely on personal/ relatives/ friends for finance (0) and units availing institutional credit (1). The estimated coefficients are presented in Table 7.2.

The organisation aspect of technology is taken in terms of quality management, which is specified as having a total quality system called ISO 9000 (1) or not (0). Total quality system like ISO 9000 enables units to supply consistent quality components and hence increasingly emphasised by vehicle industry. As discussed earlier, it is taken as a function of a subset of variables that are considered for the transformation technology, namely, scale of operation, kind of market and education of the owner-

Table 7.2: **Marginal Coefficients of Technology Functions—Auto Components Industry**

Variable	Coefficient	t–values
Dependent variable: LOM Constant	–0.4606	–2.760
SCA (scale of operation)	0.0008	1.722
INF (sources of information)	–0.1995	–1.062
FIN (sources of finance)	0.4604	2.120
LAB (labour attitudes)	–0.3474	–1.862
Dependent variable: ISO Constant	–0.4612	–3.692
SCA (scale of operation)	0.0013	2.028
Dependent variable: MCC Constant	–0.4126	–2.633
SCA (scale of operation)	0.0020	2.458

manager. Accordingly, we write our organisation function as

$$ISO = F(SCA, MKT, EDU) \quad (7.2)$$

where, ISO = ISO 9000 certification

MKT = Product Market Served

EDU = Education of owner-manager

SCA is as defined for equation (7.1)

Product market is taken as one if units are original equipment manufacturer and zero for the units serving replacement market. Education is specified as one if the owner is professional and zero for the units with non-professional owner-managers.

The other dimension of organisation that turned out to be empirically relevant, namely, work allocation is not considered for estimation purposes as it is highly related with the type of machinery than any other characteristic of the unit.

As regards information technology, modern means of communications like electronic mail and information (data) management methods involve the usage of computers and thus highly related to each other. Information management is also not totally computerised in the selected units excepting three. So, we have considered means of communication as a proxy for information technology function and specified it as

MCC = F (SCA, MKT, EDU) (7.3)

where, MCC = Means of communication

SCA, MKT, EDU are as defined for equation (7.1) and (7.2)

Communication technology too is considered as a binary variable having a value of zero and one. Units having modern communication technology like e-mail are given one and the remaining units are assigned zero. We have estimated the transformation, organisation and information technology functions using Probit method.

In this section, we present the marginal coefficients of the three technology equations estimated and analyse these results. Results show that the level of mechanisation, the transformation technology variable, is explained by the combination of scale of operation, information sources, sources of finance and labour attitudes (see Table 7.2). Of these, scale of operation, finance sources and labour attitudes show statistically significant impact on the level of mechanisation. Of these three significant variables, magnitude of influence as given by marginal coefficient is the highest for the finance variable followed by that of labour and scale of operation.

As said earlier, finance variable is specified as having zero for the units relying on personal finance and one for the units availing institutional finance. It is expected that personal funds (vis-à-vis institutional finance) are always limited and hence restrict the scope for purchasing NC machinery. This is because NC machinery requires heavy investments in relation to the manual and semi-automatic machinery. The estimated marginal coefficient, being positive, confirms the same. The estimate further indicates that the availability of institutional credit raises the probability of a unit going for NC machinery by 0.46.

Labour attitudes is having zero for the units that have reported negative labour attitudes and one for the units that have labour with positive attitudes. Attitudes of labour, as mentioned earlier, are taken in terms of their willingness to work and learn especially labour giving its best even when owner-manager is away. If the attitudes are negative, it may induce the firms when the need arises, to go for numerically controlled machines, which once set does not require workers' attention till the end of the operation. Our estimate of marginal coefficient of labour, being negative, indicates the same. Magnitude of the coefficient indicates that negative attitudes of labour enhance the probability of going for NC machinery by the magnitude of 0.35.

The marginal coefficient of scale of operation is positive and significant but smaller in magnitude. This could perhaps be due to the units of measurement of annual sales turnover, the proxy for scale of operation in the study. As discussed earlier, larger scale of operation increases the scope of exploiting indivisibilities and ensures better returns on new investment associated with the NC machinery, and thus enhances the scope for having this machinery in comparison with the small-scale operation. Positive coefficient of the scale variable confirms the same. Marginal coefficient of scale variable also indicates that a lakh rupee rise in the annual sales turnover increases the probability of going for NC machinery by 0.0008.

Statistical insignificance of information variable could possibly be due to the fact that majority of the sample units are not finding information a problem, whatever be the number of sources of information these are using. This could further be due to their location, i.e. national capital region, and majority of these units are original equipment manufacturers and hence in constant touch with the vehicle industry, which may be providing technology information to their vendors.

Both the organisation and information though taken as a function of scale of operation, kind of market served and education of the owner-manager, only scale of operation is explaining them statistically. Market served and education of owner-manager taken as important even in the case of transformation technology (i.e. level of mechanisation) could not fit in the equation statistically. This is because one of the categories of these variables is not present in both the categories of dependent variable. So, we have to leave these variables out of statistical analysis.

Acquisition of ISO 9000, the organisation variable, is primarily explained in terms of sales turnover. Positive magnitude of its marginal coefficient indicates that one lakh rupee rise in sales turnover increases the probability of acquiring the total quality system called ISO 9000 by 0.0013.

Usage of electronic mail, the proxy for information technology too is mainly explained in terms of sales turnover. The marginal coefficient in this respect shows that one unit (i.e. one lakh rupees) rise in sales turnover raises the probability of going for electronic mail by 0.0020.

In sum, transformation technology taken in terms of level of mechanisation in small auto component units is primarily influenced by the availability of institutional finance, labour attitudes and scale of operation. Both organisation (taken in terms of having total quality system like ISO 9000) and information (usage of electronic mail) technologies are mainly determined by scale of operation.

7.5 ESTIMATION OF THE IMPACT OF TECHNOLOGICAL CHANGE

We analyse the impact of technology on the competitiveness of the units by introducing technology variables directly in the production function along with the conventional inputs of capital, labour and materials. Technology is again specified in terms of relevant technological characteristics of the sample, namely, level of mechanisation, quality management, work allocations, mode of communication, and information (data) management. All these characteristics are introduced as dummy variables. Thus specified production function is estimated by Ordinary Least Squares (OLS) method. We tried various alternatives owing to econometric problems such as multicollinearity and degrees of freedom.[3] We, finally, confined to the level of mechanisation, quality of management and modes of communication as transformation, organisation and information technology variables respectively. As regards the conventional variables in the production function, we have considered the original investment in plant and machinery as capital, the total number of employees as labour and the value of materials utilised during the year. As mentioned earlier, we have taken sales turnover as dependent variable, which gives the actual size of the market served by the concerned firm. Thus, differences in sales turnover across firms can be taken as differences in their competitiveness. In effect, we specify our production function as six-input Cobb-Douglas function and write it in the log-liner form as below.

$$\ln ST = C + \alpha \ln PM + \beta \ln LAB + \gamma \ln MAT + \theta_1 LOM + \theta_2 ISO + \theta_3 MCC + \mu \quad (7.4)$$

where, "ln" refers to the logarithmic values of the variables

ST = Annual sales turnover

PM = Original value of plant and machinery

LAB = Total number of employees

MAT = Value of materials consumed during the year
LOM = Level of mechanisation; 1 for units with NC machines; 0 otherwise
ISO = Quality management system; 1 for units with ISO 9000 certification; 0 otherwise
MCC = Means of communication; 1 for units with e-mail; 0 otherwise
μ = Random error term

Equation (7.4) has been estimated through Ordinary Least Squares (OLS) method. The estimated parameters are presented below.

$$\ln ST = \underset{(6.709)^*}{0.8685} + \underset{(2.374)^*}{0.0957} \ln PM + \underset{(2.912)^*}{0.2015} \ln LAB + \underset{(14.371)^*}{0.6792} \ln MAT + \underset{(2.523)^*}{0.2471} LOM + \underset{(1.357)}{0.1325} ISO - \underset{(-1.204)}{0.1112} MCC^4$$

$$N = 29,\ R^2 = 0.9827,\ F_{6,\,22} = 208.237$$

The estimated coefficients presented above indicate that all the conventional variables, namely, plant and machinery, labour, materials and the level of mechanisation have a statistically significant and positive impact on the sales turnover. ISO 9000 certification and methods of communication with the customers are not statistically influencing the sales turnover.

ISO 9000 certification, implying total quality system, enables the units to produce the products of consistent quality and hence increases the scope for market expansion. It seems that in the case of our sample of small-scale auto component units, the expansionary effects of consistent quality have not yet started kick-in. So is the case with the electronic means of communications. This could perhaps be due to the fact that the benefits of these technologies depend on the degree of their usage, which, in turn, depends on the nature and degree of association with the customer companies. It may take some time for smaller units to tune-in with the customer companies. In addition, use of electronic means of communication is still in the initial phase and used along with the traditional methods like phone and personal visit.

With regard to the variables that show statistically significant impact on sales turnover, all these yield positive coefficients as expected. The level of mechanisation shows the highest coefficient (1.07) followed by materials (0.6792), labour (0.2015) and the plant and machinery (0.0957). In other words, the sensitivity of firms' sales turnover is the highest to the presence of NC machines. NC machinery embodies advanced technology, ensures both quality and productivity improvements, and thus increasing sales turnover. This, juxtaposed with the result that investment in the plant and machinery yields statistically significant but smaller magnitude of impact on sales, implies that it is the machine-embodied technology (or quality of machinery) rather than the stock of machinery, which has the greatest effect on improving sales turnover. Quantitatively, sensitivity of the firms' sales turnover to materials is second, meaning that availability and quality of materials have a considerable influence on the sales turnover of the automotive component units.

7.6 SUMMARY

In sum, our auto components sample shows the presence of different levels of mechanisation along with changes in machinery in some of the units. Suppliers of machinery are the primary source of transformation technology. Units purchase machinery keeping their scale of operation and product specification in mind. Sample is dominated by proprietary and partnership firms, and owner-managed units. Most of the characteristics of production organisation are turned out to be flexible in the sample units. Only work allocation and quality management practices vary across the sample. Our sample has a good number of units with computers and hence started using modern methods of communication (e-mail) and data management.

Original equipment manufacturers dominate the sample. A good number of owners in the sample are mechanical engineers but use of professional labour is limited. Most of the sample units feel market competition is intensifying and threatening their units' survival. Reasonable number of sample units obtain institutional finance and do not find information a problem. However, labour attitudes are creating a problem for a number of sample units.

Empirical results regarding the determinants of technology reveal that the level of mechnisation is determined by scale of operation, sources of finance and labour. It means larger units with access to institutional finance are in a better position to go for higher level of machinery like numerically controlled machines. Both the organisation (quality management) and information (means of communication) technologies are influenced by scale of operation.

Transformation, i.e. machine-embodied technology is turning out to be important for the competitiveness of the units taken in their sales turnover. Both organisation and information technologies are not showing any significant impact on the competitiveness of the units.

Endnotes

1. 10 lakhs = One million
2. Zero wage share means negligible share. It is there in one or two units possibly due to the small number of employees or, lower wages or, both.
3. For instance, work allocations are linked to the type of machinery. Manual machine demands constant worker presence and hence worker is tied-up to machines. On the other hand, NC machines require workers for the initial setting-up phase of operation. Once started, NC machine functions on its own till the operation is over and allows worker to attend other jobs in the interval.
4. Figures in the parentheses are t-values and * indicates the statistical significance of the relevant variables

Chapter 8 Empirical Evidence for Technological Change: *Electronics Industry*

8.1 INTRODUCTION

In this chapter, we examine the empirical evidence in the case of electronics industry, for the objectives of the study, namely, factors influencing technological change and its impact on the competitive strength of small units.

As mentioned in chapter 6 we first present the general economic features of our sample units in terms of output, inputs and some of the structural ratios based on these. Next, we discuss the evidence regarding technology and non-technology characteristics so as to deduce their relevance for the empirical analysis. Finally, using the selected econometric methods, we investigate the evidence for the determinants of technological change and the impact of technology on the competitiveness of small-scale electronics units.

8.2 FIELD IMPRESSIONS

Small-scale electronic units in and around Delhi were setup when there were heavy regulations on importing electronic items and on the entry of large-scale units into the production of numerous products. Small-scale units have been producing various electronic items at different time points essentially to earn quick profits by exploiting the immediate local demand. Some of the items that have been produced by these units at various time points are, radios, two-in-ones, TVs, TV components, calculators, push-button telephones, voltage stabilisers, invertors. For some of these products like TV components and voltage stabilisers, the components are mostly indigenous. For a majority of the products, components (at times CKD kits) are imported, assembled, tested and sold by the small-scale units mostly under the name of the company whose CKD kits they are importing such as Sony or National. Testing instruments change across the products.

In the initial days of sudden demand for electronic products such as TVs, audios, calculators and C-DOT (indigenous telecom technology) components in the eighties, or of push-button telephones, car stereos, invertors and computers in the nineties, numerous small-scale units entered into the production of these products to exploit the immediate local demand. Some of the units with a vision of expansion did establish themselves and grow beyond the local market and build proper factories with later technologies using semi-automatic and fully automatic machinery. Most of the units, however, aimed at exploiting the immediate demand. Hence, they have been shifting from the production of a product with a waning demand to a product with a growing demand. Shifting from the production of one product to another especially in the case of manual assembly is not a problem given the fact that they do not use much of the machinery except tools and testing instruments and the Indian tools and testing instruments are not costly. Some other units however are totally closing down.

In the wake of globalisation and liberalisation and the consequent entry of multinational companies like Sony (whose kits a majority of the small units have been importing), the legal enforcement of trade-mark and brand name laws (it is important as many small units give the established brand names like Sony or National or similar names for their products) and the declining cost differentials of a product produced by the fully automated plants of multinational companies and that of the small units, are threatening the survival of small-scale units in the electronics industry. Only, some of the small units realised this and are trying to get into the global chains as sales and/or service agents to the multinational companies. Most of the units still think that they can manage given the product market segmentation in India. A good number of units however are closing down their operations in the electronics area.

8.3 SALIENT FEATURES OF THE SAMPLE UNITS

For the purpose of our analysis, we have surveyed 30 small-scale industrial units located in and around Delhi and producing electronic items. A good number of these units are involved in the manufacture of consumer and industrial electronics. Some of the products that are being produced by these sample units are telephones, calculators, car stereos, tape recorders, emergency lights, inverters, voltage stabilisers, process controls, biomedical instruments, and TV tuners. For all these electronic items, design of the product comes with the printed circuit boards (PCB). Production of the item involves placement of the relevant components on PCB, fixation of electrical connections, testing for the required parameters and finally closing it in a plastic or metal cabin. Almost all these products can be produced by fully automated plant. However, in our sample, a good number of units produce these items manually. Most of the sample units usually buy the PCB and the required components, do the placement of the specified components on the PCB, give electrical connections to these components, test the piece and place it in metal cabins in their premises. Cabins are made in-house in some of the units. In majority of the sample units, machinery is due to the production of cabin making. Few of the units are using machinery in assembling of the components. Design making is seen in the units that are involved in the production of process controls for specific customers.

8.3.1 General Economic Characteristics

All the sample units excepting two were set up by owners themselves. But for five, all the sample units have only one plant. Growing units have gone for another plant due to the space constraint in the first plant. Twenty of the sample units are not registered under the Factories Act and the remaining ten units are factories. Only two of the 30 sample units availed any government assistance. But for three, none of the sample units has asked for protection to the small-scale industrial units. However, majority of the units (22) have expressed their dissatisfaction over government policies especially about fiscal policies including excise and import duties on components.

The annual sales turnover of the electronic sample ranges widely between one and 450 lakhs. The mean value of the sample for sales turnover is around 82.23 lakhs of rupees. The variation of the sample units around the mean value of sales turnover as given by the coefficient of variation, is 133 per cent. For seven units, sales turnover is less than rupees 25 lakhs. Twelve sample units have sales turnover that lies between 25 to 50 lakhs of rupees. Four units have a sales turnover that comes in the class interval of 50 to 75 lakhs of rupees. For the remaining seven units, annual sales turnover is higher than 75 lakhs. Percentage distribution of sample units in terms of sales turnover is presented in bar figure 8.1.

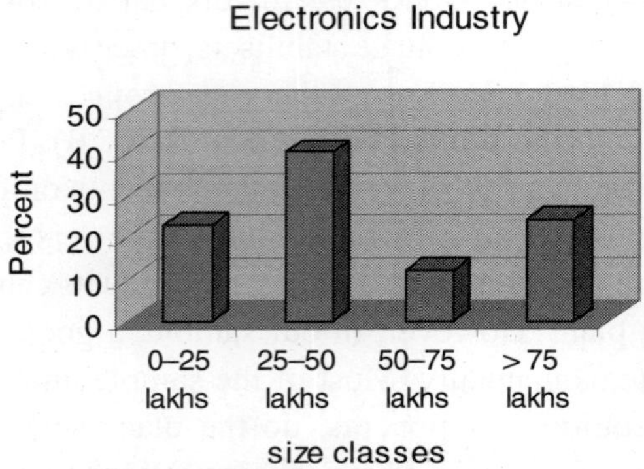

Figure 8.1 Sales Tumover

The original investment in the plant and machinery of the sample units ranges from rupees 30.000 to 97 lakhs. The mean value of the plant and machinery for the sample is around 8 lakhs and the variation around the mean as given by the coefficient of variation is 245 percent. Almost half of the units (i.e. 14) have original investment in plant and machinery that is less than or equal to 1 lakh rupees. For five units, the investment in plant and machinery falls in the range of 1 and 2 lakhs and for another six units, it lies between 2 and 5 lakhs. The remaining five units have an original investment higher than 5 lakhs rupees. Percentage distribution of the sample units in terms of plant and machinery is given in bar figure 8.2.

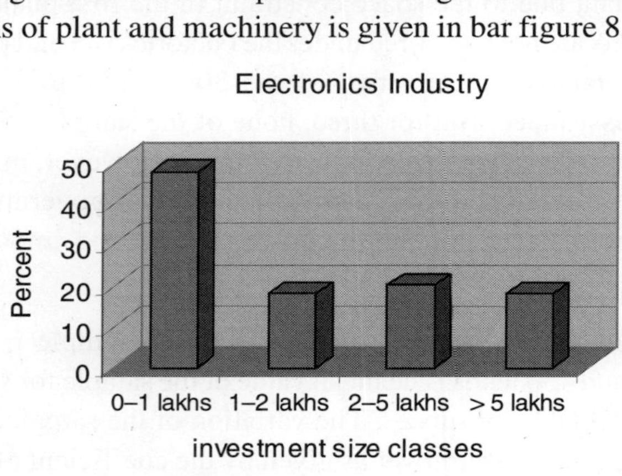

Figure 8.2 Plant and Machinery

The total employment of the sample varies between 5 and 45 persons with a mean value of around 14 persons. The variation in the employment of the sample units around the sample average is 77 per cent. More than half of the units that are surveyed (i.e. 16) have employed less than or equal to 10 persons. Another 11 units of the sample have employment that ranges between 10 and 20 persons. Only three sample units have employment that is more than 20 employees. The percentage distribution of sample units in terms of employment is given in bar figure 8.3.

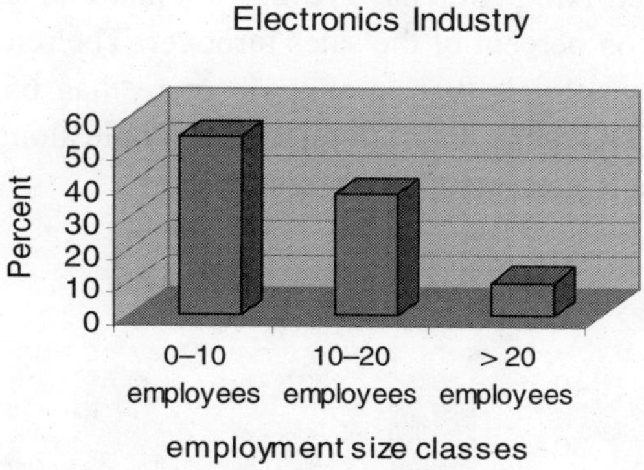

Figure 8.3 Employment Size Groups

The percentage share of the wage bill in the annual sales turnover for the sample units lies between zero[1] and 44. The mean value of the share of wages is 13 percent and the coefficient of variation is 0.73. For three units, percentage share of wage bill is less than 5. For 14 units, the share of wage bill stands between 5 and 10 percent. Five units have maintained a wage share that comes in the range of 10 to 15 percent. Rest of the sample (8) has reported a wage bill that constituted more than 15 percent of the sales turnover. Percentage distribution of units according to wage share is presented in bar figure 8.4.

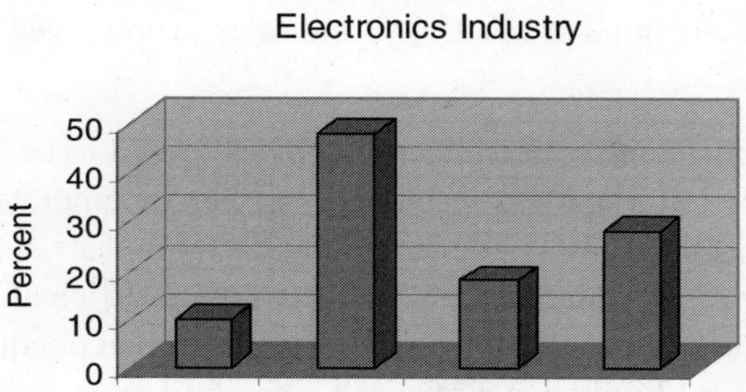

Figure 8.4 Wage Share Groups

Materials constitute a share in the annual sales turnover that ranges between zero[2] and 80 percent. The average share of materials, however, is 53 percent. The variation of sample values around this mean, as given by the coefficient of variation, is 43 percent. One-third of the sample (i.e. 10 units) have shown material share that is less than or equal to 50 percent of the sales turnover. Nine units have revealed a material share that ranges between 50 and 65 percent of the sales turnover. The remaining 11 units have consumed materials that amounts to more than 65 percent of the sales turnover. Percentage distribution of the sample along the dimension of material share is presented in bar figure 8.5.

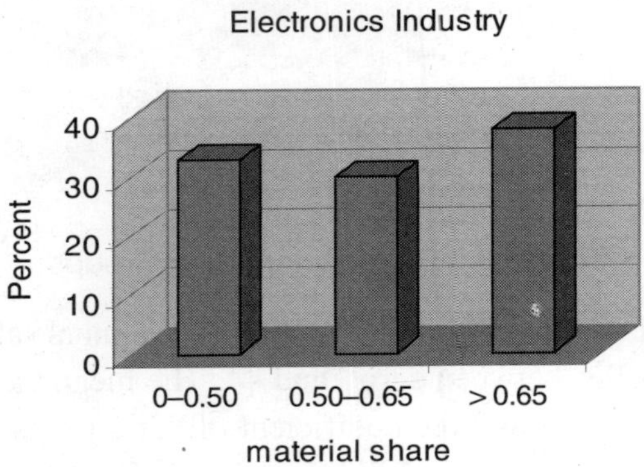

Figure 8.5 Materials Share Groups

In addition to the above-discussed variables, we have calculated some structural ratios that can be used as indicators of employment and efficiency. These ratios are capital-labour ratio (capital-intensity), sales to plant and machinery ratio (capital productivity) and sales to employee ratio (labour productivity).

The capital-intensity of the sample ranges from 3 to 645,000 rupees. The mean value of plant and machinery per person employed is around 46,000 rupees. One finds a wide variation (252%) in the sample values of capital-labour ratio, which can be seen from the coefficient of variation. Ten of the 30 units have yielded a ratio that is less than or equal to 10,000 rupees. Another 13 units have revealed a capital-labour ratio that lies in between 10 and 25,000 rupees. Only seven units have given a capital-labour ratio that is more than 25,000. The distribution of the sample units along the capital-labour ratio is given in bar figure 8.6.

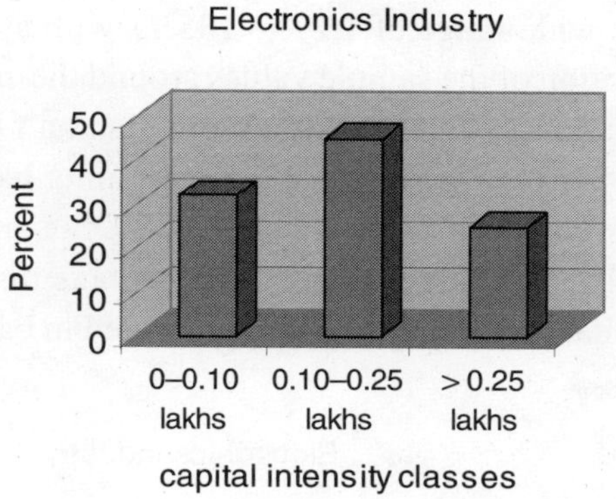

Figure 8.6 Capital Intensity

Sales per person, i.e. labour productivity for the sample units ranges between the minimum of 20,000 and a maximum of 20 lakhs of rupees. The mean value of the sales to employee ratio for the sample is around 5 lakhs of rupees. The sample values show a variation of 79 percent around the mean value. For four units, labour productivity is less than or equal to 2 lakhs of rupees. For a maximum number of the sample units (18), labour productivity lies in between 2 to 5 lakhs. The remaining eight units have yielded labour productivity that is higher than 5 lakh rupees. Percentage distribution of sample units on the labour productivity axis is given in bar figure 8.7.

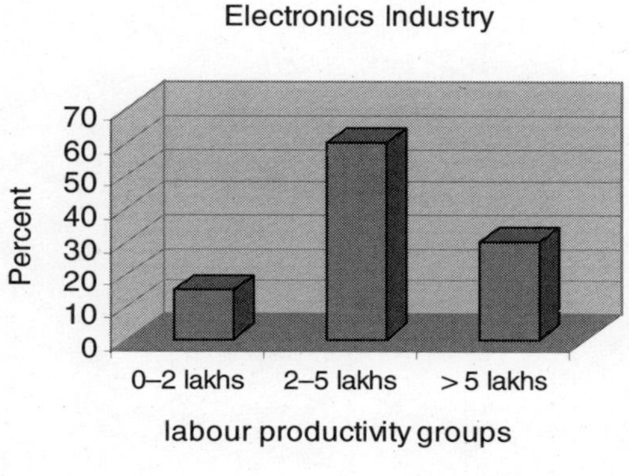

Figure 8.7 Labour Productivity

The values of sales per unit of capital, i.e., capital productivity are scattered over a wide range of 1.27 to 185.71 with a mean of 39.34. The percentage variation of the sample values around the mean as given by the coefficient of variation, is 116. Little more than half the sample (16) has values ranging between zero and 25. Seven units have revealed capital productivity that comes in the range of 25 to 50. For another seven, capital productivity values are larger than 50. Percentage distribution of sample units on the capital productivity axis is presented in bar figure 8.8.

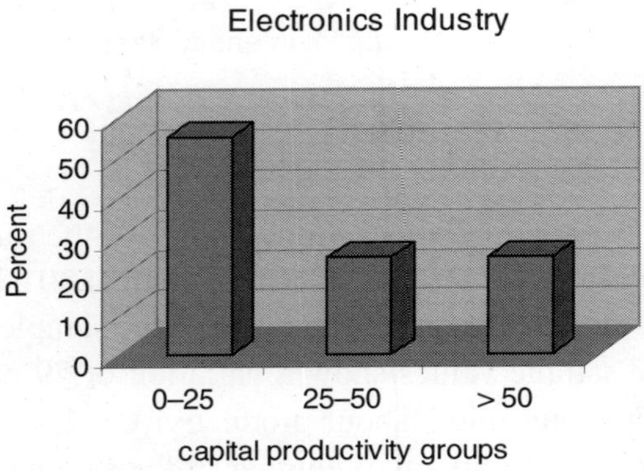

Figure 8.8 Capital Productivity

Descriptive statistics for all the continuous variables discussed above are presented in Table 8.1.

Table 8.1: **Descriptive Statistics for Output, Inputs and Their Ratios—Electronics Industry**

Variable	Mean	Minimum	Maximum	Coefficient of Variation	No. of Observations
Sales Turnover (lakhs)	82.23	1.00	450.00	1.33	30
Plant and Machinery (lakhs)	7.77	0.30	96.72	2.45	30
Total Employment (no.)	14.06	5.00	45.00	0.77	30
Owner Experience (years)	19.60	3.00	60.00	0.63	30
Share of Wage Bill	0.13	0.00	0.44	0.73	30
Share of Material Cost	0.53	0.00	0.80	0.43	30
Capital-Labour Ratio	0.46	0.03	6.45	2.52	30
Capital Productivity	39.34	1.27	185.71	1.16	30
Labour Productivity	5.01	0.20	20.00	0.79	30

Source: Field Survey

8.3.2 Technology Characteristics

The present study has, as mentioned earlier, collected information about different characteristics representing three parts of technology, namely, mechanisation, organisation and information. Thus collected information for the electronics industry is discussed in this section essentially to find the relevance of the technology characteristics considered in the study for the empirical analysis.

Of the 30 sample units, three units have used only instruments and no machinery. Six units have manually operated machines and another five units have numerically controlled machinery. Most of the units (16) have used semi-automatic machines. Twelve of the sample units have undertaken some changes in their machinery over time and the remaining 18 units remain unchanged in terms of mechanisation. Percentage distribution of the sample according to the level and changes in machinery is summed up in pie figures 8.9 and 8.10.

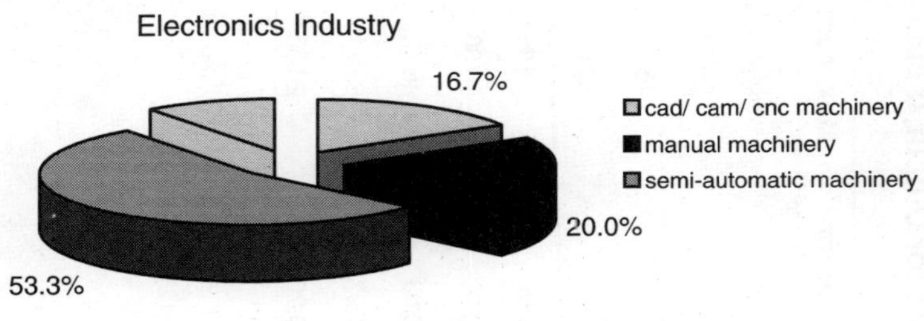

Figure 8.9 Level of Mechanisation

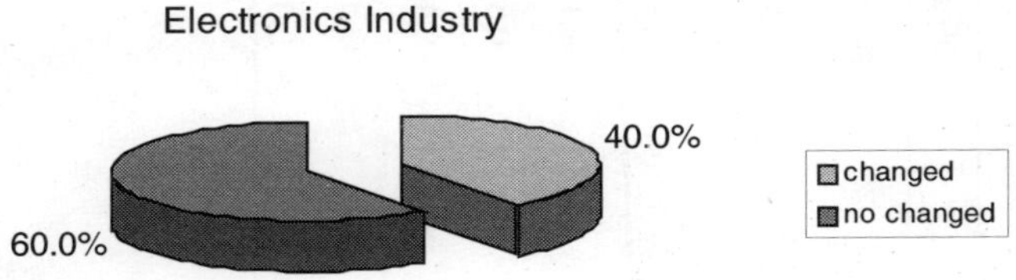

Figure 8.10 Changes in Machinery

A major source of technology for all these electronic units is again the suppliers of machinery. Twenty-three of the 30 units have employed 100 percent Indian machinery in their plants. Of the remaining 7 units, 3 units have employed totally foreign machinery and 4 units have one or two foreign instruments.

A good proportion of the sample (i.e. 19 units) does not know the alternative technologies available to produce their product. Only 11 owners are reported to be aware of the alternative technologies. Almost all the sample units have purchased their machinery mainly keeping their product characteristics in mind. Scale of operation, complementary skills, materials and the relative factor prices are just not taken into account while purchasing their technology especially the machinery. This is because most of their machinery is in the form of instruments which at a time can be used to only one piece and thus independent of scale. In view of lack of knowledge of alternatives, selection criteria in this industry too can be taken as parameters placed by the units before the suppliers of machinery to provide appropriate machinery.

As regards the business form of organisation, 19 of the 30 sample units are proprietary concerns. Only three units are partnership firms and the remaining eight units are organised as limited companies. Twenty-six of our sample units are managed by owners. Work allocation is fixed for more than half of the units (16) and the remaining units have rotated jobs for their employees. But for three units, the electronics sample has not acquired any quality management system like ISO 9000. The empirical evidence pertaining to the business form of organisation and work allocation is presented in pie figures 8.11 and 8.12. The remaining production organisation variables like production schedules and materials management are quite flexible in these small-scale units. So, for further analysis, we mainly focus on the business form of organisation and work allocation as these two variables show a reasonable variation across the sample.

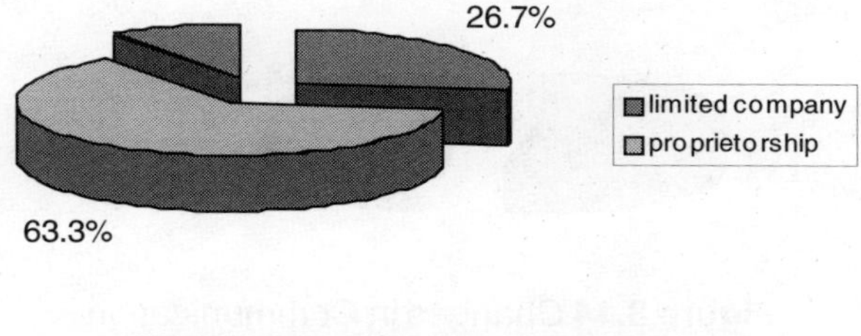

Figure 8.11 Business Organisation

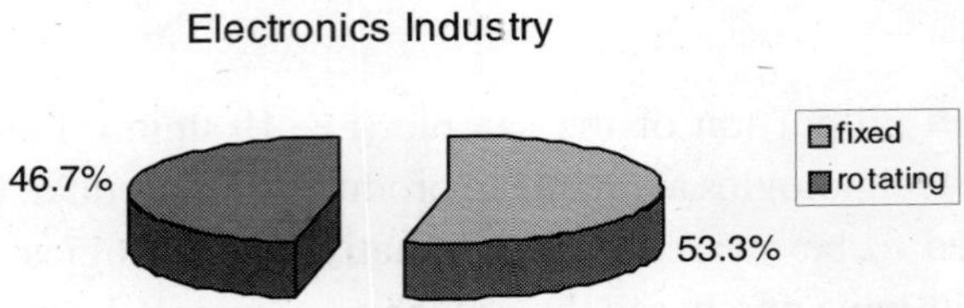

Figure 8.12 Work Allocation

As regards information technology, little more than half of the units (16) have started using electronic mail and the remaining units still use the traditional ways of communication. Fourteen of the 30 units have not made any changes in their ways of communication with the outside agents. The rest of the sample (16) has undertaken changes in the ways of communication. Eight units have been using paper files to store and process data and another eight units have shifted entirely to computers. 14 of the 30 units are in the process of computerising their data. Percentage distribution of survey units according to the means and changes in means of communication as well as data management or record keeping is presented in pie figures 8.13, 8.14 and 8.15. In sum, all the information technology characteristics show substantial variation among the sample units.

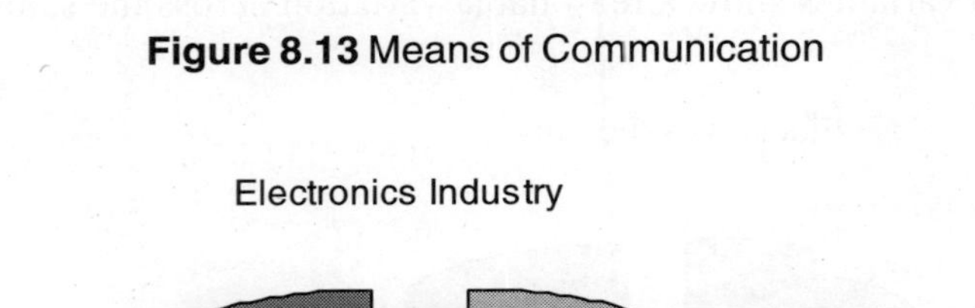

Figure 8.13 Means of Communication

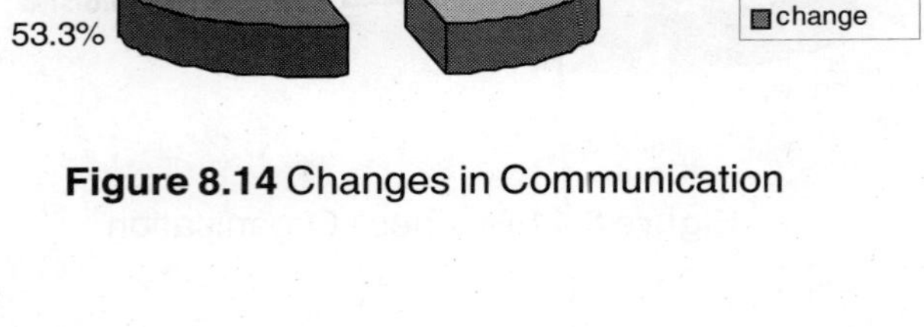

Figure 8.14 Changes in Communication

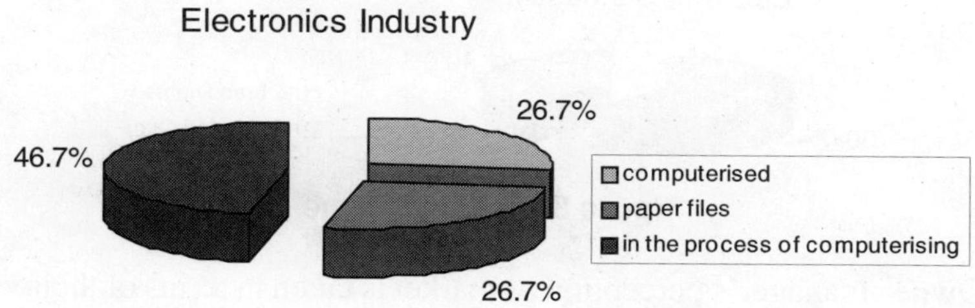

Figure 8.15 Record Keeping

8.3.3 Non-Technology Characteristics

We now examine variations in the non-technology characteristics that are taken to influence technology characteristics. We start with the product market served and the owner's perceptions about market competition.

As far as the product market is concerned, the entire electronics industry group in the sample serves the domestic market. Of a total of 30 electronics units, 16 sell their products at the national level while nine units sell only in the northern region. Five units serve specific customers. Since most of the electronic units of our sample produce consumer items, the brand name matters. However, 12 of the 30 sample units have not given any brand name to their products. Majority of the sample units (25) do not feel that payment is a problem. Units producing consumer electronics distribute their products through wholesale dealers. Percentage distribution of units according to the type of market and brand name is presented in figures 8.16 and 8.17.

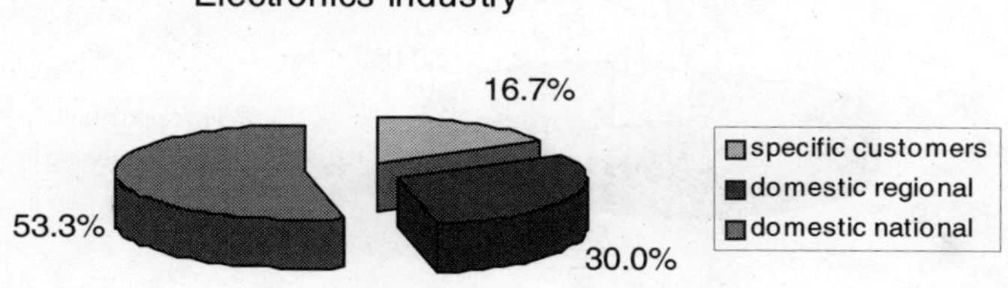

Figure 8.16 Product Market

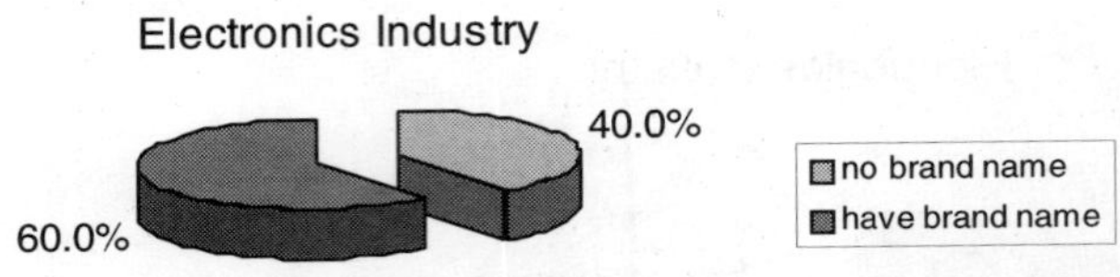

Figure 8.17 Brand Name

Owner-manager's perception of market is taken in terms of their views on market competition, its likely impact on the unit and demand for their products. Twenty-six owner-managers think that markets are increasingly competitive. Of these 26, fourteen units feel intensive competition. The remaining four units do not sense any difference in market competition. The primary reason given for the increasing market competition is the entry of multinational corporations. Regarding the consequences of market changes on the unit, 21 owners have reported that the market changes are threatening. Only nine of 30 have taken the market changes as opportunities for the growth of their units. But for four, all the sample units do not consider demand as a constraint. Empirical evidence relating to the perceptions of market competition and its impact is presented in pie figures 8.18 and 8.19.

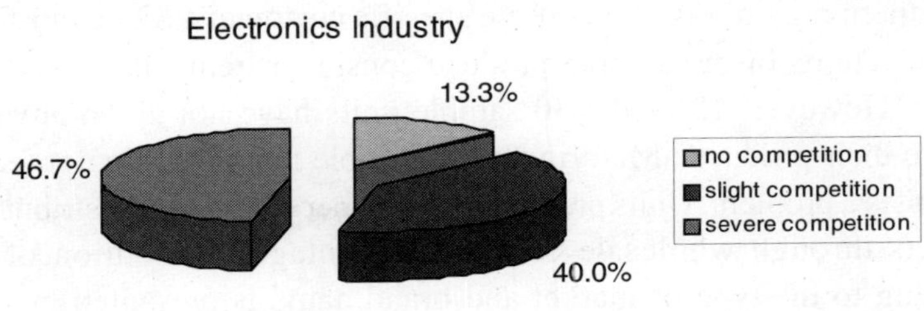

Figure 8.18 Market Competition

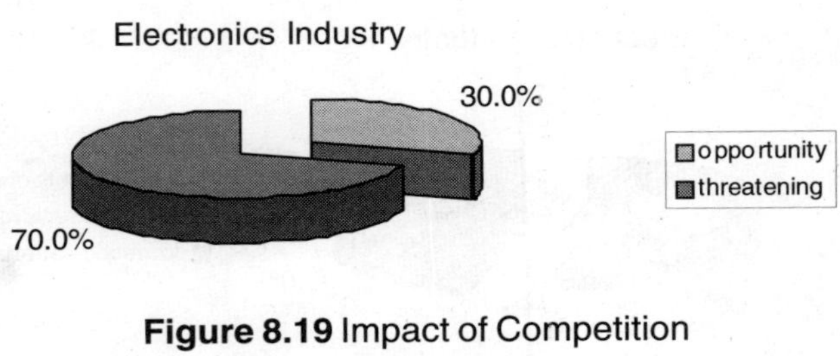

Figure 8.19 Impact of Competition

As has been mentioned earlier, the technological capabilities of the units are proxied by owner-manager's education and experience and the share of professional labour in the total labour of the unit. As far as the owner's education is concerned, a majority of the sample owners (23) are professionals mainly electronic engineers. Six of the owners in the sample had higher education but not a professional course. One owner completed only schooling.

As far as the experience of the owners is concerned, the sample minimum is 3 years and the maximum is 60 years. The mean value of the sample for the owner's experience is 19 years. The sample variation around the mean value of experience is 63 per cent. Eight owners have less than 10 years experience in the area of production. Majority of the sample has an experience that ranges between 10 to 25 years. The owner-managers of 7 units have more than 25 years of experience.

Of the 30 units surveyed, 7 units have employed entirely non-professional labour. Sixteen sample units have professional labour up to 25 percent of the total labour. Rest of the sample has more than 25 percent of their labour as professional labour. The evidence in respect of the characteristics representing technological capabilities of the firm is presented in figures 8.20, 8.21 and 8.22.

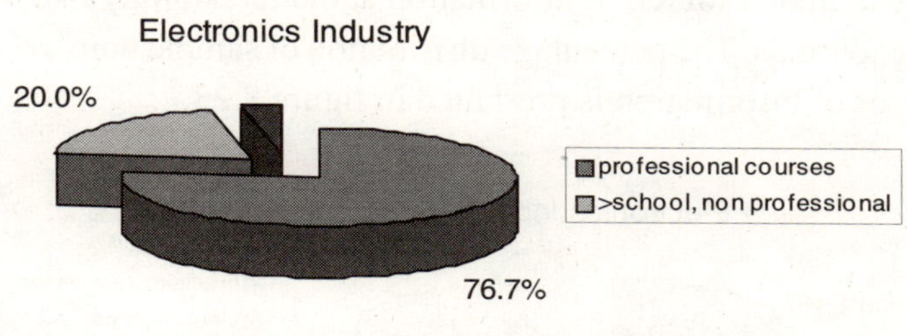

Figure 8.20 Education of Owners

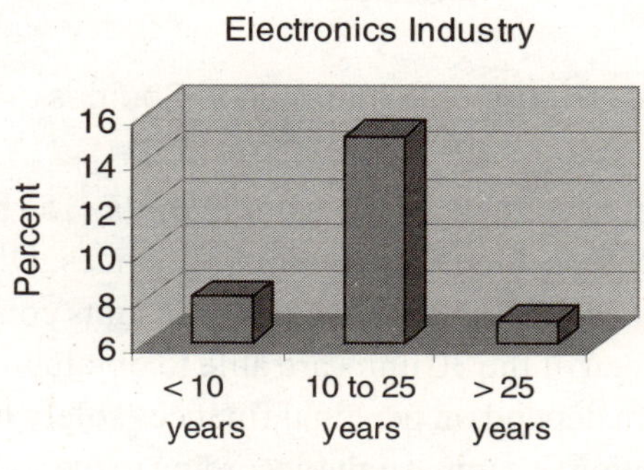

Figure 8.21 Experience of Owners

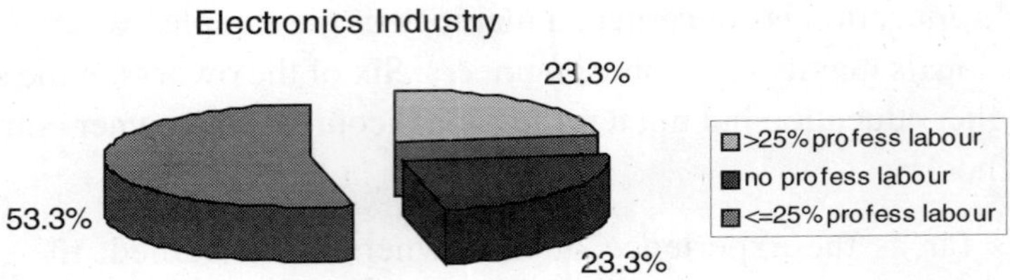

Figure 8.22 Use of Professional Labour

Scale of operation that has been considered as one of the important determinants of technology, has been represented by the annual sales turnover of the units. Survey results of the sales turnover of the electronics sample have already been discussed in section 8.3.1.

Technology information is not considered a problem by a majority of the sample units, i.e. 24. Of the remaining six units, only one feels the problem intensely. Thirteen of 30 sample units use a single source of information including their personal experience. Rest of the sample (17) has more than one source of information about technology like trade fairs and trade journals. The percentage distribution of sample units according to the sources of information is presented in figure 8.23.

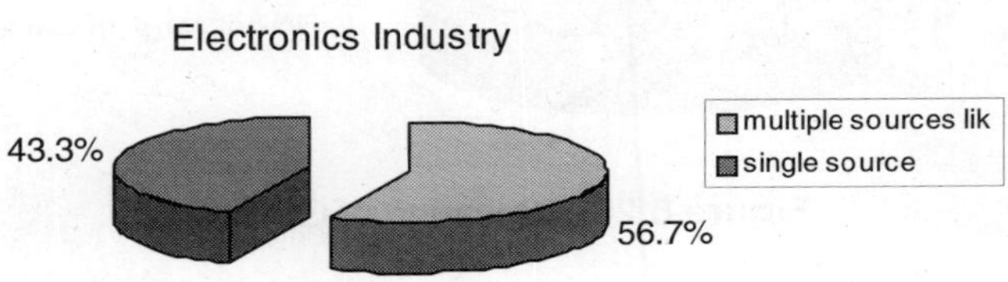

Figure 8.23 Information Sources

Regarding finances, half of the sample units (15) have reported that they do not have any problems in obtaining finances. Of the remaining 12 units that find it difficult to obtain finances, five units consider it as a severe constraint. Seventeen of the 30 units are able to obtain institutional finance and only 13 of them depend on personal finances solely to manage the unit. Percentage distribution of sample units according to the sources and problems of finances are summed up in pie figures 8.24 and 8.25.

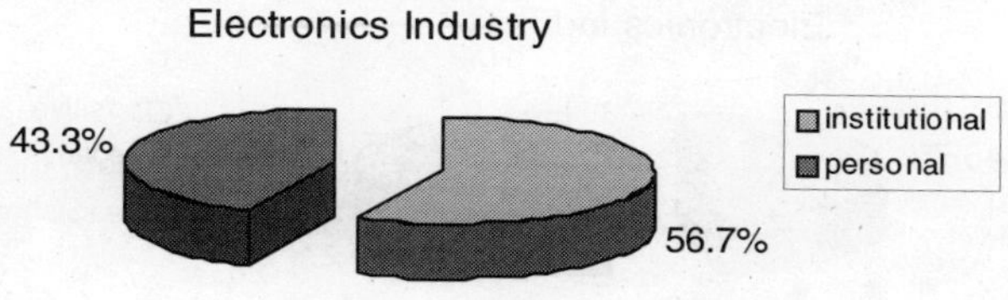

Figure 8.24 Sources of Finance

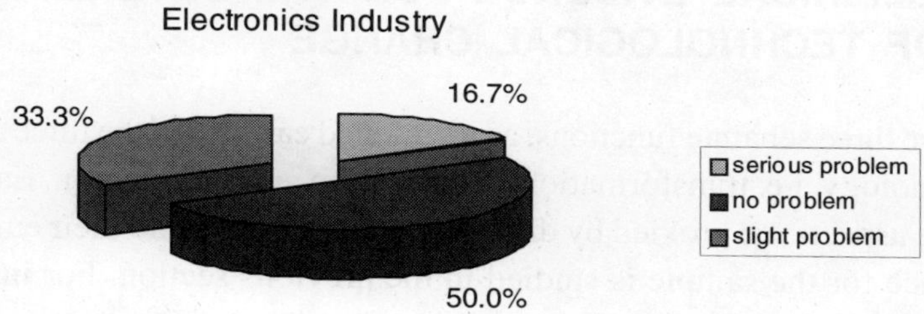

Figure 8.25 Finance Problem

Of the 30 sample units, 24 units have not complained of any problems due to labour behaviour like absenteeism, unionism and turnover. However, almost half of the sample units (14) have reported that their problems are due to negative labour attitudes. The remaining 16 units have experienced positive attitudes. Survey results in respect of labour behaviour and attitudes are summed up in pie figures 8.26 and 8.27.

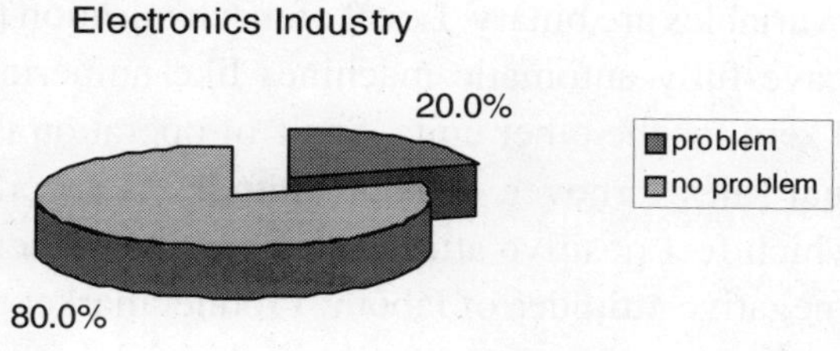

Figure 8.26 Labour Behaviour

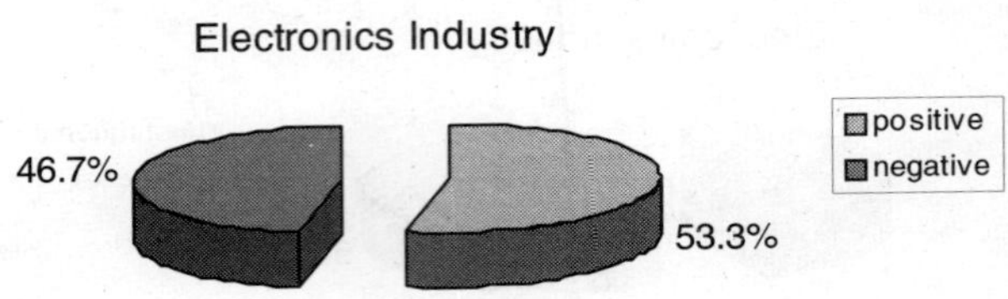

Figure 8.27 Labour Attitudes

8.4 EMPIRICAL EVIDENCE FOR THE DETERMINANTS OF TECHNOLOGICAL CHANGE

We have three separate functions, as mentioned earlier, for the three aspects of technology, i.e. transformation, organisation and information. Each one of these aspects are proxied by different characteristics and their empirical relevance for the sample is studied in the previous section. For instance, both the level and changes in mechanisation turned out to be empirically relevant in our electronics industry sample. Econometric estimation, however, could be done only with the level of mechanisation. Among the alternatives tried out with the level of mechanisation as dependent variable, equation (8.1) turned out to be better. It is given as

$$\text{LOM} = \text{F (CONST, SCA, MKT, LAB1)} \qquad (8.1)$$

where LOM = Level of mechanization
SCA = Scale of operation and
MKT = Product market served
LAB1 = Labour problems due to attitudes

All these variables are binary. Level of mechanisation takes a value of one if units have fully automatic machines like numerically controlled machines and zero for the other units. Scale of operation is considered in terms of annual sales turnover. Labour attitudes is specified as one for those units, which feel positive attitudes of labour and zero for the units experiencing negative attitudes of labour. Product market takes value one for the units serving specific customers, i.e. industrial units and zero for the units catering to the open market, where units do not personally know their final consumers. This equation is estimated using Probit model.

As regards organisation, only work allocation practices are varying across the sample units and hence considered for econometric purpose.

Variations in work allocation practices are explained by the combination of scale of operation, labour behaviour and product market. The organization function is given as

	RWA	=	F (CONST, SCA, LAB2, MKT)	(8.2)
where	RWA	=	Work allocation practices	
	LAB2	=	Labour problems due to behaviour	

SCA and MKT are as defined in the equation (8.1)

Work allocation practices is a binary variable with zero for the units that fix jobs to their workers and one for the units rotating job assignments for their workers. Labour behaviour is taken as one for the units, which do not have any labour problems like absenteeism or turnover, and zero for the units that experience these problems. This equation again is estimated in the Probit model framework as the dependent variable is binary.

Although both the means of communication and data management turned out to be relevant for the empirical analysis in the sense that these characteristics vary across the sample units, econometric estimation was possible in the case of data management only. The selected equation for the data management is given as

	RRK	=	F (CONST, SCA, REOO)	(8.3)
where	RRK	=	Record keeping/ data management	
	REOO	=	Education of owners	

SCA is as defined in the other two equations.

Record keeping/data management is defined as zero for the units using only (or mainly) paper files and one for the units storing and processing of entire data through computers only. Education of owners is zero for the units with non-professional owners and one for the units with professional owners. This equation too is specified in terms of Probit model. Results for the transformation, organisation and information technologies are tabulated in Table 8.2.

Table 8.2: **Marginal Coefficients of Technology Functions——Electronics Industry**

Variable	Coefficient	T-values
Transformation Technology		
Dependent Variable: Level of Mechanisation (LOM)		
Constant	–2.27209	–13.5.95
Scale of operation (ST)	0.0030	0.4289
Product Market (MKT)	0.0994	0.59.8
Labour Attitudes (LAB1)	–0.2306	–1.5826
Organisation Technology		
Dependent Variable: Work Allocation Practices (RWA)		
Constant	–2.2509	–11.9867
Scale of operation (ST)	0.0002	0.4969
Labour Behaviour (LAB2)	–0.1024	–1.5249
Product Market (MKT)	–0.2880	–1.0415
Information Technology Dependent Variable: Data Management (RRK)		
Constant	–2.9468	–9.0802
Scale of operation (ST)	0.0005	1.6246
Education of Owner (REOO)	0.0577	0.4220

As regards the level of mechanisation, estimates reveal that only labour attitudes are having statistically significant influence on the level of mechanisation. Both scale of operation and product market is not showing any influence on the level of mechanisation. Given the fact that most of the small electronic units are engaged in the manual assembling of the components into specific products and are hence labour-intensive, it is quite possible that labour attitudes than any other variable is affecting the units adversely. Hence, all those units feeling negative attitudes of labour may be going in for fully automatic machinery. It can be seen in the negative sign of the labour variable. The magnitude of the marginal coefficient of labour variable show that the probability of a unit going in for fully automatic machines due to negative attitudes of labour is 0.23.

Work allocation practices are mainly influenced by the labour behaviour. It can be seen from the coefficients of labour behaviour which is statistically significant. Labour behaviour such as absenteeism and turnover leads not only to immediate production loss but also disturbs the delivery schedules. Hence, labour behaviour, if problematic, prompts the units to rotate jobs among the workers so that workers have knowledge of many jobs. This enables units to shift workers on to the other jobs if the concerned worker is on leave or has left the unit. Thus, rotation of jobs among workers minimises adverse consequences of labour behaviour like absenteeism or turnover.

In the case of storing and processing of data, scale of operation turns out to be statistically significant. It only indicates that larger scale of operations makes it worth for the units to use computers for storing and processing data. It is quite possible given that the smaller units dominate the sample and mostly owners does the processing of data as they do not keep supporting staff to do it.

8.5 IMPACT OF TECHNOLOGICAL CHANGE

As mentioned in the earlier chapters, impact of technological change is studied in terms of the unit's competitiveness. Competitive strength of units is further taken in terms of their sales performance. Impact of technology on sales performance is examined in the production function framework where technology variables are taken along with the conventional inputs like capital, labour and materials. In the case of electronics, we have considered level of mechanisation, work allocation practices and data management as proxies for transformation, organisation and information technologies respectively. These technology characteristics are introduced directly in the production function as dummy variables. Our production function is specified as six-input Cobb-Douglas function and written in terms of log-linear form as

$$\begin{aligned} \text{LnST} = \; & C + \alpha \ln \text{PM} + \beta \ln \text{LAB} + \delta \ln \text{MAT} \\ & + \theta_1 \text{LOM} + \theta_2 \text{RWA} + \theta_3 \text{RRK} + \mu \end{aligned} \tag{8.4}$$

where, ln refers to logarithmic values of the variables

ST = Sales turnover

PM = Original value of plant and machinery

LAB = Total number of employees

MAT = Value of materials consumed during the year

LOM = Level of mechanisation;
1 for units with fully automatic machinery; 0 otherwise

RWA = Work allocation practices;
1 for units rotating jobs to workers; 0 otherwise

RRK = Data management;
1 for units with computerized entirely data processing;
0 otherwise

Equation (8.4) has been estimated through the Ordinary Least Squares (OLS) method. The estimated parameters of the equation are presented in Table 8.3.

Table 8.3: **Estimates of Production Function—Electronics Industry**

Variables	Coefficients	T-values
Dependent Variable: Ln (sales turnover)		
Constant	0.8700	2.927
Ln (plant and machinery)	0.0530	1.005
Ln (labour)	0.2530	1.509
Ln (materials)	0.669	7.448
Level of mechanisation	0.1630	0.989
Work allocations	0.1180	1.037
Data management	0.3850	2.805
	$R^2 = 0.922$ F = 41.496	

The estimated parameters of materials, labour and data management turn out to be statistically significant in explaining the variation in the sales turnover of electronics. Neither the coefficients of level of mechanisation nor the stock of machinery (i.e. plant and machinery) are statistically significant in the production function estimation. So is the case with the coefficient of work allocation practices. Since most of the small-scale electronic units are engaged in the manual assembling of the purchased components into specified products, labour and materials are more important for these units in comparison with the machinery. Specifically, the availability of materials, which mainly includes components is expected to be significant. Once the materials are purchased, it is the labour, which plays a significant role in assembling the components into the final product.

Statistical significance of the parameter estimates indicates the same. For the same reason that the manual assembling is a primary production operation, stock of plant and machinery as well as its level is not statistically significant. It can also be seen from the smaller amounts of original value of plant and machinery in majority of the sample units. Data management has statistically significant coefficient indicating that it also plays an important role in sales performance of the units. Data management through computers gives a clear and immediate picture of orders, production status and sales, and hence enables the unit to take prompt actions required to improve sales. It is important as most of the small-scale electronic units cater to the open market.

8.6 SUMMARY

The sample electronics units of our study are primarily involved in the assembling of consumer and industrial electronics. Majority of these units have plant and machinery worth less than or equal to five lakhs of rupees producing up to Rs. 75 lakhs. Few units have numerically controlled machinery and few units have changed their machinery over time. Main source of technology even for the electronics sample is suppliers of machinery. These units purchase their machinery from the suppliers of machinery keeping their product characteristics in mind.

Most of the sample units are proprietary and partnership firms, and owner-managed. But for work allocation practices, characteristics representing production organisation are quite flexible and do not vary much across the sample units. Reasonable number of sample units has computers and use modern methods of communication and data management.

As regards product market, few units in our sample serve specific customers and rest of them cater to the open market where they do not personally know their customers. Most of our sample units have started feeling intense competition primarily due to the entry of multinational corporations, which is threatening their survival. Almost all the owners are highly educated and a good number of them are electronic engineers. Professional labour can be seen in some of the units.

Information is not considered as a problem by the sample units. Although a good number of units have access to institutional finance, half of the sample feels finance a problem. Labour problem is experienced by a reasonable number of sample units.

Transformation technology taken in terms of level of mechanisation is primarily determined by labour attitudes in the electronics units. Negative labour attitudes towards work prompts units to go for fully automatic machinery.

Organisation technology captured through work allocation practices is explained by the behaviour of labour. Labour behavioural problems like absenteeism and turnover is influencing units to rotate job assignments for workers.

Information technology considered in terms of data management is explained by scale of operation indicating that large-scale operation makes it worth to use computers for data processing.

Sales performance, the indicator of the competitive strength of units is influenced primarily by materials, labour and information technology. Both the stock of machinery and level of mechanisation are not playing a role in enhancing the competitive strength of our sample electronics units.

Endnotes

1. Zero means negligible share. It is there in one of the sample units because of small number of employees and lower wages paid to them.
2. It is the case with the only one unit that is engaged in the job work.

Chapter 9 Technological Change in the Garments Industry

9.1 INTRODUCTION

In this chapter, we discuss the empirical evidence for the basic objectives of the study i.e. causes and consequences of technological change, with reference to the garments industry.

We, first, present the basic features of our sample units in terms of output, inputs and structural ratios like capital-labour ratio. Later, we discuss the evidence regarding technology and non-technology characteristics and their relevance for the empirical analysis. Finally, we examine the statistical relations between the technology and non-technology characteristics including the indicators of competitive strength, using econometric tools.

9.2 FIELD IMPRESSIONS

Garment units came up in Delhi mainly in response to the large-scale external demand. The rise in domestic demand later added impetus to the growth of this industry. These two components of the market remained segmented in terms of units serving, product nature and prices. Whatever be the market served, industry has come up with numerous small-scale units that can be taken more as a set of organisers in the garment business than manufacturers of garments. These units were getting specialised jobs done such as procurement of orders, procurement of materials and getting the garments made by independent tailors, and earning commissions for their jobs. Not many of the units focused on developing into a modern garments manufacturing unit, which would attempt to sell its product in the market.

By the 1990s, importers from the developed nations were well aware of the ground realities in India in the garments sector including the costs of materials, individual commissions and growing number of units that are willing to do at lower costs. Simultaneously, these importers have explored alternative countries of cheap labour to get their jobs done. Hence, they have started pressurising the exporters in India not only to have their own manufacturing facilities to ensure quality and reduce costs but also to conform to environment and labour standards.[1] The Indian exporting units have no other option except to setup a full-fledged manufacturing unit or leave.

Units that have established themselves reasonably in the business in the sense of getting regular export orders of large size over time are going in for a full-fledged manufacturing unit. Most of these units have gone for quality sewing machines imported from Japan or Germany to the extent that their finances permitted. The size of the units is not only constrained by size of the orders and finance but also by labour problems given the labour intensity of the industry and the existing labour laws. Really big exporters are going in for more than one factory keeping the potential threat from unionization of labour in mind. Some of these units have recruited professionals like textile engineers or trained fashion designers.

Numerous other units operating with smaller and irregular orders do not want to risk having their own production and hence are managing as it is or closing down their operations. A few such people after closing down their independent operations joined the management of the newly built manufacturing units. The situation is more or less similar for the employment of the hitherto independent tailors who are shifting to work in the newly set up units. Thus, the nineties witnessed a shift from the numerous small-scale organisers in the garments export business aiming at an immediate commission to the development of garment manufacturing units focussing on quality improvements and cost reduction and thus to raise their market shares. Though at a smaller level, units established in the domestic market are also slowly going in for their own manufacturing plants or raising their in-house production.

9.3 BASIC CHARACTERISTICS OF THE GARMENTS SAMPLE

We have surveyed 31 garment units in order to study the technological change, factors affecting it and its consequences in the garment industry.

The surveyed units produce all types of garments, i.e., garments for men, women and kids. However, most of the units are involved in the production of women's garments. As has already been discussed in section 5.3, the garment industry is currently undergoing transformation to fully in-house production of garments. Hitherto, a major production operation like tailoring was mostly farmed out to fabricators. Now, the garment units are increasingly turning to in-house tailoring. This means more machinery and changes in the production organisation of the units. Another feature of the industry that is relevant for the study is that there have not been any technological developments in sewing machines and hence tailoring, the major production operation in the industry, is still done by manually operated power driven machines internationally. There exists, however, wide differences in the quality of machines that are available. The usage of computerised machines can be seen only in the pre-assembly stages like design, pattern making and in value added activities like embroidery. For the purpose of the study, we have confined ourselves to design making, pattern marking, cutting, tailoring and finishing operations as these are the basic operations that are involved in the production of every garment.

9.3.1 General Economic Characteristics

But for 3, none of the sample units availed any government assistance. Twenty-one of the total 31 units have expressed their views about government policies. But they are so wide ranging that it is not possible to group them in one or the other category. It includes export procedures, availability of quality fabric, import duties, quota implementation, infrastructure, labour etc. But for 5 units, none of the sample units have any brand name of their own. Seventeen of the sample units have registered under the Factories Act and the remaining 14 units are non-factories. The garments sample is also dominated by units (28) that were set up, not inherited, by the current owners.

As regards the annual sales turnover, the mean sales turnover of our sample is around 576 lakhs of rupees. The sales turnover of the sample units shows a variation of 134 per cent around the sample mean and within the range of 1.80 (minimum) to 3032 (maximum) lakhs. Twelve units have a sales turnover that is less than 100 lakhs. Eight units are in the range of 100 to 500 lakhs. Six of the sample units fall in the range of 500 to 1000 lakhs of sales turnover and another five units have a sales turnover that is greater than 1000 lakhs. Percentage distribution of the sample units along the lines of sales turnover is presented in bar figure 9.1.

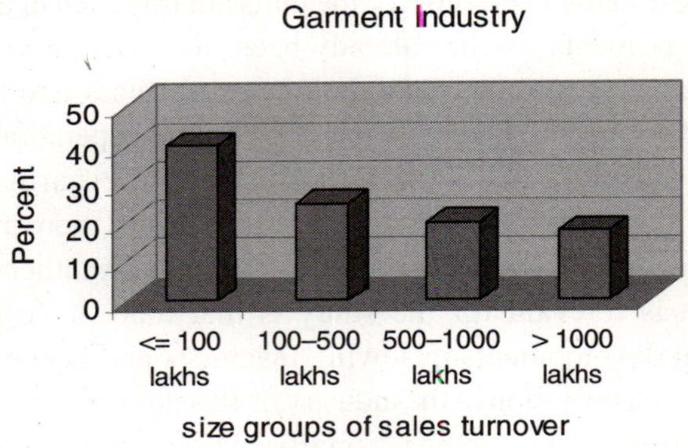

Figure 9.1 Sales Turnover

As has been noted earlier in the section, garment industry has the practice of farming out their main production operation namely, tailoring. This practice has been changing and the garment units are slowly going in for in-house production. In this context, it is important to know how much of the sales come from their in-house production. So, we have collected information relating to their in-house production, which is presented here. Nine of the 31 sample units have farmed out the entire tailoring operation to fabricators and thus do not have any in-house production facilities in this respect. Eight units of the sample, produce less than or equal to 50 percent of their total production in-house. Another six units have in-house production that amounts to 50 to 90 percent of the total production. Eight of the 31 sample units have 100 percent in-house production. Percentage distribution of sample units according to the in-house production is reported in bar figure 9.2.

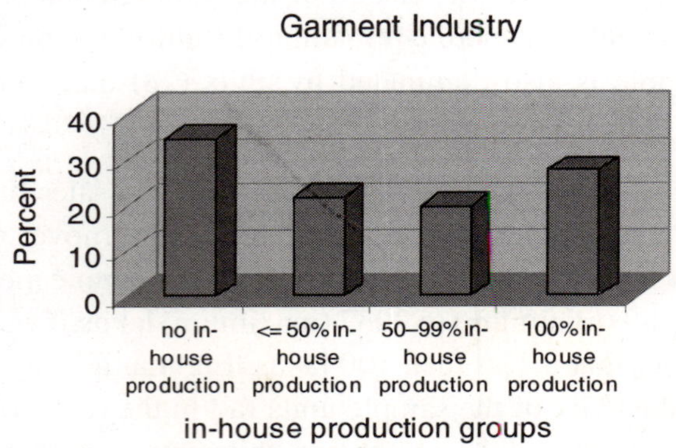

Figure 9.2 Percentage of In-house Production

The original investment on plant and machinery of the sample units ranges between rupees 0.01 to 200 lakhs with a mean value of 38.38 lakhs of rupees. The variation of sample values around the mean is 143 percent. A little more than half (i.e. 16 units) have plant and machinery that is less than or equal to 15 lakhs. The rest of the sample (15 units) has plant and machinery that is more than 15 lakhs.

Minimum employment of the sample is 3 and the maximum is 500 persons. The mean value of the employment of the sample is 92 persons and the variation around the mean as given by coefficient of variation is 140 percent. Eleven of our sample units have an employment up to 10 persons. Another 8 units have an employment in the range of 10 to 50 employees. The remaining 12 units have employed more than 50 persons. Percentage distribution of sample units along the dimensions of plant and machinery and employment is shown in bar figures 9.3 and 9.4.

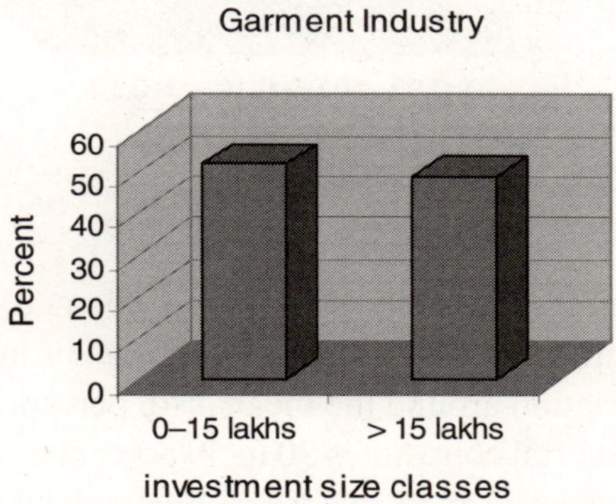

Figure 9.3 Plant and Machinery

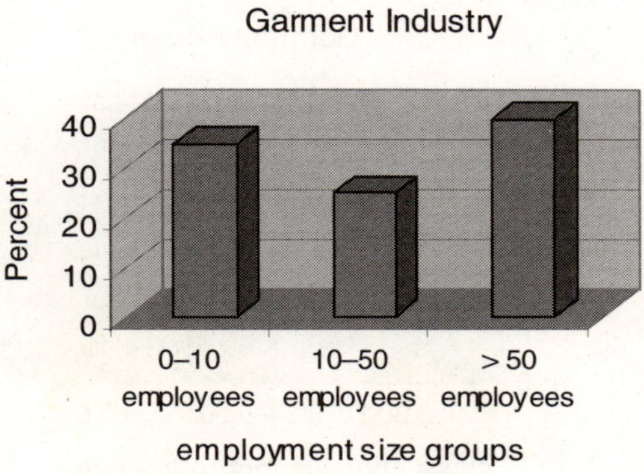

Figure 9.4 Total Employment

The share of wage bill in the sales turnover in the sample units ranges from 0.03 to 0.80 with a mean value of 0.16. Variation around the mean that is given by coefficient of variation is 105 percent. Only 5 units have a wage share that is less than 5 percent of their sales turnover. 12 units display a wage bill that lies in the range of 5 to 10 percent. The wage share of the remaining 14 units is more than 10 percent of the sales turnover. Percentage distribution of sample units according to the percentage share of wage bill is given in bar figure 9.5.

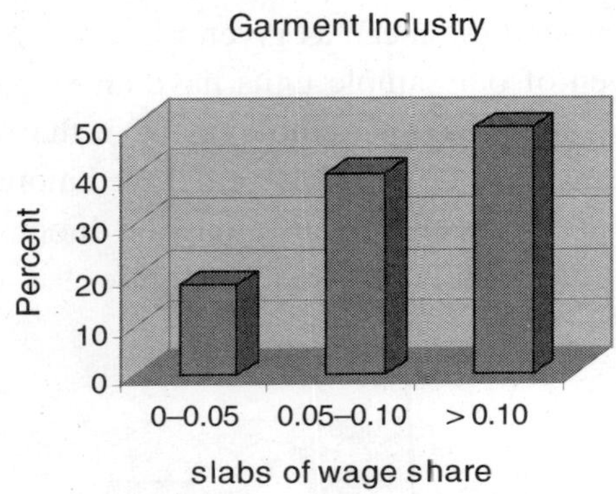

Figure 9.5 Wage Share

As far as material share of the sample is concerned, it oscillates in the range of 0 to 75 percent.[2] The sample mean value of material share is 43 percent and the variation around the mean is 46 percent. For a majority of the sample (14), material constitutes 30 to 50 percent of the sales turnover. Eight units have a material share that is less than or equal to 30 percent and 9 units have more than 50 percent. Percentage distribution of sample units according to the percentage share of materials is given in bar figure 9.6.

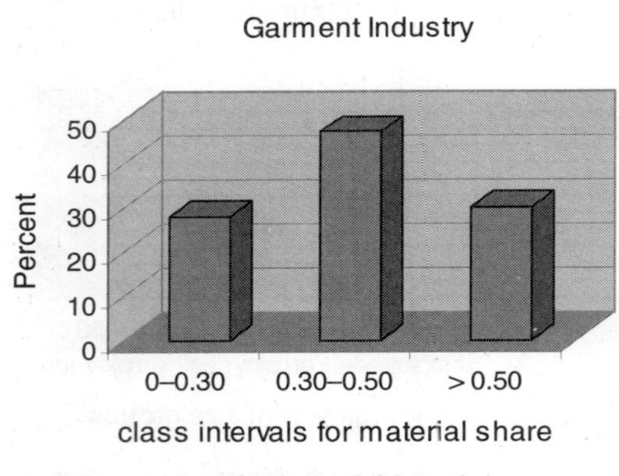

Figure 9.6 Share of Materials

Evidence with respect to the structural ratios indicates that all the three ratios vary widely. Capital-intensity taken as the ratio of plant and machinery to employment varies from 0.01 to 6.67 in the sample. The mean of the sample is 0.49 and the variation around the mean is as high as 237 percent. A good proportion of sample (12) shows capital intensity that is less than 0.10. Another 11 units have yielded a capital intensity that is more than 0.40. The rest of the sample (8 units) falls in between the two groups. Percentage distribution of sample units according to their capital intensity is reported in figure 9.7.

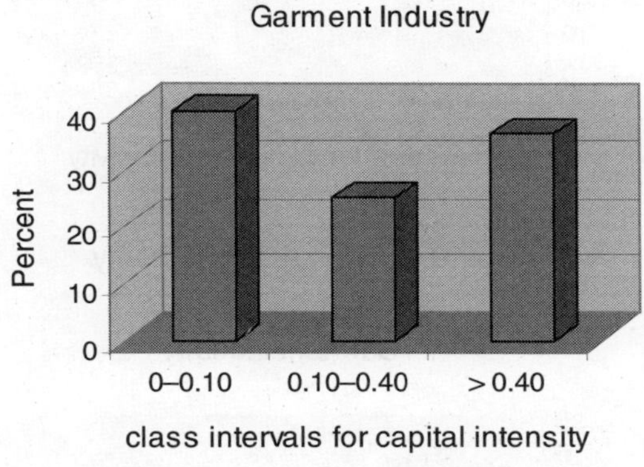

Figure 9.7 Capital Intensity

As regards the factor productivities, capital productivity measured as a ratio of sales to plant and machinery ranges between a minimum of 1.43 and a maximum of 2727.27. The mean value of the capital productivity comes around 158.56. The variation in the sample values as given by the coefficient of variation is 3.18. Eight units revealed a capital productivity that is less than or equal to 10. Another 16 units displayed a capital productivity that lies in between 10 and 50. The remaining seven units yielded capital productivity that is greater than 50.

Labour productivity is measured as the ratio of sales to employment. It varies widely across the sample from 0.18 to 50. The sample mean for labour productivity is 7.47 and the coefficient of variation is 1.21, which essentially indicates that the percentage variation of sample values around the mean value is 121 percent. The maximum number (i.e. 16) has yielded a labour productivity that lies in the range of zero to 5 lakhs of rupees. Seven units have labour productivity in the range of rupees 5 to 10 lakhs and the other eight units have labour productivity that is more than 10 lakhs. The sample variation in the two productivities can be seen in bar figures 9.8 and 9.9.

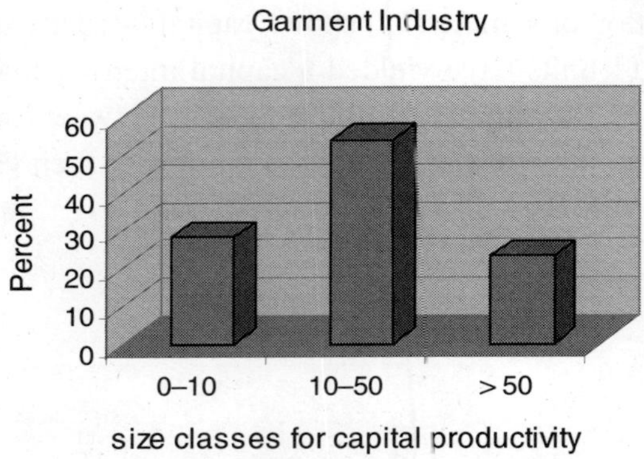

Figure 9.8 Capital Productivity

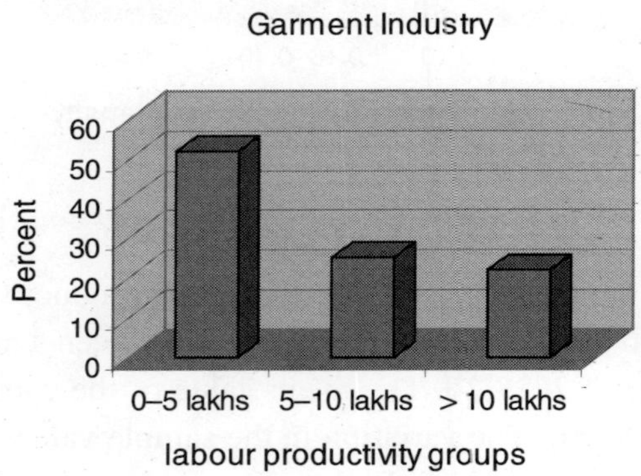

Figure 9.9 Labour Productivity

Descriptive statistics for all the continuous variables are presented in Table 9.1.

Table 9.1: **Descriptive Statistics for Output, Inputs and Their Ratios—Garment Industry**

Variable	Mean	Minimum	Maximum	Coefficient of Variation	No. of Observations
Sales Turnover (lakhs)	576.57	1.80	3032.00	1.34	31
Plant and Machinery (lakhs)	38.38	0.10	200.00	1.43	31
Total Employment (no.)	92.48	3.00	500.00	1.40	31
Owner Experience (years)	13.23	3.00	30.00	0.58	31
Share of Wage Bill	0.16	0.03	0.80	1.05	31
Share of Material Cost	0.43	0.00	0.75	0.46	31
Capital-Labour Ratio	0.49	0.01	6.67	2.37	31
Capital Productivity	158.56	1.43	2727.27	3.18	31
Labour Productivity	7.47	0.18	50.00	1.21	31

Source: Field Survey

9.3.2 Technology Characteristics

As mentioned earlier, we have considered numerous characteristics of industrial units that represent mechanisation, organisation and the information parts of the technology of these units. Here, we examine these characteristics with respect to the garment sample.

As far as the level of mechanisation is concerned, of the 31 sample units, seven have instruments only and the remaining 24 units have manually operated machines. Units which have farmed out 100 percent of their tailoring operations, are expected to have only cutting and ironing machines which are no more than tools. As regards the change, 19 units have changed their machinery for betterment. Only 12 units have reported no such change in their machinery. The percentage distribution of sample units in these categories can be seen from pie figures 9.10 and 9.11.

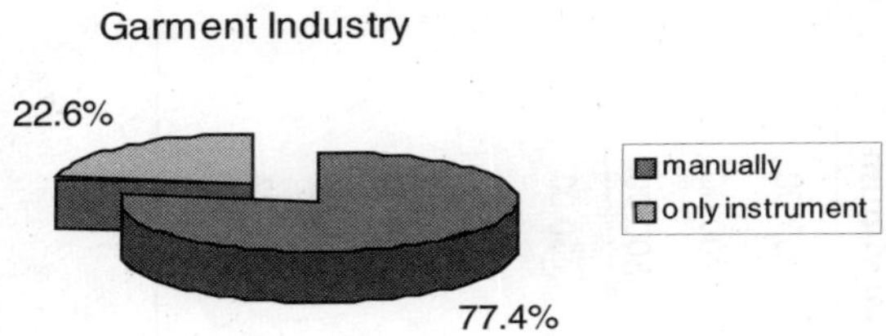

Figure 9.10 Level of Mechanisation

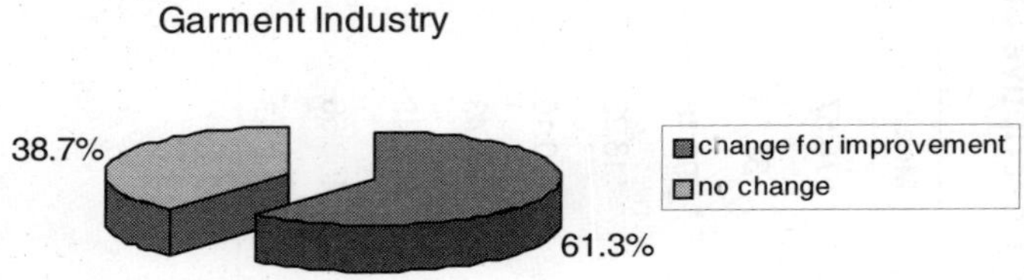

Figure 9.11 Changes in Machinery

Suppliers of machinery are the major source of technology even for the garment industry. One finds a good presence of foreign machinery in the industry while a few units have foreign machinery only. All the machines are first-hand. Thirteen units do not have any foreign machine especially stitching machines in their units while one finds the presence of foreign machines in the remaining units. The percentage distribution of sample units according to the presence or absence of foreign machines is given in pie figure 9.12.

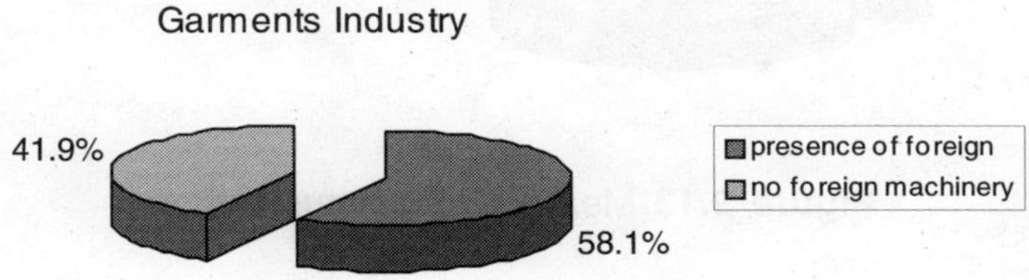

Figure 9.12 Presence of Foreign Machinery

All the sample units are aware of at least, the presence of alternative machinery like Juki and Brother of Japan, Sunstar of Korea, in addition to the Indian based Meritt and Singer stitching machines. Of all the foreign companies, Juki is fairly established in the Indian garment industry. Units have gone for a foreign machine like Juki stitching machine for quality reasons. Availability of finance and the cost of machine given the lower scale of operation are some of the reasons given by the units that have not bought good machines like Juki. Availability of complementary skills and materials, and relative factor prices are turned out to be unimportant.

With respect to the means of communication with outside agents, most of the sample (i.e. 22 units) have an e-mail in addition to the traditional ways of communication like personal visit or post or phone. The remaining units (9) still use the traditional ways of communication. While 20 of the 31garment units that have been surveyed, have changed their ways of communication over time, the rest of the sample (11 units) has not made any changes over time in their ways of communication with the outside agents like customers. As regards record keeping or data management, only five units have computerised the entire data. A good proportion of the sample (16) is in the process of computerising information. Ten units, however, still use paper files for storing and processing the information. Percentage distribution of sample units according to the three dimensions of information technology is reported in pie figures 9.13, 9.14 and 9.15.

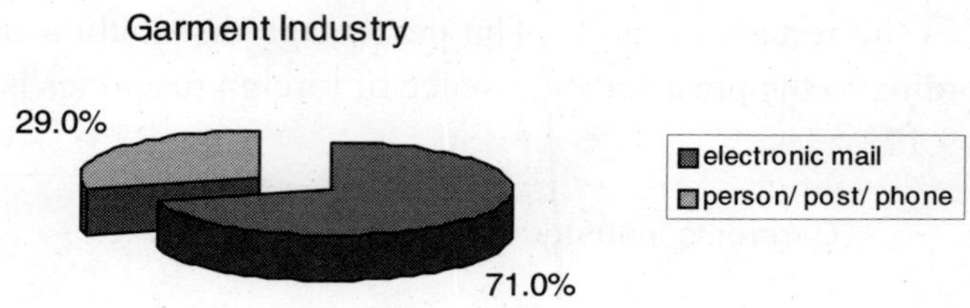

Figure 9.13 Means of Communication

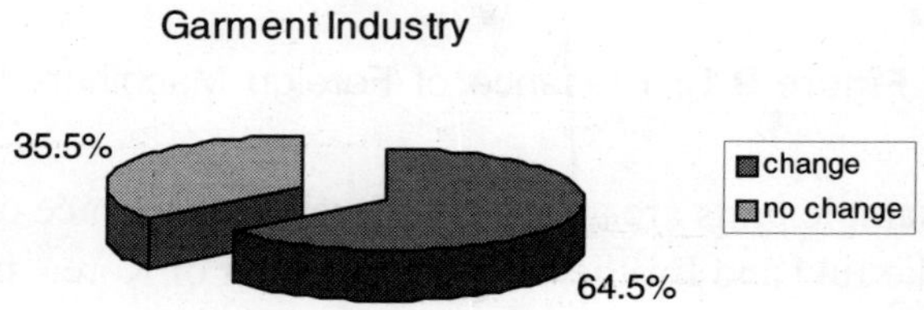

Figure 9.14 Changes in Communication

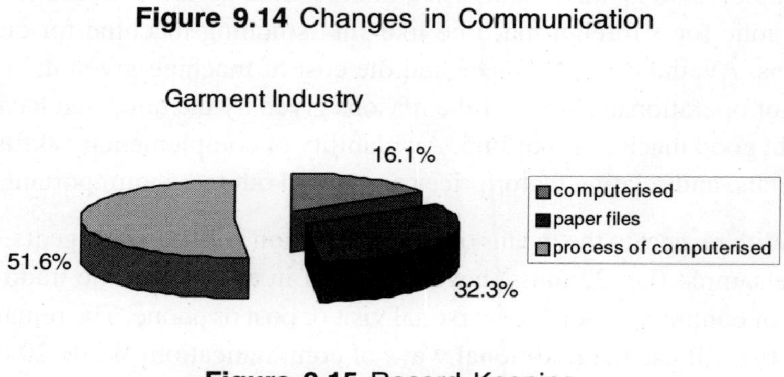

Figure 9.15 Record Keeping

As regards the characteristics of production organisation, namely, plant layout, production schedules and materials management, the surveyed units have quite a flexible system and hence these are not considered for further analysis. The units in the garment industry so far have not started following any standard quality management systems like ISO 9000 and have fixed jobs for their employees. The only characteristic that seems relevant in this regard is the facility of in-house production given the nature of garment industry where subcontracting tailoring operation has been the common form. The status of in-house production in our sample units is already discussed in the previous sub-section.

A little more than half of the surveyed units (16) are proprietary concerns. The remaining sample has 8 partnership firms and 7 limited companies. A good number of sample units (24) has been managed by the owners themselves. One finds non-owner managers only in 7 units. The percentage distribution of the sample units along the lines of business form of organisation and the type of management are summarised in pie figures 9.16 and 9.17.

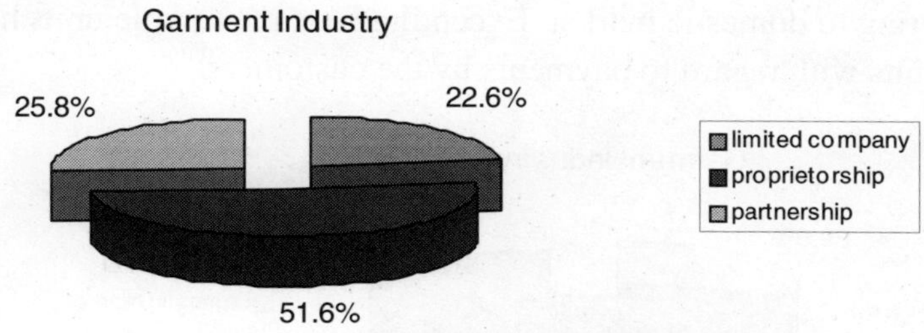

Figure 9.16 Business Organisation

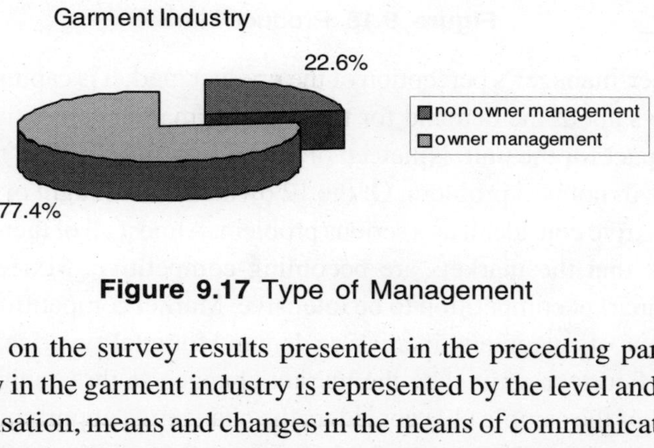

Figure 9.17 Type of Management

Based on the survey results presented in the preceding paragraphs, technology in the garment industry is represented by the level and changes in mechanisation, means and changes in the means of communication, data management, business organisation, type of management and in-house production facility. The other characteristics representing the production organisation are turned out to be irrelevant for the empirical analysis.

9.3.3 Non-Technology Characteristics

Let us now examine the evidence for the characteristics that are taken to influence the technology characteristics of the unit, namely, product market served, owner's perception of the market, education and experience of the owner-manager, professional labour component, scale of operation, sources of information and finance, and owner-manager's views about their availability, availability of complementary skills and materials, relative factor prices and labour.

We start with the nature of the product market served by our garment sample units. Of the total 31units surveyed, 22 are exporting and the remaining 9 units are catering to the domestic market. This can be seen from pie figure 9.18. All the seven units, which have their own brand name, are catering to domestic market. Excepting five, the sample units have no complaints with regard to payments by the customers.

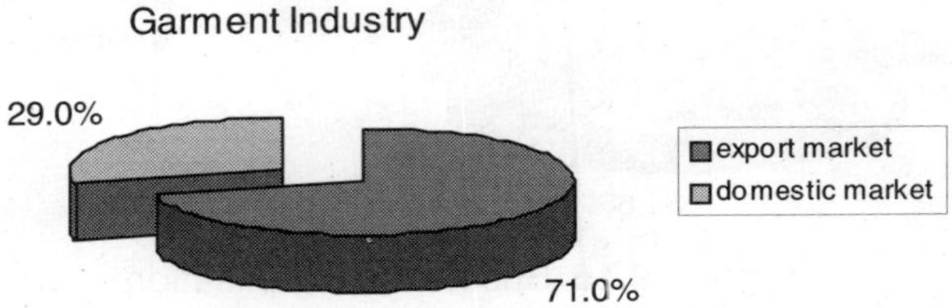

Figure 9.18 Product Market

Owner-manager's perception of the product market is captured through their views about the demand for the product, market competition and its likely impact for the unit. Nineteen of the 31 sample units feel that market demand will not be a problem. Of the 12 owners that thought of demand as a problem, five consider it as a serious problem. Almost all of them excepting two think that the markets are becoming competitive. Sixteen of them consider market competition to be intensive. Market competition is mostly felt in terms of customers' increasing demand for quality, price and timely delivery. Fourteen units take the market changes as threatening for their unit. Rest of the sample (17) considers the changes as opportunities for the unit. These results are presented in pie figures 9.19, 9.20 and 9.21.

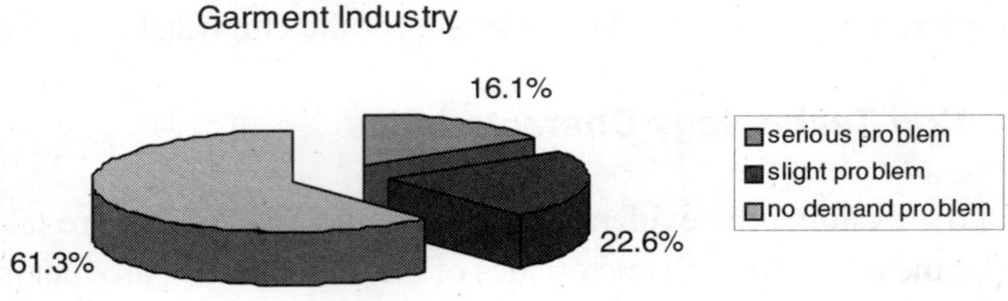

Figure 9.19 Demand Problem

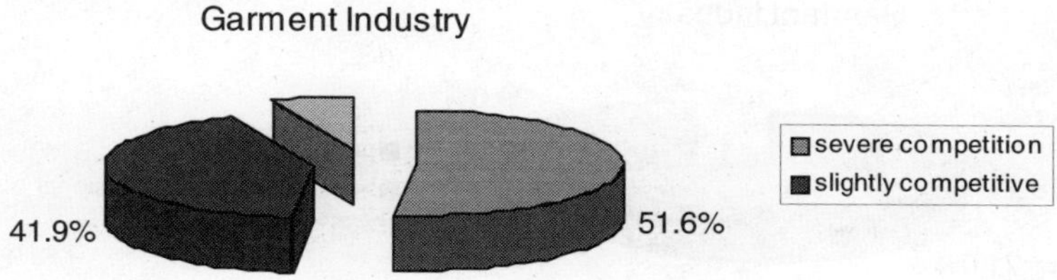

Figure 9.20 Market Competition

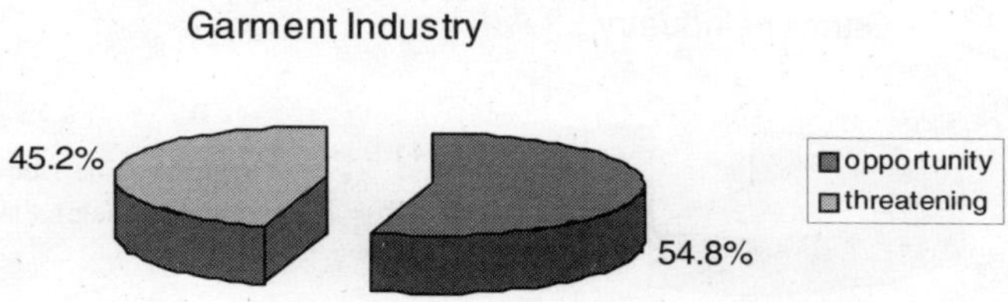

Figure 9.21 Impact of Market Competition

As regards the education of owner-managers, 22 of them have higher education that is above schooling but of non-professional nature. In the remaining units, owner-managers are professionals. The survey results indicate that 18 units have not had any professional employees and the other 13 units have few professional employees in their plants. Professional employees are mainly recruited at the higher levels such as merchandise managers.

As far as the owner-manager's experience is concerned, the average experience of the sample is almost 13 years. Experience of the owner-managers in the sample shows a variation of 58 percent (coefficient of variation) around the mean and within the range of 2 (minimum) and 30 years (maximum). Thirteen of them have an experience that is less than or equal to 10 years. The experience of the owner-manager in 13 units lies between 10 and 20 years. In the remaining 5 units, the experience of owner-manger is more than 20 years. Survey results relating to these three proxies of technological capabilities are presented in pie figures 9.22, 9.23 and 9.24.

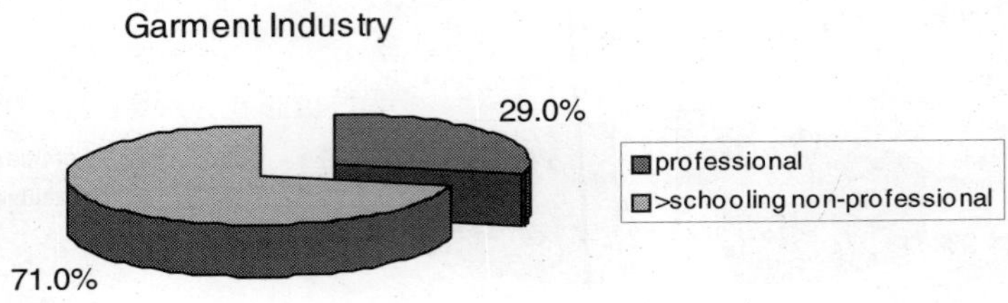

Figure 9.22 Education of Owners

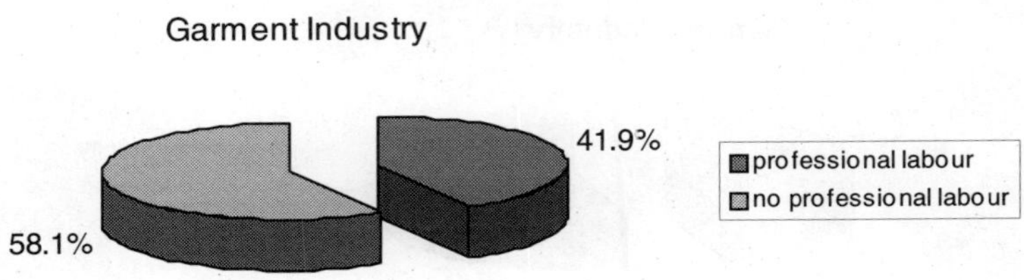

Figure 9.23 Professional Labour

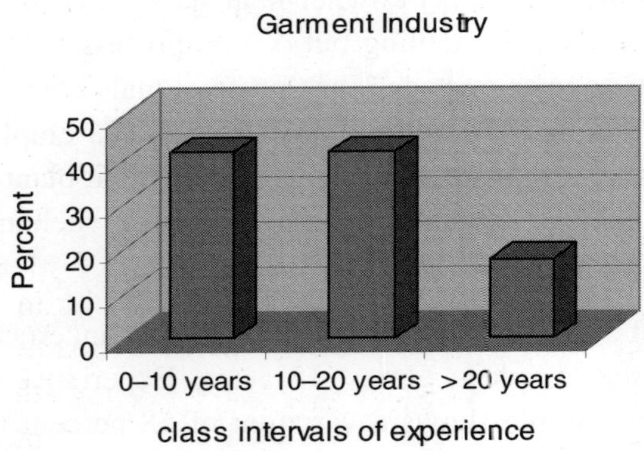

Figure 9.24 Experience of Owners

One of the basic determinants of the technology characteristics has been the scale of operation. It is captured through the annual sales turnover of the units in our study. Survey results pertaining to sales turnover have already been discussed in section 9.3.1

As far as the accessibility to information and its sources are concerned, a majority of the sample units (23) have no such problems. Of the remaining eight units that have experienced information problems, only 2 considered it to be serious. Fourteen of the 30 units have only one source of information such as trade fairs, trade journals or business associates. The other 17 units have been using more than one source of information about technology. Evidence about the information is given in figures 9.25 and 9.26.

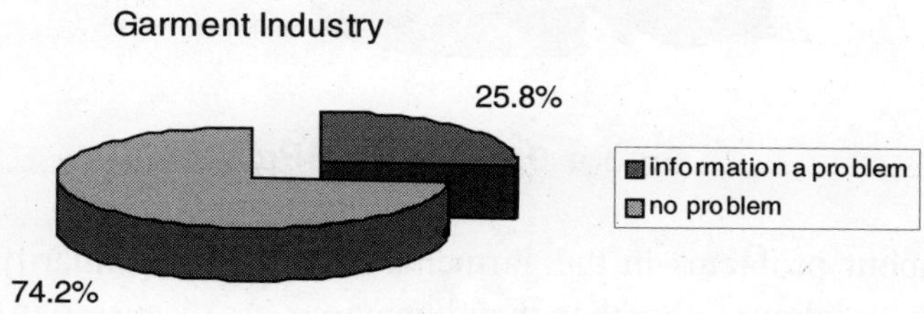

Figure 9.25 Information Problem

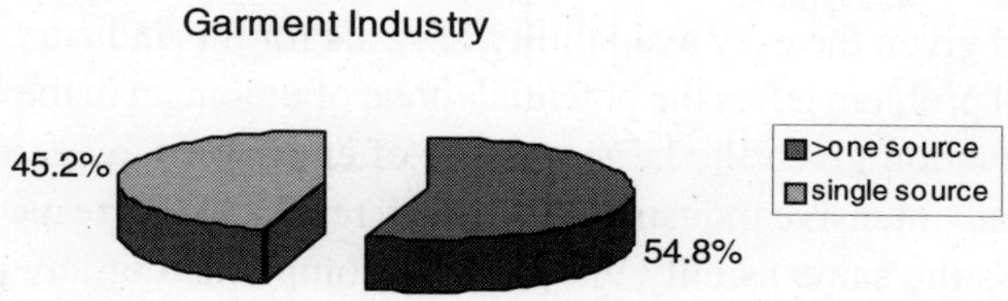

Figure 9.26 Information Sources

The empirical evidence relating to the sources of finance and problems in obtaining it reveal that a little more than half of the units (16) have used personal resources. The other 15 units have borrowed from the institutions like commercial banks. Thirteen sample units do not feel finance as a problem. The remaining eighteen units have reported that finance is a problem for them. Of these, seven units take it as a serious problem. Sources of finance and the intensity of its problem for the sample units are summed up in pie figures 9.27 and 9.28.

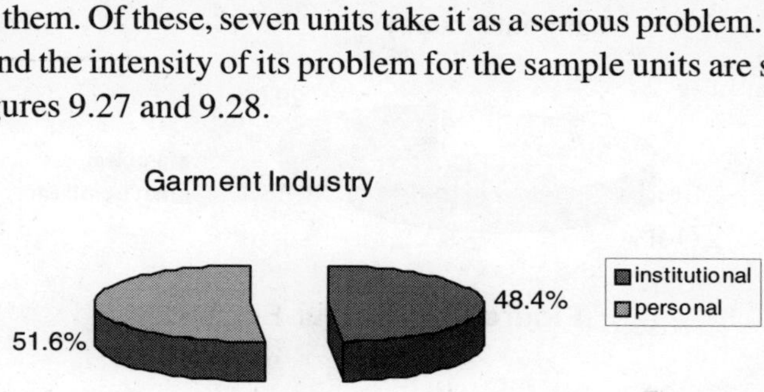

Figure 9.27 Sources of Finance

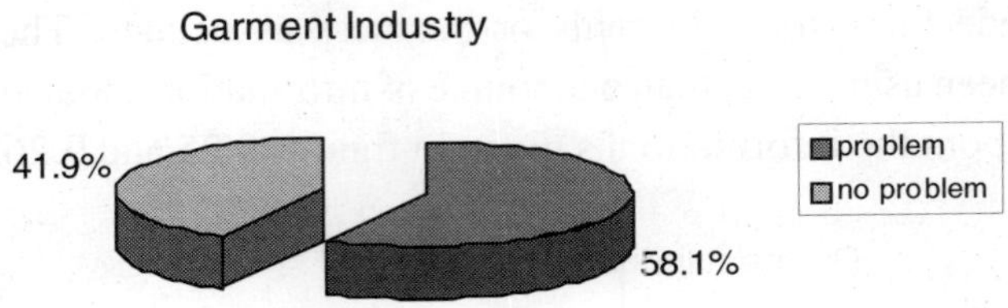

Figure 9.28 Finance Problem

Labour problems in the garments industry are primarily due to the attitudes of labour rather than their behaviour. As discussed in sections 5.3 and 5.4, labour in the garments industry is hired on contract and paid on a piece rate basis. This practice has contained behavioural problems like absenteeism and turnover. Problem of turnover of workers is otherwise also limited given the easy availability of skills for this industry. The only behavioural problem left is the potential threat of unionism in the case of in-house production given the large number of employees, as garments is a highly labour-intensive industry. Our survey results in this respect indicate more or less the same as only 9 units have complained of any problems. The rest of the sample (22) does not report any labour problems. Labour attitudes again are to be interpreted differently in the case of the garment industry. Here, we take it as attitudes towards maintaining quality and timely delivery of the product. In this respect, 13 of the 31 units have reported that the attitudes of labour are negative. The remaining 18 units feel that labour attitudes are positive. The percentage distribution of sample units in respect of labour problems and attitudes are presented in pie figures 9.29 and 9.30.

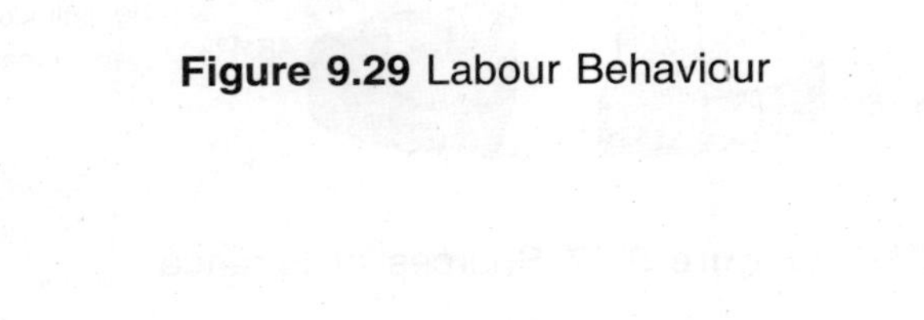

Figure 9.29 Labour Behaviour

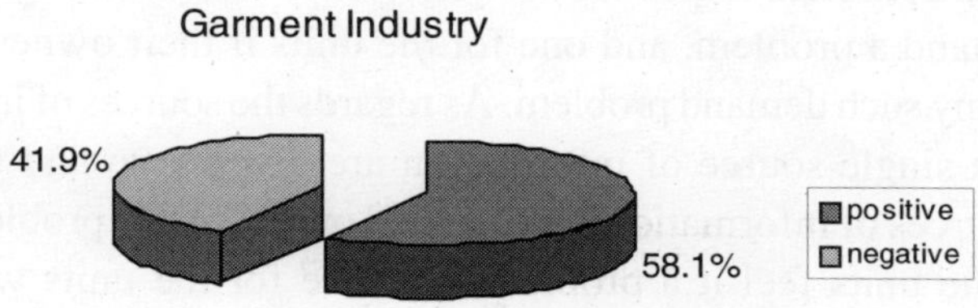

Figure 9.30 Labour Attitudes

In sum, all the non-technology characteristics except relative factor prices and the availability of materials and skills are found to be relevant in the case of garment industry. The statistical association among these and technology characteristics are examined in the next section.

9.4 DETERMINANTS OF TECHNOLOGICAL CHANGE

As in the case of the other two selected industries, we have estimated three separate functions for three dimensions of technology: transformation, organization and information technologies. Transformation technology is taken in terms of level of mechanisation even in the garments industry. Level of mechanisation, however, is represented by the presence of foreign machinery in this industry. As discussed in the earlier section, foreign machinery (especially sewing machines) is reasonably present in the industry and it is superior to Indian machinery in terms of quality of stitch and enables tailor to do many types of stitching, etc. although it costs heavily. The transformation technology function that is finally used is given as

$$PFM = F(CONST, SCA, RDP, RSTI, RFP, LAB) \quad (9.1)$$

where PFM = Presence of foreign machines
SCA = Scale of operation
RDP = Demand problem
RSTI = Sources of information
RFP = Finance problem
LAB = Labour problem

All the variables except scale of operation are binary variables. Presence of foreign machinery is defined as zero for the units, which do not have any foreign machine and one for the units that have some foreign machines. Scale of operation is represented by annual sales turnover of the units. Demand problem is zero for the units where owner-managers perceive market demand a problem, and one for the units if their owner-managers do not feel any such demand problem. As regards the sources of information, units with a single source of information are given zero and units using multiple sources of information are assigned one. Finance problem is taken as zero if the units feel it a problem, and one for the units without any finance problem. Similarly, we define labour problem to take zero if the units find labour a problem or, one if there is no such problem.

Given the nature of garments industry, we have taken organisation in terms of having in-house production and specified it as follows.

INP = F (CONST, SCA, RDP, RSTI, RFP, LAB) (9.2)

where INP = In-house production

All the other variables are as defined in the equation (9.1)

In-house production is a binary variable with zero for the units, which do not have any in-house production arrangement and one for the units that are involved in some proportion (or, full) of in-house production.

As far as information technology is concerned, we have selected equations representing the changes in both communication and data management methods. Both these indicators of information technology are taken as a function of scale of operation, product market, experience/education of owner-managers. These functions are given below.

CIC = F (CONST, SCA, MKT, EOO) (9.3)

where CIC = Changes in communication technologies

MKT = Type of market

EOO = Education of owner-managers

SCA is as defined in the earlier equations.

Changes in communication is defined as one for the units that have changed their means of communication over time and zero for the units that did not change their communication methods. Education of owner-managers is specified as one if they are professionals and zero for non-professionals. Product market variable is assigned one if the unit is exporting and zero if the unit is serving domestic market.

$$\text{RRK} = \text{F (CONST, SCA, MKT, ROE)} \quad (9.4)$$

where RRK = Data management
ROE = Experience of the owner-managers

Data management is defined as one for the units which store and process their data mainly through computers and zero for the units that manage data on paper files. Experience of owner-managers is taken in terms of number of years.

All these equations are estimated through Probit model. The estimated marginal coefficients of these equations are presented in Tables 9.2 and 9.3.

Table 9.2: **Marginal Coefficients of Transformation and Organisation Technology Functions—Garments Industry**

Variables	Coefficients	T-values
Transformation Technology Dependent Variable: Presence of Foreign Machinery (PFM)		
Constant	–2.0497	–6.6243
Scale of operation (SCA)	0.0001	0.8952
Demand problem (RDP)	0.1823	2.0388
Information sources (RSTI)	–.0812	–0.7729
Finance problem (RIFP)	0.0477	0.4727
Labour attitudes (LAB)	0.0158	0.1482
Organisation Technology Dependent Variable: Having In-house Production (INP)		
Constant	–2.0859	–6.6110
Scale of operation (SCA)	0.0001	0.7027
Demand problem (RDP)	0.1144	1.3589
Information sources (RSTI)	–0.1065	–1.1580
Finance problem (RIFP)	–0.0189	–0.2108
Labour attitudes (LAB)	0.2125	2.0090

Level of mechanisation taken in terms of the presence/absence of foreign machinery is explained only by the owner-managers' perception of market demand. None of the other characteristics considered for the estimation, namely, scale of operation, sources of information, finance and labour problems are statistically significant. It suggests that garment units go for foreign machinery, which is quite costly compared to Indian

Table 9.3: **Marginal Coefficients of Information Technology Functions—Garments Industry**

Variables	Coefficients	T-values
Dependent Variable: Changes in Communication Methods (CIC) Constant	–2.3910	–6.5179
Scale of operation (SCA)	0.0001	0.7813
Product Market (MKT)	0.2132	1.5214
Owners' education (REOO)	0.0367	0.4444
Dependent Variable: Changes in Data Management (RRK) Constant	–2.3378	–6.5217
Scale of operation (SCA)	0.0001	1.5594
Product Market (MKT)	0.0247	0.2440
Owners' experience (ROE)	0.0720	1.5555

machinery, only when they are sure of demand for their product. Demand uncertainty is more with the exporting units that dominate our sample. This is because majority of the exporting units in the industry do not produce and sell in the market. Rather these units undertake production as and when there is an export order. Export orders need not be continuous and units are not sure of their next order in terms of time and amount. Given this uncertainty of demand, units think of purchasing foreign machinery only when they have continuous orders and do not feel demand a problem. Selection parameters stated by the owners (refer to earlier section), namely, scale of operation and availability of finance comes later.

The parameter estimates of organisation technology indicate that in-house production facility is primarily influenced by labour problems. As discussed in chapter 5, garment industry has the practice of subcontracting tailoring, the basic production operation, to fabricators. These fabricators essentially do the stitching of the cut fabric as per the sample piece using their own sewing machine. Here, labour problems come in the form of quality of stitching and maintaining delivery schedules. Our results suggest that these labour problems are prompting the units to have their own production facility.

As mentioned earlier, information technology is represented by the changes in communication and data management methods in the case of garment industry. Parameter estimates given in Table 9.3 indicate that the changes in communication means are mainly influenced by the nature of product market that units are serving. Exporting units may have shifted quickly to electronic mail as it facilitates communication with their importers better. Units serving domestic market through dealers may not feel the need for modern methods of communication.

Changes in data management are statistically influenced by scale of operation and experience of owner-managers. It seems units are finding it worthy to go for computerisation of the records and processing of data at larger scale of operation. Similarly, experienced owners must have realised the benefits of computer processing of data, which enables units to know their situation, whatever be the parameters they consider, clearly and quickly. It is quite possible that scale and experience matter in the garment industry as this industry has truly large units (see sales turnover) and is dominated by exporting units.

9.5 IMPACT OF TECHNOLOGICAL CHANGE

The impact of technological change, as in the case of the other two industries, is taken in terms of competitive strength of units. Competitive strength of the units is further considered as sales performance. This impact of technology is examined in the production function framework where technology variables are introduced directly along with the conventional inputs. We have used the presence of foreign machinery, having in-house production and changes in the means of communication to represent transformation, organisation and information technologies. All the three technology variables enter production function as dummy variables. Original value of plant and machinery, number of employees and value of materials are taken as a part of conventional inputs. For the purpose of estimation, we have considered six-input Cobb-Douglas function. The log-liner form of our production function is written as

$$\begin{aligned} \text{LnST} &= C + a \ln \text{PM} + b \ln \text{LAB} + d \ln \text{MAT} \\ &\quad + q_1 \text{PFM} + q_2 \text{INP} + q_3 \text{CIC} + m \end{aligned} \tag{9.4}$$

where, ln refers to logarithmic values of the variables

ST	=	Sales turnover
PM	=	Original value of plant and machinery
LAB	=	Total number of employees
MAT	=	Value of materials consumed during the year
PFM	=	Presence of foreign machinery;

1 for units having foreign machinery; 0 otherwise

INP = In-house production;
1 for units having in-house production facility;
0 otherwise

CIC = Changes in communication methods;
1 for units using electronic mail; 0 otherwise

Equation (9.4) has been estimated through the Ordinary Least Squares (OLS) method. The estimated parameters of the equation are presented in Table 9.4.

Table 9.4: **Estimates of Production Function—Garments Industry**

Variables	Coefficients	T-values
Dependent Variable: Ln (sales turnover)		
Constant	0.8490	1.138
Ln (plant and machinery)	–0.0990	–0.722
Ln (labour)	0.4060	2.804
Ln (materials)	0.6630	4.820
Foreign machinery	–0.0890	–1.304
In-house production	–0.0870	–1.162
Changes in communication methods	0.7690	0.799
$N = 31, R^2 = 0.910, F = 37.076$		

Parameter estimates presented in Table 9.4 show that only labour and materials are influencing sales performance of the units in the garments industry. None of the coefficients of technology variables are statistically significant indicating that they have not started having influence over sales performance. So is the case with the plant and machinery. These results suggest that garment units are depending on labour and material management to improve the sales performance and hence the competitive strength. It is quite possible given the fact that most of our garment industry is serving the lower end market especially exports where cost competitiveness matter. Materials (mainly fabric) and labour are the primary determinants of cost competitiveness of the Indian garment industry. This is because the industry is both labour- and materials-intensive and India has comparative advantage in these factors. Cotton cloth sourced from powerlooms is considered as cheap along with labour.

9.6 SUMMARY

Garment sample of the study is dominated by proprietary concerns that are owner-managed. We have both factory and non-factory units in equal number. As regards the basic inputs and output, sample shows wide variation. Good presence of foreign machines can be seen in the sample units. Suppliers of the machinery are the primary source of technology. All the sample units are aware of the availability of foreign machinery. Machines, however, are purchased keeping scale of operation and availability of finance in mind. A good number of sample units have computers and hence use electronic methods of communication and data processing. Most of the owners have higher education though they are not professionals. Exporting units outnumber the units serving domestic market in our sample. Majority of the sample units feel market competition is increasing and threatening their survival. Information is not considered a problem by most of the sample units. Although good number of units avail institutional finance, sample units, at large, feel finance a problem. Labour problems are felt mainly in terms of threat of unionisation and indifference of labour to quality and timely delivery.

Transformation technology considered in terms of presence of foreign machinery is mainly determined by owner-managers' perception of market demand. Organisation taken in terms of in-house production facility is influenced by negative attitudes of labour. Information technology represented by the changes in communication and data management towards modern electronic methods is influenced by the nature of product market, scale of operation and experience of owner-managers. Competitiveness of the unit specified in terms of sales performance is still influenced by labour and materials than capital (stock of machinery) or technology.

Endnotes

1. Under each category, so many conditions exist, which the importers want their exporting units to fulfil. For instance, they ask the units whether there is any child labour or prison labour employed, the number of hours workers are working uninterruptedly, time limits on the usage of women labour and so on. One of the companies showed the author the list of the conditions to be fulfilled by the units in order to procure export orders.

2. It is the case with one or two units involved in the job work.

Chapter 10 Summary Findings and Policy Suggestions

10.1 INTRODUCTION

In this study, we have tried to conceptualise the process of firm-level technological change, to examine the factors influencing this process, the impact of technological change on the competitive strength of the units, and the differences in the last two across the selected industries belonging to the small manufacturing sector. This chapter summarises the empirical findings of the study and tries to bring out their policy implications. The unique feature of this study is that it attempts to develop a comprehensive analytical framework, drawing on different literature, which enables us to study technological changes in the context of Indian small-scale industries.

10.2 ANALYTICAL FEATURES

Literature on technological change in the industrial units confines to the major technological changes (i.e. innovations) that too in the physical processes of transformation including materials and output characteristics whereas technology transfer literature deals with the formal modes of transfer such as licensing. Both do not suit the Indian small-scale industries as majority of these units are imitators (not innovators) and obtain their technology through informal means. The existing literature, thus, does not provide a suitable framework to study technological changes in the small-scale units. As a result, we made an attempt to develop an analytical framework, following an *eclectic* approach, which permits us to study the technological change in the Indian small-scale units (sections 4.2 and 4.3).

In this respect, we have drawn on the relevant concepts from the evolutionary economics, economics of technological change, technological capabilities and organisation theories (Chapter 3).

We take *industrial unit* as an economic organisation engaged in the production of a given set of goods and services. It operates in a *business environment* that is constituted by the other units of the industry, markets and other macroeconomic institutions such as factor markets, consultancy organizations and government policies. All these change continuously shifting the business environment and hence the barometers of the success for firms. Industrial units have to strive continuously to succeed i.e. to maintain and improve their commercial viability in the changing business environments. We treat the changes in technology as one of the strategies of industrial units to operate effectively in the changing environment.

For the purpose of study, we focus on the three elements of an industrial unit, namely, technology (that undergoes change), decision-maker (who undertakes change) and technological capabilities (pre-requisite for change). *Technology is defined to include the physical processes of transformation of inputs into output, organisational methods that structure these processes, and information flows required to carry out these processes.* Thus, the study considers three dimensions of technology, i.e., transformation, organisation and information. The *transformation* technology refers mainly to mechanisation. The *organisation* part is taken to include the form of business organisation and type of management at the structural level, and plant layout, materials management, quality management, production schedules and work allocations at the operational level. The *information* aspect includes the means of communication with outside agents like customers and suppliers, and the methods of storing and processing of information (information/data management) within the unit. Of these, mechanisation is considered as 'core' technology. *Technological changes refer to the changes in any one or a combination of the three dimensions of technology that are undertaken by the industrial unit to improve its competitive strength.* As the study deals with the Indian small-scale units most of which are imitators, *technological changes are taken as the changes in their existing technology either in the form of addition or replacement by a later vintage technology.*

Owner-manager is the sole decision maker in the small-

scale units. So, the unit level technological change depends on the owner-manager's perception of the environment and the changes in it. Again, it is the *owner-manager* who is expected to *possess investment, linkage and part of production capabilities* in the Indian small-scale industrial units and the *labour needs to have the production capabilities required to operate and maintain production systems*. These capabilities further depend on the formal education and training as well as the experience of the concerned individuals.

We consider the *technological change at a firm level as a eliberately initiated process of search, selection, execution and absorption*. To accomplish change, concerned individuals have to seek it and *search* for available alternative technologies. If alternatives exist, unit has to *select* among the alternatives and acquire the selected technology. *Execution* involves modification if need be, and installation of the new machinery or implementation of the acquired organisation methods such as total quality management. With the execution, *physical change* of technology occurs. However, installation of a new machine or implementation of a new method does not automatically ensure its utilisation. Workers take time to know the machine or, to acquire an ability to operate it smoothly or, to get used to the new method. The process of technological change is completed only when the acquired changes are mastered, i.e., *absorbed*. Thus, it is the execution followed by absorption that ensures the attainment of the purpose of change in technology, namely, improvements in the competitive strength of firm (section 4.2).

Analysis of the study (section 4.3) brings out the possible factors influencing the process of technological change in the small-scale units as: *product market; owner-manager's perception of the product market; technological capabilities; scale of operation; availability of information; finance; complementary skills and materials; relative factor prices and labour*. These factors are further considered (section 5.4) in terms of the unit-level factors, namely, *product market served, owner-manager's views about market demand and its competitiveness, education and experience of the owner-manager, extent of the use of professional labour, sales turnover, unit's sources of information and finance, owner-manager's opinions about the availability of information, finance, materials, skills, and attitudes and behaviour of labour*. All these factors primarily apply to the core part of technology, i.e. mechanisation. The organisation and information technologies are determined by a subset of these factors. For instance, quality management system is supposed to be determined by scale of operation, product market and education of owners. So is the case with the changes in the means of communication with the outside agents towards electronic media (like e-mail or internet). For example, in the case of the auto components industry, larger units supplying original equipment to big vehicle manufacturers have a greater chance of adopting the total quality management system like ISO 9000 or latest information technologies using electronic media as their customers are expected to exert pressures to do so. Work allocation practices depend mainly on the nature of production processes and labour.

The consequences of technological changes are taken in terms of its impact on competitive strength of the unit which in turn represented by its sales performance. Technology makes higher sales possible in many ways: through the introduction of a new and superior product; by improving the quality of existing products or, through the efficient utilisation of resources (productivity improvements) resulting in cost reduction; by improving access to customers or a combination of these. In other words, technology enables firms to raise their sales by making it possible for them to supply increasing quantities of quality goods at cheaper prices.

We have examined the basic objectives of our study with reference to the three selected industries, namely, auto components, electronics and garments that are located in the national capital region of Delhi. The required information is collected through an intensive survey of 30/31 industrial units, selected on the basis of the purposive sampling, for each one of the three industries (section 5.5).

To study the causes or determinants of technological change, we have specified three separate functions for the three aspects of technology i.e., transformation, organisation and information. Since our technology characteristics are specified as binary variables, technology functions are taken in the form of Probit model and estimated through maximum likelihood method. Impact of technology on sales performance is studied in the production function framework. Technology characteristics are directly introduced in the production function as dummy variables along with the conventional inputs like capital (plant and machinery), labour and materials. We have taken our production function to be six-input Cobb–Douglas and estimated it through ordinary least squares method (sections 6.4 and 6.5).

10.3 GENERAL CHARACTERISTICS OF THE SELECTED INDUSTRIES

We have done intensive survey of 31 auto component units, 30 electronic units and 31 garment units. Of the three sets of industrial units, garments units are larger in the scale of operation as represented by sales turnover, electronic units are smaller and auto component units are placed in the middle (see tables 7.1, 8.1, and 9.1 for the average sales turnover of the three industries). Accordingly, auto component and garment samples are dominated by factory units whereas non-factories dominate electronics sample. While auto components is a relatively capital intensive industry, both electronics and garments have been labour intensive industries (see tables 7.1, 8.1, and 9.1 for the average capital-labour ratio of the three industries). In the three samples, very few units availed any government assistance or in favour of protection to small-scale units.

Transformation technology is mainly machine-embodied in our sample units and thus represented by the level of mechanisation in the three industries. In this regard, one finds all four categories, namely, only tools and instruments, manual, semi-automatic and numerically controlled machines in the electronics industry, the last three categories in the auto components sample, and only the first two groups in the garments industry. The presence of only tools and instruments, and manual machinery in the garments industry can be explained in terms of the practice of subcontracting the core production process i.e. tailoring, and the fact that sewing machines are yet to experience radical changes like becoming fully automatic machine at the international level. The proportion of units that have undergone changes in machinery and means of communication are comparatively large in the garment industry. This is mainly due to total transformation of the majority of garment units from having zero to significant percentage of in-house production. In the other two industries of the study, production operations are undertaken within the units from the beginning, and the changes are additions or replacement of the existing machinery.

Suppliers of machinery have been the primary source of transformation technology for almost all the sample units in the three selected industries. Garment units have shown a greater awareness of alternative available machines compared to the other two groups of industrial units. It is perhaps due to the reason that sewing machines are common for all the garment units and thus allowed machine suppliers to do intensive advertisement, which is not the case with the other two industries. Notwithstanding their lack of awareness of alternative machines, auto component units informed that they have selected their machinery based on their scale of operation and product specification, and electronics units used product specification to select their machinery. In view of lack of knowledge about the available alternatives, we take selection criteria as the parameters that small units place before the suppliers of machinery to provide them appropriate machinery. We interpret this result as small units are not aware of available alternatives although they are clear about their selection parameters. Garment units have informed that they select machinery based on the scale of operation and availability of finance.

Another important result is that none of the units in the selected industries considered availability of materials and skills and relative factor prices in their selection of machinery. It does not support the maintained hypotheses of neoclassical theory of production according to which industrial units are aware of alternative available technologies and select one among these based on the relative factor prices.

All the three forms of business organisation, namely, proprietorship, partnership and limited companies are present in more or less equal numbers in the auto components industry sample whereas in the other two industry samples proprietary concerns outnumber the other forms of business organisation. Non-owner management is reasonably present in the garment sample whereas the other two sample units are mostly owner-managed. This is perhaps necessitated by the exporting operations that many garment units are engaged in, and a good number of owners in the industry are non-professionals.

Most of the production organisation characteristics such as production schedules and materials management are quite flexible in the sense that these can be changed as per the need of the hour in all three selected industries. Quality management and work practices vary in the auto component industry, and only work practices differ in the electronics industry. One finds reasonable number of auto component units having total quality system like ISO 9000. This can be explained by the fact that a majority of the sample units are original equipment manufacturers for the vehicle industry which are required to supply consistent quality components to their customers.

A reasonable number of units rotate jobs to their workers in the case of auto component units and electronics industries whereas garment units assign fixed jobs to their workers. This is due to the nature of production operation and the consequent skills required by the workers. Machinery plays a primary role in the production process of auto components. In the electronics industry, role of machinery is dependent on the extent of mechanisation in the production process. In the mechanised production process, workers' skills are mainly related to the operation of machinery, to be trained within the plant. Consequently, it is in the interests of the unit to train workers in the operation of more than one type of machine to avoid any production losses due to absenteeism and turnover. It is further necessitated by the presence of semi-automatic and fully automatic machines that enable workers to work on more than one machine at a time. However, workers in the garments industry require job-specific skills that are more important than the operation of a machine. For instance, the operation of a sewing machine is not a big job and it is only a necessary condition. The sufficient condition is the job-specific skills that are embodied in the persons. Also, the skills required to check the fabric are totally labour embodied. In such a situation, the assignment of fixed jobs to workers enables them to improve job-specific skills and thus contribute more to the production.

Both auto components and electronic units are owned and managed, in majority of the cases, by engineers. In the case of garment industry, owner-managers are non-professionals although highly educated. Similarly, labour in a number of electronic units and half of the auto components industries is professional meaning they have formal education/ training in the relevant area of production. In the garments industry, professional labour is limited to a few large exporting units. Tailoring, the basic production operation in the garments industry, is a traditional skill that is passed on from one generation to another informally within families or, among the neighbours and hence easily available.

The product market has two distinct segments both for the auto component and garment samples. In the case of auto component industry, vehicle manufacturers, the market for original equipment manufacturers, emphasise different parameters such as quality as their market structure and behaviour is totally different from that of the replacement market. The product market for garment units is segmented into exports and domestic market both of which differ widely from each other. The product market for the electronic units cannot be grouped explicitly although they have some units catering to specific customers and the rest serve open market.

A large number of sample units depend solely on personal resources in the garment industry compared to the other two industries, which have a good number of units that are availing institutional finance. Limited fixed capital requirements due to subcontracting together with the easy availability of required materials on a credit basis seem to make garment units to manage with personal finances.

In all the three samples, labour problems due to their behaviour like absenteeism, turnover and unionisation are limited because they are small units. Of these, turnover is considered as an immediate problem given the casual nature of employment. Unionization is taken as a potential problem for the growing units given the existing labour laws. These behavioural problems of labour are largely taken care of, in the garment industry, by hiring them on contract and paying them on piece rate basis. In the other industries, labour problems are limited due to the close and informal relations with the labour that is made possible by their small numbers.

Labour attitudes in the three industries, however, are viewed as negative creating problems. Attitudes are taken in terms of labour giving their best even when the owner-manager is not around and their willingness to learn on new machines in the auto components and electronics industries where there is in-house production. In the garments industry where a substantial number of workers operate independently outside the factory premises, attitudes of labour are taken in terms of maintaining quality and delivering the product on time.

10.4 CAUSES & CONSEQUENCES OF TECHNOLOGICAL CHANGE

As regards the determinants of transformation technology, it is influenced by the sources of finance, labour attitudes and scale of operation in the auto component industry, by labour attitudes in the electronics industry and by demand prospects in the garments industry. Level of mechanisation, the representative of transformation technology is taken in terms of having/ not having numerically controlled (or fully automated) machines in the auto components and electronics industry. In these industries, our results suggest that negative attitudes of labour towards work is prompting units to go for numerically controlled machines. In addition, auto component units, being capital-intensive (plant and machinery), require large-scale operation and access to institutional finance to have fully automatic machinery. In the case of garments industry, level of mechanisation is specified in terms of having/not having foreign sewing machines, which are considered superior to Indian machinery. Demand uncertainties are high for garment units especially exporting units that dominate our sample. Hence, these units are not thinking of foreign machines unless they are sure of market demand (i.e. having continuous orders) for their product.

Organisation technology is captured through total quality management system (ISO 9000) in the auto components industry and it is influenced by scale of operation. It implies that large-scale auto component units are going for the acquisition of ISO 9000 certification, which enables these units to supply consistent quality components. Work allocation practices turned out to be empirically relevant production organization variable for the electronics industry. It is influenced by labour behaviour. Labour behaviour plays an important role in the case of electronics units as most of them are involved in manual assembling of products. In order to minimise the ill effects of labour behavioural problems like turnover and absenteeism, it seems electronic units rotate job assignments to workers. Each worker can do more than one job through the rotation of jobs, and can be shifted easily across the jobs in the event of absence or turnover of any worker. In the case of garments industry, organisation is considered in terms of having/not having in-house production facility and it is explained mainly by labour attitudes. Labour here includes fabricators who work from outside the factory premises, and their indifference towards quality of garment and delivery schedules seems to force garment units to have in-house production facility, which can be monitored easily.

Information technology taken in the form of means of communication is determined by scale of operation in the auto component industry. In the electronics industry, data management represents information technology, which is influenced by scale of operation. Means of communication may have been important for the auto component units as majority of these units serve the specific producers of vehicles. Importance of data management in the electronics industry is perhaps due to the reason that most of them serve open market and need to know the status of market through the processing of data together with the fact that owner-managers process the data. Large-scale operations may be making it worth for these units to go for computerised data processing. Changes in the communication means and data management towards electronic methods have become important for the garment units. The former is influenced mainly by product market while the latter by scale of operation and experience of owners.

For the competitiveness of the units taken in terms of their sales performance, level of mechanisation along with the conventional inputs, namely, materials, labour and plant and machinery are turning out to be important in a capital-intensive industry like auto components. In the labour-intensive industries i.e. electronics and garments, neither level of mechanisation nor stock of machinery (plant and machinery) are important in explaining sales performance. In these industries, it is the materials and labour that influence the units' performance in terms of sales.

10.5 IMPLICATIONS FOR THE INDUSTRY AND POLICY

Extensive interactions with the promotional agencies and units reveals that a large number of urban small-scale units have taken note of the ongoing changes in the business environment such as the rising importance of markets and the significance of technological upgradation in dealing with these changes. Yet, *there are many more small-scale units, which are still to grasp the shifts in the business environment and the importance of new technologies.* These numerous small-scale units have been operating with the older technologies.

The use of obsolete technologies is partly due to the outlook of small producers and partly because of the lack of awareness of available alternatives. Most of the small producers do not visualise their units as industrial units aspiring to grow and establish themselves in the specified field of production. Their focus is on immediate profits/earnings for which they keep shifting from sunset to sunrise activities. Hence, they never paid attention to technology. Rather, they may not like to have technological upgradation as it involves investments and thus set rigidities for moving across the activities. It is essential for the promotional agencies including associations to separate this type of units from the genuine industrial units and focus on the latter.

Our study provides useful insights into the technological upgradation of the genuine small industrial units.

In the majority of small units, one finds only transformation technology that is machine-embodied. Small units are yet to adopt formal and modern organisation methods such as total quality management systems, and information technologies. Although some of the urban small units are going in for electronic means of communication with the customers, these are yet to be integrated firmly with the production operations.

Despite the fact that majority of our sample units constitute the better off segment of the small manufacturing sector in terms of location and owner-manager's education, few knew available alternative technologies. For the machine-embodied technologies, small units primarily depend on the suppliers of machinery to provide them appropriate technology i.e. machinery. This implies the need for increasing the awareness of small units regarding the available technologies in the case of mechanisation. Promotional agencies can involve suppliers of machinery in this respect. Equally important is to convince small units to adopt formal organisational methods as well as information technologies given their significance in the globalised world.

As regards the determinants of technological upgradation in terms of higher level of mechanisation, these factors differ from industry to industry. Certainty of demand is a necessary condition, and larger scale of operation and availability of finances are sufficient conditions for having higher level of mechanisation in the industries where machinery involves larger amounts of investment. Labour problems matter in the case of labour-intensive production operations with limited mechanisation. Larger-scale of operation is also required to go for formal organisation methods and information technologies.

Higher level of mechanisation (i.e. quality of machinery) than the stock of machinery is important, in a capital-intensive industries, for the sales performance in addition to materials and labour. However, only materials and labour explain the sales performance of small units in the case of labour-intensive industries.

In sum, technological upgradation is imperative in the current context of globalisation and liberalisation. Small units should be made aware of this fact along with the available alternative technologies. Promotional agencies have an important role to play in this respect. To be effective, these agencies need to focus their efforts on the genuine industrial units belonging to the specified industries. Cluster approach will be an appropriate one in this respect. However, agencies instilling trust in the small units, is the most important pre-condition.

We feel that the scope for co-existence of small labour-intensive processes (like that of manual assembling of electronic products) along with the highly mechanised processes is shrinking due to rapid technological developments, liberalisation and globalisation phenomena. These units have to slowly move towards mechanisation.

Our sample units, being in the national capital region, do not find information a problem. Technological upgradation especially mechanisation in these units is mainly constrained by their smaller scale of operation and availability of finance. Both are substantially influenced by the existing policies. These policies could not succeed in improving the access of small units to institutional finance and other infrastructure facilities despite numerous promotional policies. But the existing policies created perverse incentive to these units in remaining small through protection. Hence, technological upgradation in small units urgently requires *total revamp of the existing policies for the small-scale industries so as to make them grow and facilitate their growth through providing adequate capital.* Another important policy implication relates to the amendments to labour laws. Given the existing labour laws, larger scale of operation (especially in labour-intensive industries like garments) creating potential threat from labour. This requires a *revamp of labour laws.*

Appendix - A

Table A.1: **Official Definition of Small Scale Industries over the Years**[1]

Year of Revision	Small Scale unit	Ancillary unit	Tiny unit
1966[2]	Up to 0.75	Up to 1.00	–
1975	Up to 1.00	Up to 1.50	–
1977			Up to 0.10
1980	Up to 2.00	Up to 2.50	Up to 0.20
1985	Up to 3.50	Up to 4.50	Up to 0.20
1991	Up to 6.00	Up to 7.50	Up to 0.50
1997	Up to 30.00		Up to 2.50
1999	Up to 10.00		Up to 2.50

1. 1966 onwards official definition is in terms of the original value of plant and machinery. The figures given in the table are million rupees.
2. Before 1966, small-scale industries are defined using different criteria like value of total capital assets with and without a combination of employment. The criterion of definition has been changed to the original value of plant and machinery in 1966, which has been maintained till now.

Table A.2: **Contribution of Different Segments of the VSI Sector Over Time**

Industry	Production (In rupees crores)[1]					Employment (In lakhs No.)[2]					
	73-74	79-80	84-85	89-90	2000-01[3]	73-74	79-80	84-85	89-90	95-96	2000-01
Traditional Industries											
Khadi and Village Industries	155 (1.14)	440 (1.31)	928.56 (1.41)	1304 (1.14)	6346	18.11 (10.27)	27.33 (11.69)	36.99 (11.74)	46.26 (12.03)	57 (10.61)	60 (11.36)
Handlooms	840 (6.18)	1740 (5.19)	2880 (4.38)	3377 (2.95)	—	52.10 (29.54)	61.50 (26.31)	74.66 (23.70)	76.00 (19.77)	128 (23.83)	124 (23.47)
Handicrafts	1065 (7.83)	2050 (6.11)	3500 (5.32)	7067 (6.18)	16340	15.00 (8.51)	20.30 (8.69)	27.40 (8.70)	42.15 (10.96)	66 (12.29)	57 (10.79)
Sericulture	63 (0.40)	131 (0.39)	316.57 (0.48)	493 (0.43)	—	12.00 (6.80)	16.00 (6.85)	20.00 (6.35)	50.00 (13.00)	60 (11.17)	54 (10.22)
Coir	60 (0.44)	86 (0.26)	100.50 (0.15)	128 (0.11)	—	5.00 (2.84)	5.59 (2.39)	5.90 (1.87)	5.50 (1.43)	5.12 (0.95)	5.30 (1.00)
Total	2183 (16.05)	4447 (13.26)	7725.63 (11.75)	12369 (10.82)	—	102.21 (57.96)	13072 (55.93)	164.95 (52.37)	219.91 (57.19)	316.12 (58.85)	300.3 (56.84)
Modern Industries											
Small Scale Industries	7200 (52.94)	21635 (64.51)	50520 (76.86)	92080 (80.55)	609024	39.65 (22.48)	67.00 (28.67)	90.00 (28.57)	119.60 (31.10)	153 (28.49)	186 (35.26)
Powerlooms	1980 (14.56)	3250 (9.69)	6223 (9.47)	7457 (6.52)	—	10.00 (5.67)	11.00 (4.71)	32.19 (10.22)	45.00 (11.70)	68 (12.66)	42 (7.95)
Total	9180 (67.50)	24885 (74.20)	56943 (86.63)	99537 (87.07)	—	49.65 (28.15)	78.00 (33.37)	122.10 (38.76)	164.60 (42.80)	221 (41.15)	228 (43.16)
Others	2237 (16.44)	4206 (12.54)	1061.37 (1.61)	2408 (2.10)	—	24.50 (13.89)	25.00 (10.70)	27.86 (8.84)	—	—	—
VSI Sector	13600 (100.00)	33538 (100.00)	65730 (100.00)	114314 (100.00)	—	176.36 (100.00)	233.72 (100.00)	315.00 (100.00)	384.51 (100.00)	537.12 (100.00)	528.3 (100.00)

Notes: 1. Production for the year 1995-96 is given in physical units for majority of the groups and hence not reported here.
2. Employment includes both part-time and full-time employees. It may overestimate the employment generation in the traditional industries since most of them are taken up as part-time jobs.
3. Production figures for the year 2000-01 are not available for most of the groups.
4. Figures in parentheses are percentage shares of the respective groups in the total of the VSI sector.

Source: Seventh, Eighth, Ninth and Tenth Five Year Plan Documents.

Table A.2a: **Exports Contribution of Different Segments of the VSI Sector**

Industry	73-74	79-80	84-85	89-90	95-96	2000-01
Traditional Industries						
Khadi and Village Industries	–	–	3.65 (0.08)	5.05 (0.03)	–	– –
Handlooms	89.50 (10.50)	290.41 (12.73)	348.86 (7.65)	342.00 (2.31)	1491.00 (3.32)	2127 (2.52)
Handicrafts	195.00 (22.87)	854.00 (37.45)	1700.00 (37.30)	6400.00 (43.22)	4980.00 (11.10)	9271 (10.99)
Sericulture	14.00 (1.64)	49.00 (2.15)	129.05 (2.83)	400.61 (2.71)	846.00 (1.89)	2480 (2.94)
Coir	16.00 (1.88)	37.21 (1.63)	26.00 (0.57)	33.32 90.23)	207.00 (0.46)	314 (0.37)
Total	314.50 (36.89)	1230.62 (53.96)	2207.56 (48.44)	7180.98 (48.50)	7524.00 (16.77)	14192 (16.82)
Modern Industries						
Small Scale Industries	538.00 (63.11)	1050.00 (46.04)	2350.00 (51.56)	7626.00 (51.50)	34065.00 (75.94)	59978 (71.09)
Powerlooms	–	–	–	–	–	10200 (12.09)
Total	538.00 (63.11)	1050.00 (46.04)	2350.00 (51.56)	7626.00 (51.50)	34065.00 (75.94)	70178 (83.18)
Others	–	–	–	–	–	– –
VSI Sector	852.50 (100.00)	2280.62 (100.00)	4557.56 (100.00)	14806.98 (100.00)	44857.00 (100.00)	84370 (100.00)

Notes : Figures in parentheses are percentage shares of the respective groups in the total of the VSI sector.
Source: Seventh, Eighth, Ninth and Tenth Five Year Plan Documents.

Table A.3: **Growth of the Small Scale Sector in India: Pre-Reform Period**

S. No.	Year	Units		Production[1]		Exports		Employment	
E		Lakhs	Growth rate[2]	Rs. crores	Growth rate	Rs. Crores	Growth rate	No. in lakhs	Growth rate
1.	1973-74	4.1		7200		393		39.7	
2.	1974-75	5.0	21.95	9200	27.78	541	37.66	40.4	1.76
3.	1975-76	5.5	10.00	11000	19.57	532	-1.66	45.9	13.61
4.	1976-77	5.9	7.27	12400	12.73	766	43.98	49.8	8.50
5.	1977-78	6.7	13.56	14300	15.32	845	10.31	54.0	8.43
6.	1978-79	7.3	8.96	15790	10.42	1059	25.33	63.8	18.15
7.	1979-80	8.1	10.96	21635	37.02	1226	15.77	67.0	5.02
8.	1980-81	8.7	7.41	28065	29.72	1643	34.01	71.0	5.97
9.	1981-82	9.6	10.34	32600	16.16	2071	26.05	75.0	5.63
10.	1982-83	10.6	10.42	35000	7.36	2097	1.26	79.0	5.33
11.	1983-84	11.6	9.43	41620	18.91	2159	2.96	84.1	6.46
12.	1984-85	12.4	6.90	50520	21.38	2553	18.25	94.0	11.77
13.	1985-86	13.5	8.87	61228	21.20	2785	9.09	96.0	2.13
14.	1986-87	14.6	8.15	72250	18.00	3648	30.99	101.4	5.63
15.	1987-88	15.8	8.22	87300	20.83	4535	24.31	107.0	5.52
16.	1988-89	17.1	8.23	106400	21.88	5490	21.06	113.0	5.61
17.	1989-90	18.2	6.43	132320	24.36	7626	38.91	119.6	5.84

1. Production and export values are given in current prices
2. These are annual growth rates in percentages terms

Source: *Handbook of Industrial Policies and Statistics 1997*. Ministry of Industry, Government of India, New Delhi.

Table A.4: **Growth of the Small Scale Sector in India: Post-Reform Period**

Year	Annual Growth Rates (%)				
	Units	Employment	Exports	Production (1990-91 prices)	
				SSI Sector	Industry Sector
(1)	(2)	(3)	(4)	(5)	(6)
1990-91	6.86	4.77	26.74	–	–
1991-92	6.88	3.59	43.65	3.1	0.6
1992-93	7.88	3.3	28.11	5.6	2.3
1993-94	6.32	4.0	42.29	7.1	6.0
1994-95	7.66	5.2	14.86	10.1	9.4
1995-96	5.95	4.1	25.50	11.4	12.1
1996-97	4.88	4.8	7.61	11.3	7.1
1997-98	5.5	4.5	11.97	8.4	5.8
1998-99	3.5	2.6	11.45	7.7	4.0
1999-2000	–	4.0	10.66	–	–

Source: *Handbook of Industrial Policy and Statistics* 2000 (pp. 359 & 360), 2002 (p. 150), Ministry of Commerce and Industry, Government of India, New Delhi.

Table A.5: **Industrial Growth Rates of Select Asian Economies (%)**

Country	1994	1995	1996	1997	1998	1999
Bangladesh	7.8	8.4	5.3	36.	8.1	4.0
Bhutan	13.9	16.9	8.4	4.9	6.0	–
China	18.4	13.9	12.1	10.8	8.9	8.5
Indonesia	11.2	10.4	7.4	5.6	–15.6	1.7
Korea Rep.	9.0	10.0	7.4	5.6	–7.5	13.0
Maldives	6.6	8.4	9.0	9.7	12.3	5.0
Nepal	9.0	4.0	8.3	3.5	0.2	5.7
Pakistan	4.5	4.8	5.4	1.0	6.2	3.8
Srilanka	8.1	7.8	5.6	7.9	–	4.6
Singapore	13.2	9.5	6.5	6.6	–	4.4
Thailand	10.1	10.5	7.0	–0.1	–12.1	8.3

Source: *SIDBI Report on Small-scale Industries Sector 2001*, Small Industries Development Bank, Lucknow

Table A.6: **Size Distribution and Structure of the SSI Sector**

Size Criteria Class	% of Units	% of Production	% of Employment	% of Investment	Lab. Productivity[1]	Cap. Productivity[2]
Investment in P&M						
≤ 1 lakh rupees	82.8	28.1	53.9	33.2	61,082	0.25
➤ 1 lakh rupees	17.2	71.9	46.1	66.8	1,82,889	4.98
Workers						
≤ 4 workers	64.5	11.7	22.4	21.5	60,934	0.40
> 4 workers	35.0	88.3	77.6	78.5	1,35,509	5.20

1. Lab. Productivity = Production per employee in rupees.
2. Cap. Productivity = Production per rupee investment
3. % refers to the percentage shares of the respective size classes in the total of the SSI sector.

Source: Report of the All-India Census of Small Scale Industrial Units, 1992

Table A.7: **Plan Outlays on the Village and Small Industries Sector (in crores of rupees)**

S. No	Industry	1951-56[1]	1956-61	1962-66	1969-74	1978-83	1980-85	1985-90	1992-97	1997-2002
	Traditional Industries									
1.	Khadi and Village Industries	12.50 (40.06)[2]	55.50 (27.75)	92.40 (35.00)	100.97[4] (34.45)	390.00 (27.56)	547.09 (30.73)	636.25 (23.11)	–	–
2.	Handlooms	11.10 (35.58)	59.50 (29.75)	34.00 (12.88)	29.58 (10.09)	290.00 (20.49)	310.93 (17.46)	512.26 (18.61)	–	–
3.	Handicrafts	1.00 (3.21)	9.00 (4.50)	8.60 (3.26)	13.46 (4.59)	57.00 (4.03)	110.90 (6.23)	122.86 (4.46)	–	–
4.	Sericulture	1.30 (4.17)	5.00 (2.50)	7.00 (2.65)	10.39 (3.54)	70.00 (4.95)	164.56 (9.24)	309.96 (11.26)	–	–
5.	Coir	0.10 (0.32)	1.00 (0.50)	3.20 (1.21)	5.03 (1.72)	17.00 (1.20)	26.72 (1.50)	39.13 (1.42)	–	–
	Total	26.00 (83.33)	130.00 (65.00)	145.20 (55.00)	159.43 (54.39)	824.00 (58.23)	1160.20 (65.16)	1620.46 (58.87)	–	–
	Modern Industries									
6.	Small Scale Industries	5.20 (16.67)	55.00 (27.50)	114.80 (43.48)	123.33 (42.07)	585.00[5] (41.34)	616.10 (34.60)	1120.51 (40.71)	–	–
7.	Powerlooms	–	15.00 (7.50)	4.00 (1.52)	9.77 (3.33)	6.00 (0.42)	4.15 (0.23)	11.77 (0.43)		
	Total	5.20 (16.67)	70.00 (35.00)	118.80 (45.00)	133.10 (45.41)	591.00 (41.77)	620.25 (34.84)	1132.28 (41.13)		
	VSI Sector	31.20 (100.00)	200.00 (100.00)	264.00 (100.00)	293.13[6] (100.00)	1415.00 (100.00)	1780.45 (100.00)	2752.74 (100.00)	6334.20	136100.00[7]
		1.3[3]	4.1	2.8	1.5	1.5	1.8	1.5	1.5	

1. Years given in this row indicate the time periods corresponding to the First, Second, Third, Fourth, Fifth, Sixth, Seventh, Eighth and
2. Ninth Five year plan periods respectively.
3. Figures in parentheses are percentage shares in the total outlay for VSI sector.
4. This row gives the percentage shares of the VSI sector in the total development plan outlays of the respective plans.
5. This figure includes 4.50 crores outlay on rural industries project.
6. Of this amount, 60 crore rupees are for the schemes of craftsmen and apprentice training programme.
7. This figure includes apart from the above specified outlays, 0.60 crores of rupees for the collection of statistics. Hence, the percentage shares of the groups are not added up to 100.
8. Ninth Five Year Plan figures refer to projected but not the actual outlay.
9. 1 Crore = 10 million

Sources: Various Five Year Plan documents and Economic Survey 1998-99.

Table A.8: **Relative Contribution of Different Segments of the Electronics Industry (Hardware) Over Time (Production in Rs. Millions)**

Segment/ Year	71-72	81-82	1988	1989	1990	1991	1992	1993	1994	1995	1996	1997
Consumer Electronics	52.5 (30.3)	260 (29.4)	23,320 (37.7)	28,250 (34.1)	29,710 (32.4)	30,240 (31.3)	33,840 (29.8)	39,290 (30.2)	45,070 (29.2)	55,590 (32.0)	64,960 (33.2)	74,500 (34.5)
Instrumentation and Industrial Electronics	13.0 (7.5)	165 (18.6)	9,370 (15.1)	12,310 (14.6)	14,040 (15.3)	14,160 (14.7)	16,140 (14.2)	17,200 (13.2)	20,250 (13.1)	25,610 (14.7)	31,850 (16.3)	31,200 (14.5)
Data Processing Systems	–	35 (4.0)	5,760 (9.3)	8,490 (10.2)	10,220 (11.2)	9,650 (10.0)	12,000 (10.6)	13,420 (10.3)	17,770 (11.5)	20,160 (11.6)	25,010 (12.8)	27,000 (12.5)
Communication and Broadcasting Equipment	39.5 (22.8)	165 (18.6)	9,060 (14.6)	14,330 (17.3)	16,310 (17.8)	19,360 (20.0)	25,290 (22.3)	31,500 (24.2)	35,010 (22.7)	30,300 (17.4)	26,050 (13.3)	32,000 (14.8)
Strategic Electronics	28.0 (16.2)	75 (8.5)	3,900 (6.3)	5,030 (6.1)	5,700 (6.2)	5,190 (5.4)	4,020 (3.5)	3,580 (2.8)	6,000 (3.9)	7,750 (4.5)	12,000 (6.1)	9,370 (4.3)
Electronic Components	40.0 (23.12)	185 (20.9)	10,440 (16.9)	14,620 (17.6)	15,660 (17.1)	18,020 (18.7)	22,270 (19.6)	25,180 (19.3)	30,280 (19.6)	34,480 (19.8)	35,940 (18.4)	41,800 (19.4)
Total Electronics -Hardware	173 (100)	885 (100)	61,850 (100)	82,850 (100)	91,640 (100)	96,9620 (100)	113,560 (100)	30,170 (100)	154,380 (100)	173,890 (100)	195,810 (100)	215,870 (100)

Notes: Figures in parentheses are percentage shares of the respective segments in the industry
Source: *Guide to Electronics Industry in India 1999.* Department of Electronics, Government of India, p. 5.1

Table A.9: **The Relative Contribution of the Small Scale Sector in the Electronics Industry in the year 1997**

Sector/ Variable	No. of Units	%age Share	Production (Rs. Millions)	%age Share	Employment (in numbers)	%age Share
Public Sector	97	2.5	42,020	20.0	86,000	25.0
Organised Private Sector	625	17.5	98,120	45.0	95,000	27.5
Small Scale Sector	2800	80.0	75,730	35.0	164,000	47.5
Total Electronics Industry	3522	100	215,870	100	345,000	100

Source: Guide to Electronics Industry in India 1999. Department of Electronics, Government of India, pp. 1.16 and 1.20

Table A.10: **Segment-wise Contribution of the Small Scale Sector in the Electronics Industry for Two Time Points**

Segment	Production in Rs. Crores for the Year 1981			Production in Rs. Crores for the Year 1997			Growth Rates (%)	
	Orgd. Sector	Small Sector	% S. Sector	Orgd. Sector	Small Sector	% S. Sector	Orgd. Sector	S. Sector
Consumer Electronics	135	120	47.1	3097	4353	58.4	21.5	25.2
Instrumentation and Industrial Electronics	105	55	34.74	2100	1020	32.7	20.6	20.0
Data Processing Systems	29	2	6.5	2133	567	21	30.7	42.3
Communication and Broadcasting Equipment	144	10	6.5	2921	279	8.7	20.6	23.1
Strategic Electronics	69	0	–	850	86	9.7	17.0	–
Electronic Components	128	58	31.2	2912	1268	30.3	21.4	21.1
Total Electronics	610	245	28.7	14013	7573	35.1	21.6	23./8

Source: Guide to Electronics Industry in India 1999. Department of Electronics, Government of India, p. 1.16

Table A.11: **Readymade Garment Exports of India (in Rs. Crores)**

Years (1)	Garment Exports (2)	Total Exports (3)	% Share of (2) in (3) (4)
1981-82	669.80	7798	8.59
1982-83	629.30	8788	7.14
1983-84	734.60	9738	7.54
1984-85	948.30	11705	8.10
1985-86	1096.10	10847	10.10
1986-87	1503.00	12417	12.10
1987-88	1999.50	15611	12.81
1988-89	2278.10	20148	11.31
1989-90	3472.20	27681	12.54
1990-91	4639.64	32555	14.25
1991-92	6282.35	44042	14.26
1992-93	8840.75	53688	16.47
1993-94	11648.06	69752	16.70
1994-95	13921.62	82609	16.85

Source: Compendium of Textile Statistics 1995. Textile Commissioner

Appendix - B

B1: LIST OF RESERVED PRODUCTS IN THE SELECTED INDUSTRIES

B1.1 Automotive Components

1. Truck Body Building Wooden Structure (374201005)[1]
2. Seats for Buses and Trucks (374202001)
3. Wiring Harness except Integrated Wiring Harness (374616000)
4. Grease Nipples (37470600x)
5. Gun Metal Bushes (374708002)
6. Bulb Horns (374714002)
7. Hub Caps-Auto (374721009)
8. Hose Pipes and Radiator Hoses-Auto (374721009)
9. Horn Buttons (374722005)
10. Shackle Pins-Automobile Use (374726019)
11. Auto Leaf Springs Excluding Tapered Leaf Springs (37472802x)
12. Luggage Carrier (37472900x)
13. Ornamental Fittings-Auto (374737002)
14. Break and Pedal Pads-Auto (374749000)
15. Automobile Radiators Except Aluminium Radiators (374749000)

16. Radiator Grills-Auto (374752001)
17. Seat Cushion (374759006)
18. Sun Shades-Auto (374778000)
19. Side Lamps Assembly-Auto Excluding Combination Lamp Assembly (374780005)
20. Spot Lamp Assembly-Auto (374782008)
21. Tail Lamp Assembly-Auto (37478700x)
22. Ash Trays-Car Fittings (374804001)
23. Battery Cables and Fittings (374811008)
24. Battery Cell Tester (374812004)
25. Electrical Fuse Boxes-Auto (374869006)
26. Electrical Fuses-Auto (374870004)
27. Exhaust Mufflers-Auto Other Than Double Coil (37487400x)
28. Fuel Tank Caps-Auto (374883009)
29. Break Pedals (374994013)
30. Clutch Pedals (374994021)
31. Dust Covers (37499403x)
32. Wiper Blade Components (374994048)
33. Wind Screen Beedings (374994056)
34. Door Channels (374994064)
35. Rubber Beeding (374994072)

Products numbering 29 to 35 are Auto Rubber Components. Of these automotive components, six products, namely, Hub Caps-Auto, Ornamental Fittings-Auto, Stop Lamps Assembly-Auto, Stop Lamps Assembly-Auto, Tail Lamp Assembly-Auto and Ash Tray-Car Fittings are de-reserved from April 1997 onwards. For the remaining products the ceiling limit has been raised to fifty million rupees recently following the recommendations of a study group.

B1.2 Electronics

1. AA Conductors up to and including 19 strands (38391501x)
2. ACSR Conductors up to and including 19 strands (383916018)
3. Radio/Car Radio low cost up to Rs. 250 each (364201010)
4. TV Antennas (364302003)
5. TV Tuners Excluding Electronic Tuners (36430300x)
6. TV Booster Amplifiers (364802006)
7. Amplifiers for Entertainment and Public Address System (364903007)
8. Air Break Off Load Isolators 11kw (366202014)
9. Electronic Fan Regulators (366206001)
10. Telescopic Aerials for Radio Receivers (369601009)

B1.3 Garments

Ready-made Garments (264104005) has been reserved for the exclusive production in the small-scale units but the ceiling limit for the plant and machinery has been raised initially in 1993 up to 30 million rupees and later in August 2000 up to 50 million rupees keeping the export potential of the industry. Recently, garment industry was de-reserved totally.

B2: FIRM-LEVEL CHARACTERISTICS REPRESENTING TECHNOLOGY AND ITS DETERMINANTS

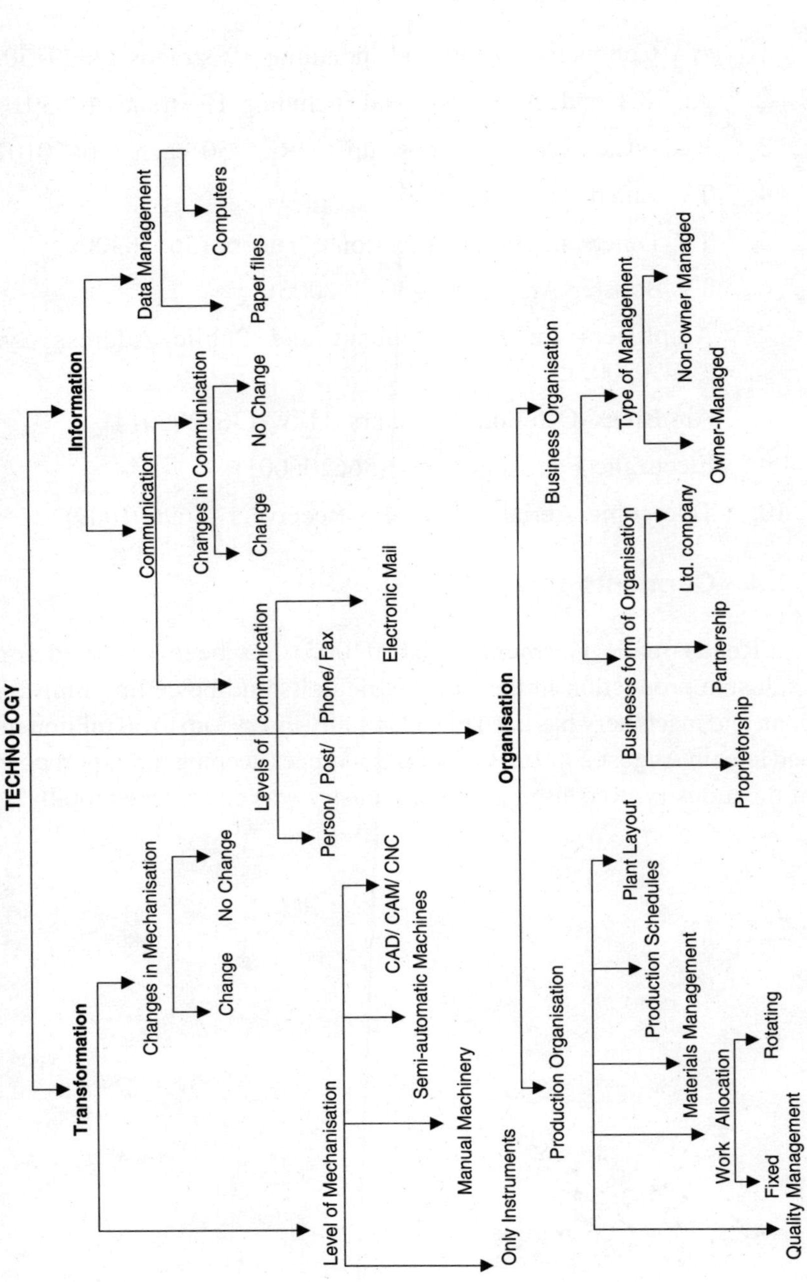

B2 *Contd.*

B2.1 Non-Technology Characteristics

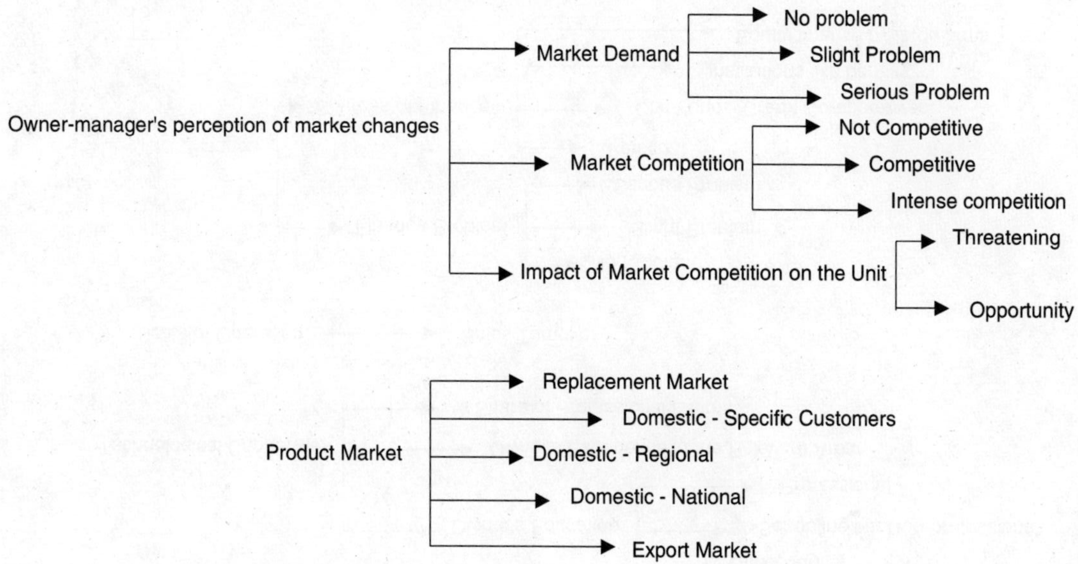

B2 *Contd.*

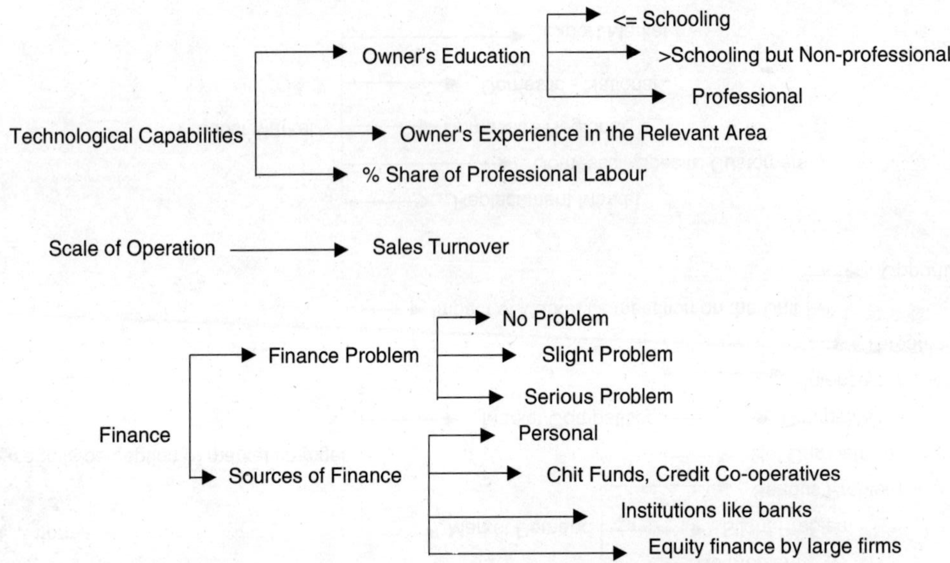
Technological Capabilities
Owner's Education
<= Schooling
>Schooling but Non-professional
Professional
Owner's Experience in the Relevant Area
% Share of Professional Labour
Scale of Operation
Sales Turnover
Finance
Finance Problem
No Problem
Slight Problem
Serious Problem
Sources of Finance
Personal
Chit Funds, Credit Co-operatives
Institutions like banks
Equity finance by large firms

B2 *Contd.*

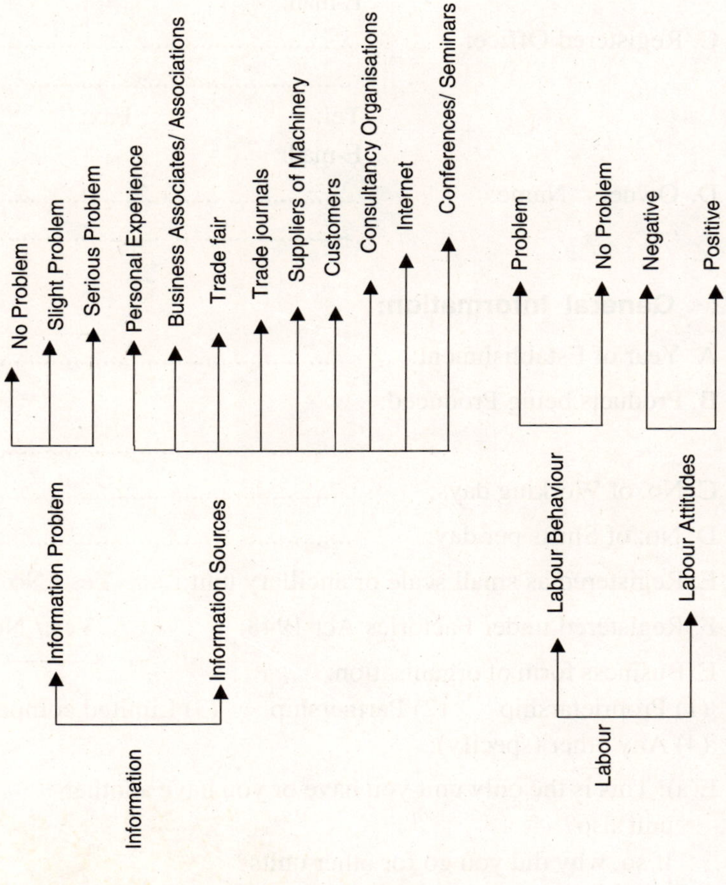
Information
Information Problem
No Problem
Slight Problem
Serious Problem
Information Sources
Personal Experience
Business Associates/ Associations
Trade fair
Trade journals
Suppliers of Machinery
Customers
Consultancy Organisations
Internet
Conferences/ Seminars
Labour
Labour Behaviour
Problem
No Problem
Labour Attitudes
Negative
Positive

B3: QUESTIONNAIRE USED FOR URBAN SMALL-SCALE INDUSTRIES

B3.1 Company's Identification:

A. Name of the Company: ....

B. Address: Plant: ....

....

Tel: Fax:

E-mail:

C. Registered Office: ....

....

Tel: Fax:

E-mail:

D. Owners' Name: ....

....

B3.2 General Information:

A. Year of Establishment: ....

B. Products being Produced:

....

C. No. of Working days: ....

D. No. of Shifts per day: ....

E. Registered as small scale or ancillary unit: Yes / No

F. Registered under Factories Act 1948: Yes / No

E. Business form of organisation:

(1) Proprietarship (2) Partnership (3) Limited company

(4) Any other (specify):

E(a): This is the only unit you have or you have another unit also?

If so, why did you go for other units?

Do you do jobwork or production?

H. Owners are full time involved in the management: Yes / No

If yes, what is their designation: ....

Nature of management:

General / specialised: ....

B3.3 **Outputs and Inputs:**

A. Value of production: ....
(Annual sales turnover)

B. Value of capital: ....
Plant and machinery: ....
(Purchase value)

C. Employment:

	No.	Av. Wage (p.m)	Av. Experience
Total:	....	....	....
Professional:	....	....	....
Non-professional:	....	....	....
Above schooling:	....	....	....
Schooling + vocational Training:	....	....	....
Schooling:	....	....	....
Women:	....	....	....
Regular/permanent:	....	....	....
Casual:	....	....	....

D. Value of raw materials:

Name	Value (% in sales turnover)
....	....
....	....
....	....

E. Main source of energy:

Name	Value (% in sales turnover)
....	....
....	....

F. Total Cost of Production:

G. Profits: ....

Garments: Production: In-house (%) Fabricators (%)

B3.4 Existing Technologies:

A. Main Processing: Assembly type/Flexible manufacturing /any other

B. Is there any name for the type of technology that is in use?

....

C. Do you use CAD/CAM/CNC? Yes/No
Semi-automatic ( ) Manual ( )

D. Technologies in material handling and packing are: Manual/ Mechanised

E. Work allocations: Fixed/Rotating Single/Multiple

F. Inventories: Few months stock/few weeks stock/few days stock
Imported ( ) ( ) and Indian materials ( ) ( )
Reason for importing: Cheaper/quality/non-availability/any other
Materials obtained through cash/credit/advance

G. Quality management: Total/sample basis/none
Did you obtain any standards for quality of the product or system like ISO 9000?
If yes, specify:

H. Communication: Card/messenger (word of mouth or paper)/ phone/fax/e-mail/any other (specify):
Within plant: ....
Suppliers: ....
Customers: ....
With other services like banks: ....

I. Do you have MIS? Yes/No

J. Have you hooked to any business network? Yes/No

K. How do you store and process information?
Records/ computers

B3.5 Any Changes in the Technologies over time?

(any additions to the original machinery)

A. Added any machinery? Yes/No if yes, when?
If yes, specify: ....
....

Whenever you bought the machine did you (have to) make any modifications to it?

If so, what type of modifications did you do? ....

Why did you do so? ....

B. Any changes in production schedules? Yes /No if yes, when?

If yes, specify: ....

C. Any changes in work allocations? Yes/No if yes, when?

If yes, specify: ....

D. Any changes in material inventories? Yes/No if yes, when?

If yes, specify: ....

E. Any changes in ways of communication? (refer to IV. 8)

Within the plant: Yes/No if yes, when?

If yes, specify: ....

With suppliers: Yes/No if yes, when?

If yes, specify: ....

With customers: Yes/No if yes, when?

If yes, specify: ....

F. Do you frequently change plant level organisation like work allocations?

If yes, how frequently? ....

Any specific change after 1991? Yes/No

If yes, specify:

G. Why did you go for change?

To increase the speed of production process so as to increase the amount of output,

To increase the flexibility,

To improve the quality of product,

To reduce the cost of production,

Product diversification

Any other

H. Were you able to do whatever you want to do? ....

Do you think that you should go for technological upgradation or not?

B3.6 Owner / Manager's Profile:

A. Number of owners: ....

B. Age of owners: ....

C. Educational qualification: ....

D. Any further training: ....

E. Business started or inherited by the current owner? ....

F. Any previous employment? Yes/No

If yes, specify the nature of employment and the number of years worked

....

Do you often travel in connection with your business?

Manager's qualification:

.... Experience: within the unit: Before that:

B3.7 Market Profile:

A. Is the unit exporting? Yes/ No

B. If exporting, specify: ....% of exports

Destination countries: ....

C. Domestic market is: Local/regional/national/specific customers

Specify the locality/ region:

Specify the customers:

Are you an original equipment manufacturer?

....

D. Do you have any payment problems like delays in payment or rejecting the product after delivery?

Usual payment period:

E. Distribution through: retail/wholesale/direct to customers/any other

....

F. Do you have your own brand name? Yes/ No

If yes, specify: ....

G. Do you think demand is constrained?

If so, how severe do you rate it? (0, 1, 2) ....

H. How competitive do you think markets are? (0, 1, 2) ....

I. What do you think are the reasons for markets being competitive?
(Rate the following reasons in order of preference)
Number of suppliers increasing,
Capacities of the existing suppliers are enhanced,
Number of substitutable/new products are increasing,
Large-scale companies or multinational companies entered,
customers are demanding in terms of quality/cost

J. How do you view the changing markets?
Opportunity to grow/threatening/risky to the business
Whatever be the way you consider it how do you go about it?

....

K. Do you have any regular practice of collecting market information about products, customers and distribution arrangements? Yes/ No
If yes, how frequently do you collect? ....

L. Do you expect expansion of market for your product? Yes/No
If yes, how are you going about it? By i.e. strategy
Cutting down costs,
Increasing quality,
Improving delivery schedules,
Improving after sales service

M. Are you availing any government assistance in marketing like preferential government purchase?
If yes, specify ....

B3.8 Sources of Information with regard to Technology

Do you treat getting information is as a big problem? (0, 1, 2) ....

A. What are your sources of information regarding technology?
Trade fairs/trade journals/seminars and conferences of professionals/associations/business associates/ suppliers of machinery/customers/consultancy organisations/
What is the major source of information?

B. Do you regularly participate in/attend trade fairs?
If yes, specify the number of times: ....

C. Do you subscribe to trade/technology related journals regularly?

D. Have you ever attended any technology related seminars/ conferences?
If yes, are they organised by government or business associations or professional bodies ....

E. If you had gone to consultancy organisations, are they private or government?

....

B3.9 Sources of Technology

A. What are your sources of technology?
consultancy organisations/suppliers of machinery/other private enterprises/government R&D labs/customers/own R&D

B. If you availed your technology through consultancy organisation,
Is it private or government? ....

C. If the source of technology is suppliers of machinery, are they Indian or foreign?

....

D. Did you buy first- or second-hand machinery? ....

E. Any government assistance like hire-purchase of machinery or any concessional government finance to buy technology or subsidising consultancy fee? Yes/No
If yes, specify: ....

B3.10 Sources of Finance

Do you feel finance is a serious problem for you? (0, 1, 2) ....
If yes, is it in respect of fixed capital or working capital?

A. What are your sources of finance?
Personal, relatives and friends/financial institutions/ development banks/commercial banks/equity finance by other firms/credit co-operatives or chit funds

B. If equity participation by other firms, are they Indian or foreign firms?

what is the percentage of equity holding by other firms? ....

C. Specify the percentage of each of the following:
Financial institutions ( ), development banks ( ), commercial banks ( ),
Personal ( ), relatives ( ), friends ( )

D. Are you a member of any chit funds or co-operative credit societies? Yes/No
Do you make use of these sources regularly? ....

E. Any government assistance either as small-scale unit or in general like subsidised interest rates? Yes/No
If yes, specify: ....

B3.11 Selection of Technology

A. How did you select your technology i.e. plant and machinery first time and
Whenever you added machinery?
(Give your order of preference in the case of more than one reason)
Consultant advised,
Thought it is better because it reduces costs or improve quality,
Thought it suits your product requirements,
Thought it suits your scale of operation,
Thought it suits the available raw materials, labour skills,
Selected keeping energy supply in mind
Selected keeping capital costs, labour price or raw material or energy prices

B. Were you aware of alternative technologies available? Yes/No

C. Have you ever felt constrained, otherwise you could have gone for better technology?
If yes, what are your constraints?
(Specify in order of preference in case of more than one reason)
Finance/existing labour/demand constraint/government policies

B3.12 Ways of Acquisition of Technology

A. How did you acquire your technology?
Outright purchase
License fees
Royalty payment
Equity participation
Purchase of machinery (First-/second-hand)

B3.13 Technical Personnel working at the Plant

A. Details of technical personnel: See Q III

B. Any intermittent training programmes for technical personnel? Yes/No
If yes, how frequently do you have these programmes? ....

C. Is turnover of personnel a problem: Yes/No
If yes, non-workers (0, 1, 2), Workers (0, 1, 2)

D. Is absenteeism a problem? Yes/No
If yes, non-workers (0, 1, 2), Workers (0, 1, 2)

E. Are the workers unionised? Yes/No
If yes, are they strong and troublesome? ....

F. What are their main demands? Wages or any other (specify):

G. Are the workers willing to learn whenever they have to work on a new machine? Yes/No

Do workers give the same output whenever you are outside the factory?

H. Whenever you buy a new machine do you train your existing labour to handle?
or do you let them practice on it without having any training?
or do you recruit new people with the knowledge of new machines?

....

B3.14 Government Policy Measures

A. What do you think about changing government policies?
(Rate them in order of preference)
Are they giving you more freedom to take decisions?

Do you still feel government regulating?
Do you think government is not protecting enough small units?
Did you ever think government policies are useful?
If not, why did you think so? ....

B4: LIST OF ORGANISATIONS VISITED

1. Dy. Development Commissioner and Jt. Commissioner (Technology), from the Office of the Development Commissioner, Small Scale Industries, Ministry of Industries, New Delhi
2. Small Industries Service Institute, New Delhi
3. Directorate of Industries, Delhi Administration, Delhi + local offices of some of its Industrial Estates
4. Small Industries Development Bank of India, New Delhi
5. Technology Bureau for Small Enterprises, New Delhi
6. The National Small Industries Corporation Ltd., New Delhi + its Regional office for Delhi and Haryana at Gurgaon and for Uttar Pradesh at Noida
7. Automotive Components Manufacturers Association, Delhi
8. Electronics Component Industries Association, New Delhi
9. Garment Exporters Association, New Delhi
10. Apparel Exporters and Manufacturers Association, New Delhi
11. Confederation of Indian Industry, New Delhi
12. PHD Chamber of Commerce and Industry, New Delhi
13. Okhla Industries Association, New Delhi
14. Flatted Factory Entrepreneurs Association Okhla, New Delhi
15. Faridabad Small Industries Association, Faridabad
16. Noida Small and Tiny Industries Association, Noida

Endnote

1. The numbers in the parentheses are National Industrial Classification 1987 numbers for the concerned product.

References

ACMA (1997). *Facts and Figures : Automative Inductry of India 1996-97*. Automotive Component Manufacturers Associations of India, Delhi.

A TSQ - A T Kearney Study (1998). "How Indian Firms Fare on Sourcing" in *The Strategist*, October-December, 1998, pp. 5-13

Ahluwalia, I.J. (1988). "Industrial Policy and Performance in India" in Lucas, R.E.B. and G.F. Papanek (eds.) (1988). *The Indian Economy: Recent Development and Future Prospects*. Delhi: Oxford University Press, pp. 151-162

Ahluwalia, I.J. (1991). *Productivity and Growth in Indian Manufacturing*. Delhi : Oxford University Press.

Ahluwalia, I.J. (1996). "India's Opening up to Trade and Investment" in I.J. Ahluwalia, Rakesh Mohan and Omkar Goswami *Policy Reform in India*. Edited by Charles Oman. Paris: OECD, pp. 17–41

Ahluwalia, M.S. (1999). "India's Economic Reforms: An Appraisal" in Sachs, J.D., A. Varshney and N. Bajpai (eds) (1999). *India in the Era of Economic* Reforms. Delhi: Oxford University Press, pp. 26–80

Ahmad, Q.K. (1996). "Problems and Prospects of Small and Micro Enterprises in the Process of Economic Liberalisation in South Asia" in R. Islam (ed) (1996). *Small and Micro Enterprises in a Period of Economic Liberalisation: Opportunities and Challenges*. New Delhi: ILO-SAAT, pp. 16–51

Bagchi, A.K. (1995). "Introduction: Coping With Technological Change" in Bagchi, A.K. (ed). *New Technology and the Workers' Response: Microelectronics, Labour and Society*. New Delhi: Sage, pp. 12–26

Bagchi, A.K. (ed) (1995). *New Technology and the Workers' Response: Microelectronics, Labour and Society*. New Delhi: Sage

Bardhan, P. (ed) (1989). *Conversations Between Economists and Anthropologists*. Delhi. Oxford University Press.

Beckmann, M.J. (1995). "Economic Growth in a Central Place System" in Giersch, H. (ed). *Urban Agglomeration and Economic Growth.* New York: Springer, pp. 107–116

Bell, M. and K. Pavitt (1992). "Accumulating Technological Capabilities in Developing Countries" in the *Proceedings of the World Bank Annual Conference on Development Economics*, pp. 257–282.

Berry, V.K. (1997). *A Background Paper on the Technological Changes and Changes in Women's Employment in Garment Industry*. IAMR working paper no. 3/1997.

Bhagwati, J.N. and P. Desai (1970). *India: Planning for Industrialisation*. Delhi: Oxford University Press

Bhalla, A.S. (1996). *Facing the Technological Challenge*. London: Macmillan Press Ltd.

Bhavani, D.A. (1989). Some Economic Aspects of the Modern Small Scale Industries in *India*. Ph.D. Thesis. University of Delhi, Delhi

Bhavani, T.A. (2001): *Technological Change in the Indian Small Scale Industries: Its Causes and Consequences*. IDPAD Project Report, Institute of Economic Growth, Delhi.

Bhavani, T.A. (2001).""*Towards Developing an Analytical Framework to Study Technoloogical Change in the Small Units of the Developing Nations"*, Working Paper Series No. E/216/2001, Institute of Economic Growth, Delhi, 2001.

Bhavani, T.A. (2002)."Small-scale units in the Era of Globalisation: Problems and Prospects", *Economic and Political Weekly*, vol. XXXVII, No. 29, July 20, 2002

Bhavani, T.A. (2002)."*Employment, Efficiency and Technology in the Indian Small Enterprises: A Re-examination of the Basic Issues*" published in the NISTADS News, Vol. 4(2), October 2002, pp. 26–33

Bhavani, T.A. (2002)."*Impact of Technology on the Competitiveness of the Indian Small Manufacturing Sector: A Case Study of the Automotive Component Industry*". Discussion Paper No. 2002/76, WIDER, United Nations University, Helsinki, 2002.

Bhavani, T.A. (forthcoming). "An Examination of Determinants of Employment Generation in the Indian Small-scale Industries" in Odaka, K., and Kiyokawa, Y. (ed) *Small and Medium-Sized Industries in India, 1990-1995: A Comparative Perspective with Japan*, New Delhi: Allied Publishers

Bhavani, T.A. and Suresh D. Tendulkar (2000): "Determinants of Firm-Level Export

Performance: A Case Study of Indian Textile Garment Industry", *Journal of International Trade and Development*, Vol. 10, no.1, pp. 65–92

Biersteker, T.J. (1995). "The "Triumph" of Liberal Economic Ideas in the Developing World" in Stallings, B. (Ed). *Global Change and Regional Response: The New International Context of Development*. Cambridge, UK: Cambridge University Press, pp. 174–198

Biggs, T., Manju Shah and Pradeep Srivastava (1995). *Technological Capabilities and Learning in African Enterprises*. World Bank Technical Paper No. 288, Africa Technical Department Series.

Bos, Antonio, and William, Cole (1994). "Management Systems as Technology: Japanese, US and National Firms in the Brazilian Electronic Sector" in *World Development*, vol. 22 (2), pp. 225–236.

Carlton, D.W., and J.M. Perloff (1990). Modern Industrial Organisation. Glenview (USA): Scott, Foresman and Company

Chandra, P., and Sastry, T. (1998) "Competitiveness of Indian Manufacturing: Findings of the 1997 Manufacturing Futures Survey" in in *Vikalpa the Journal for Decision Makers*, Vol. 23, no.3, July-September, pp. 25–36

Chatterjee, S. (1998). "Focus Turns to Exports" in *The Hindu Survey of Indian Industry*, Chennai, pp. 141–143

Chatterjee, S. and Rakesh Mohan (1993). "Indian Garment Exports" in *Economic and Political Weekly*. Vol. 28 (35), August 28, pp. M-95–M-120

Chhachhi, A. (1999). *Gender, Flexibility, Skill and Industrial Restructuring: The Electronics Industry in India*. Working Paper Series No. 296, Institute of Social Studies, The Hague

Cohen, W. (1995). " Empirical Studies in Innovative Activity" in Stoneman, Paul (ed) (1995). *Handbook of Economics of Innovation and Technological Change*. Oxford: Blackwell, pp. 182–264

Cohen, W.M and R.C. Levin (1989). "Empirical Structure of Innovation and Market Structure" in Schmalensee, R and R.D. Willig (ed). *Handbook of Industrial Organisation*. Vol. II, Amsterdam: North-Holland, pp. 1059-1107

EIB (1996). *Consumer Electronics: A Sector Study*. Occasional Paper No. 43, Export-Import Bank of India, 1996

Coombs, R., P. Saviotti and V. Walsh (1987). *Economics and Technological Change*. London: Macmillan

Cooper, C. (1994). "Relevance of Innovation Studies to Developing Countries" in

Cooper, C. (ed). *Technology and Innovation in the International Economy*. England: Edward Elgar

Dahlman, C.J and F.C. Sercovich (1984). "Exports of Technology from Semi-industrial Economies and Local Technological Development" in *Journal of Development Economics*, vol. 16, nos. 1-2, (September-October), pp. 62–100.

Dahlman, C.J., Bruce Ross-Larson and L.E. Westphal (1987). "Managing Techological Development: Lessons from the Newly Industrialising Countries" in *World Development.* Vol. 15 (6), pp. 759–775

Dahlman, Carl and Larry Westphal (1982). "Technological Effort in Industrial Development" in Stewart, Frances and Jeffrey James (eds). *The Economics of New Technology in Developing Countries*. London: Pinter Publishers, pp. 105–137.

Dahmen, D. (1993). "Semiconductors" in Wellenius, B., A. Miller and C. J. Dahlman (eds). *Developing the Electronics Industry*. The World Bank, Washington, D.C., pp. 31–42

Delhi 1999: A Fact Sheet. National Capital Region Planning Board, New Delhi

Desai, A.V. (1984). "Achievements and Limitations of India's Technologyical Capability" in Fransman, M., and Kenneth King (Eds) (1984). *Technological Capability in the Third World.* London: Macmillan Press, pp. 245-261.

Desai, A.V. (1988). "Technology Acquisition and Application: Interpretations of the Indian Experience" Lucas, R.E.B. and G.F. Papanek (eds.) (1989). *The Indian Economy: Recent Development and Future Prospects*. Delhi: Oxford University Press, pp. 163–184

Desai, A., and N. Taneja (1990). *The Role of Small- and Medium-Scale Industries in the Industrial Development of India*. Asian Development Bank, New Delhi

Dhar, P.N. (1979). "Some Observations on Small Scale Enterprise" in Rao, C.H. and P.C. Joshi (eds). *Reflections on Economic Development and Social Change: Essays in Honour of Prof. V.K.R.V. Rao*. New Delhi: Allied, pp. 169–86

Dobb, M. (1960). *An Essay on Economic Growth and Planning*. London: Routledge and Paul

Dosi, G. (1982). "Technological Paradigms and Technological Trajectories" in *Research Policy*, vol. 11 (3), June, pp. 147–161.

Dosi, G. (1988a). "Sources, Procedures, and Microeconomic Effects of Innovation" in *Research Policy*, vol. 26, September, pp. 1120–1171.

Dosi, G. (1988b). "The Nature of the Innovative Process" in Dosi, G., Freeman, C.,

Nelson, R., Silverberg, G., and Soete, L. (Eds) (1988). *Technical Change and Economic Theory*. London: Pinter Publishers. Pp. 221–239.

Dosi, G. and L. Orsenigo (1988). "Co-ordination and Transformation: An Overview of Structures, Behaviours and Change in Evolutionary Environments" in Dosi et.al. (eds). *Technical Change and Economic Theory*.

Dosi, G. and Franco Malerba (eds) (1996). *Organization and Strategy in the Evolution of the Enterprise*. London: Macmillan Press.

Dosi, G., and R.R. Nelson (1994). "Evolutionary Theories in Economics" in *Journal of Evolutionary Economics*, vol. 4, pp. 152–171.

Dosi, G., Freeman, C., Nelson, R., Silverberg, G., and Soete, L. (Eds) (1988). *Technical Change and Economic Theory*. London: Pinter Publishers.

Dosi, G., D.J. Teece and J. Chytry (ed) (1998). *Technology, Organisation, and Competitiveness: Perspectives on Industrial and Corporate Change*. New York: Oxford University Press.

Douma, S., and Hein Schreuder (1998). *Economic Approaches to Organizations*. Second edition, London: Prentice-Hall.

Edgren, Gus (1989). "Structural Adjustment: The Enterprises and the Workers" in Edgren, Gus (ed). *Restructuring, Employment and Industrial Relations: Adjustment Issues in Asian Industries*. Geneva: ILO (ARTEP), pp. 1–21

Egan, M.L., and A. Mody (1992). "Buyer-Seller Links in Export Development" in *World Development*, Vol. 20 (3), pp. 321–34

EIB (1995). *Electronic Components: A Sector Study*. Occasional Paper No. 42, Export-Import Bank of India, 1995

Elster, J. (1983). *Explaining Technical Change*. Cambridge: Cambridge University Press.

Ernst, D. and D. O'Connor (1992). *Competing in The Electronics Industry: The Experience of Newly Industrialising Economies*. Paris: OECD

ESCAP (1991). *Industrial Restructuring In Asia and The Pacific: In Particular With a View To Strengthening Regional Co-operation*. United Nations, Bangkok

"Factory of the Future" in *The Economist*, May 30, Vl. 303 (7500), 1987.

Finik, A. (1995). *How to Sample in Surveys*. London: Sage

Finik, A. (1995). *The Survey Handbook*. London: Sage

Flamm, K. (1993). "The Computer Industry" in in Wellenius, B., A. Miller and C. J. Dahlman (eds). *Developing the Electronics Industry*. The World Bank, Washington, D.C., pp. 43-56

Fransman, M. (1984). "Technological Capability in the Third World: An Overview and Introduction to Some of the Issues Raised in this Book" in Fransman, M., and K. King (eds) (1984). *Technological Capability in the Third World*. London: Macmillan.

Fransman, M. (1998). "Information, Knowledge, Vision, and Theories of Firm" in Dosi, G., D.J. Teece and J. Chytry (ed) (1998). *Technology, Organisation, and Competitiveness: Perspectives on Industrial and Corporate Change*. New York: Oxford University Press.

Fransman, M., and K. King (eds) (1984). *Technological Capability in the Third World*. London: Macmillan.

Gadgil, D.R. (1973). *The Industrial Evolution of India in Recent Times 1860-1939*. Second Edition. Delhi: Oxford University Press

Galbraith, J.K. (1957). *American Capitalism: The Concept of Countervailing Power*. Revised Edition. London: Hamish Hamilton

Garud, R., Nayyar, P.R., and Shapira, Z.B. (eds) (1997). *Technological Innovation: Oversights and Foresights*. Cambridge: Cambridge University Press.

Gereffi, G. (1995). "Global Production Systems and Third World Development" in Stallings, B. (Ed). *Global Change and Regional Response: The New International Context of Development*. Cambridge, UK: Cambridge University Press, pp. 100-142

Goldar, B.N. and D.B. Gupta (1989). *Industrialising India's North Eastern Region: A Study of District Industry Centres*. Institute of Economic Growth and National Institute of Public Finance and Policy, Delhi.

Goldman, M., and H. Ergas (1997). *Technology Institutions and Policies: Their Role in Developing Technological Capability in Industry*. World Bank Technical Paper N0. 383. Washington, D.C: The World Bank

Gowen, G and D. Hefler (1993). "The Electronics Industry in India: Past Problems, Recent Progress, Future Outlook" in Wellenius, B., A. Miller and C. J. Dahlman (eds). *Developing the Electronics Industry*. The World Bank, Washington, D.C., pp. 209–222

Griliches, Z. (1996), 'The Discovery of the Risidual : A Historical Note'. Journal of Economic Literature, XXXIV: 1324.30

Griliches, Z. (1995). 'R.D. and Productivity : Econometric Results and Measurement Issues' in Paul Stoneman (ed). *Handbook of the Economics of Innovation and Technological Change. Oxford, UK: Balackwell.*

Guide to Electronics Industry in India 1999. Department of Electronics, Government of India, New Delhi

Gulati, M. (1997). *Restructuring and Modernisation of Small Medium Enterprise Clusters in India: A Report.* UNIDO.

Gumaste, V.M. (1988). *Technological Self Reliance in the Automobile and Ancillary Industries in India.* Institute for Financial Management and Research, Madras.

Garg, Charu, S.K. Sanyal, S.T. Nagarathinam and K.R. Pandit (1990): *Central Fiscal Incentives and Concessions to Small Scale Industries: Impact on Growth and Structure*. National Institute of Public Finance and Policy, New Delhi.

Hamilton, C.B. (ed) (1990). *The Uruguay Round, Textiles Trade and the Developing Countries.* The World Bank, Washington, D.C.

Hart, J.A. (1993). "Consumer Electronics" in Wellenius, B., A. Miller and C. J. Dahlman (eds). *Developing the Electronics Industry*. The World Bank, Washington, D.C., pp. 57–74

Hayek, F.A. (1945). "The Use of Knowledge in Society" in the *American Economic Review*, vol. 35 (4), september, pp. 519 - 530.

Hicks, J.R. (1932). *The Theory of Wages*. London: Macmillan

Hodgson, G. (1982). "Theoretical and Policy Implications of Variable Productictivity", *Cambridge Journal of Economics*, V0l. , pp. 213-226

Hoffman, K. and H. Rush (1988). *Micro-Electronics and Clothing: The Impact of Technical Change on a Global Industry.* New York: Praeger

ICRA (1999). *The Indian Automotive Components Industry*. ICRA Industry Watch Series. New Delhi.

IDE (1995). *The Automotive Industry in Asia: The Great Leap Forward*? Institute of Developing Economies, Tokyo.

Islam, R. (1996). "Policy Environment for Small and Micro Enterprises in a Period of Economic Liberalisation: An Overview of the Asian Scenario" in R. Islam (ed) (1996). *Small and Micro Enterprises in a Period of Economic Liberalisation: Opportunities and Challenges*. New Delhi: ILO-SAAT, pp. 1–15

Jain, Rajeev (1990). *Absenteeism and Labour Turnover: A Study of Textile Industry in Rajasthan.* Jaipur: Aalekh Publishers

James, J. (1992). *Microelectronics and the Third World*. UNU/INTECH Working Paper No. 2.

Jeffrey James and A.K. Bhalla (1995). "Microelectronics, Flexible Specialisation and Small-Scale Industrialisation in the Third World" in Bagchi, A.K. (ed). *New Technology and the Workers' Response: Microelectronics, Labour and Society*. New Delhi: Sage, pp. 216–256

Joseph, K. J. (1995). "Output Growth, Technology Behaviour and Employment: Indian Electronics Industry Under Liberalization" in Bagchi, A.K. (ed). *New Technology and the Workers' Response: Microelectronics, Labour and Society*. New Delhi: Sage, pp. 123–144

Joshi, V. and I.M.D. Little (1996). *India's Economic Reforms* 1991-20001. Delhi: Oxford University Press

Kanji, G.K., and M. Asher. (1996). *100 Methods for Total Quality Management*. New Delhi: Sage

Kaplinsky, R. (1994). "From Mass Production to Flexible Specialisation: A Case Study of Microeconomic Change in a Semi-Industrialised Economy", *World Development*, Vol. 22(3), March, pp. 337–53

Karshenas, M and P. Stoneman (1995). "Technological Diffusion" in Stoneman, Paul (ed) (1995). *Handbook of Economics of Innovation and Technological Change*. Oxford: Blackwell, pp. 265–294

Kathuria, S.(1992). "Transfer of Small-Scale Industrial Technology from India to Africa and Other Less Developed Regions-Experience and Potential" in Islam, R. (ed) (1992). *Transfer, Adoption and Diffusion of Technology for Small and Cottage Industries*. Geneva: ILO-ARTEP, pp. 109–35

Katsoulacos, Y.S. (1986). *The Employment Effect of Technical Change*. Sussex: Wheatsheaf Books

Khan, M.U. (1997). *India and Korea: A Comparison of Electronic Technology Policy*. New Delhi: Har-Anand

Khanna, S.R. (1991). *International Trade in Textiles: MFA Quotas and a Developing Country*. New Delhi: Sage

Kimmel, C. (1993). "Trends in Worlwide Sourcing in the Electronics Industry" " in Wellenius, B., A. Miller and C. J. Dahlman (eds). *Developing the Electronics Industry*. The World Bank, Washington, D.C., pp. 151–160

Kmenta, J. (1971). *Elements of Econometrics*. New York: Macmillan

Koopmans, T.C. (1957). *Three Essays on the State of Economic Science*. New York: McGraw-Hill

Koshy, D.O. (1997). *Garment Exports: Winning Strategies*. New Delhi: Prentice-Hall of India

Krishna Sridhar (2001):"Phasing Out of Import Licensing: Impact on Small-Scale Industries", *Economic and Political Weekly*, Vol. 36, No.27, July 7, pp. 2545–2550.

Kumar, Anil (2000). "World Trade Organisation Agreement: Its Impact on Small

Scale Sector" in *Laghu Udyog Samachar*, vol. XXIV (6-8), Jan-March, 2000, pp. 28–39

Kumar, N and N.S. Siddharthan (1997). *Technology, Market Structure and Internationalisation: Issues and Policies for Developing Countries*. London: Routledge

Lal, K. (2000). *Adoption of Information Technology and Its Consequences in a Development Context*. Rotterdam: Erasmus University Rotterdam

Lall, Sanjaya (1987). *Learning to Industrialize*. London: Macmillan

Lall, Sanjaya (1992). "Technological Capabilities and Industrialization" in *World Development*, vol. 20 (2), pp. 165–186.

Lall, Sanjaya (2001). *Competitiveness, Technology and Skills* Cheltenham, UK, Edward Elgar.

Langlois (1997). "Cognition and Capabilities: Opportunities Seized and Missed in the History of the Computer Industry" in Garud, R., Nayyar, P.R., and Shapira, Z.B. (eds). *Technological Innovation: Oversights and Foresights*. Cambridge, UK: Cambridge University Press. Pp. 71– 94

Langlois, R.N., T.A. Pugel, C.S. Haklisch, R.R. Nelson and W.G. Egelhoff (1988). *Micro-Electronics: An Industry in Transition*. Boston: Unwin Hyman

Liebetrau, A.M. (1983). *Measures of Association*. A Sage University Paper, Quantitative Applications in Social Sciences. Thousand Oaks, California: Sage

Link, A.N. (1997). *Technological Change and Productivity Growth* London: Harwood Academic Publishers.

Little, I.M.D, Mazumdar, D and J.M. Page (1987). *Small Manufacturing Enterprise*. New York: Oxford University Press

Lucas, R.E.B. (1988). "India's Industrial Policy", Lucas, R.E.B. and G.F. Papanek (eds.) (1988). *The Indian Economy: Recent Development and Future Prospects*. Delhi: Oxford University Press, pp. 185–203

Lucas, R.E.B. and G.F. Papanek (eds.) (1988). *The Indian Economy: Recent Development and Future Prospects*. Delhi: Oxford University Press

Mahalanobis, P.C. (1963). *The Approach of Operational Research to Planning in India*. Bombay: Asia Publishing House

Mansfield, E. (1961). "Technical Change and the Rate of Imitation" first published in *Econometrica* (October). Later reproduced in Rosenberg, N. (Ed) (1971). *The Economics of Technological Change*. Baltimore: Penguin Books. Pp. 284–316.

Marathe, S.S. (1989). *Regulation and Development: India's Policy Experience of Controls over Industry*. Second Edition. New Delhi: Sage Publications Ltd.

Mashelkar, R. (1998). "Manufacturing Technology in India: The New Challenges" in *Vikalpa the Journal for Decision Makers*, Vol. 23, no.3, July-September, pp. 15–23

McGuickin, R.H., M.L. Streitwieser, and M.E. Doms (1996). *'The Effect of Technology use on Productivity Growth'*. Discussion paper. Washington D.C: Centre for Economic Studies.

"Meet the Global Factory" in *The Economist*, June 20, 1998.

Meyanathan, S.D. (ed) (1994). *Managing the Restructuring in the Textile and Garment Subsector: Examples from Asia*. EDI Seminar Series. The World Bank, Washington, D.C.

Meyanathan, S.D., and J. Ahmed (1994). "Managing Restructuring in the Textile and Garment Subsector: An Overview" in Meyanathan, S.D. (ed) (1994). *Managing the Restructuring in the Textile and Garment Subsector: Examples from Asia*. EDI Seminar Series. The World Bank, Washington, D.C. pp. 1–30

Miller, A. (1993). "Building a Modern Electronics Industry" in Wellenius, B., A. Miller and C. J. Dahlman (eds). *Developing the Electronics Industry*. The World Bank, Washington, D.C., pp. 15–28

Minami, R., K.S. Kim, F. Makino and J.Seo (eds.) (1995). *Acquiring, Adapting and Developing Technologies: Lessons From the Japanese Experience.* New York: St. Martin's Press

Mintzberg, H. (1979). *The Structuring of Organizations*. Englewood Cliffs, N.J: Prentice-Hall.

Mody, A. (1993). "Alternative Strategies for Developing Information Industries" in Wellenius, B., A. Miller and C. J. Dahlman (eds). *Developing the Electronics Industry*. The World Bank, Washington, D.C., pp. 223-238

Mody, A., and Carl Dahlman (1992). "Performance and Potential Information Technology: An International Perspective" in *World Development*, vol. 20 (12), pp. 1703–1719.

Mody, A., Rajan Suri and Jerry Sanders (1992). "Keeping Pace With Change: Organizational and Technological Imperatives" in *World Development,* vol. 20 (12), pp. 1797–1816.

Mody, A., and D. Wheeler (1987). "Towards a Vanishing Middle: Competition in the World Garment Industry" in *World Development*, Vol. 15 (10/11), pp. 1269–84

Mohan, Rakesh (2002): "Small-Scale Industry Policy in India: A Critical Evaluation" in Anne O. Krueger (ed). *Economic Policy Reforms and the Indian Economy*, Oxford University Press, New Delhi, pp. 213–302

Morris, Sebastian, Rakesh Basant, Kesab Das, K.Ramachandran and Abraham Koshy (2001). *The Growth and Transformation of Small Firms in India*, Oxford University Press, New Delhi

Mowery, D. and Rosenberg, N. (1979). "The Influence of Market Demand Upon Innovation: A Critical Review of Some Recent Empirical Studies", *Research Policy*, Vol. 8, pp. 102–53

Myrdal, G. (1968). *Asian Drama: An Inquiry in to the Poverty of Nations*. Vol. 2, Ch. 25. London: Allan Lane The Penguin Press

Narayana, D. (1989). *The Motor Vehicle Industry in India*. Occasional Paper Series, Centre for Development Studies, Trivendrum

NCAER (1993). *Spurious Automotive Components: Market Size and Consequences*. Sponsored by Automotive Components Manufacturers Association and Confederation of Indian Industry. New Delhi.

NCAER (1999). *Spurious Automotive Components: Market Size and Consequences*. Sponsored by Automotive Components Manufacturers Association. New Delhi.

Nelson, R. and S.G. Winter (1977). "Dynamic Competition and Technical Progress" in Balassa, B. and R. Nelson (eds). *Economic Progress, Private Values, and Public Policy: Essays in Honour of William Fellner*. Amsterdam: North-Holland

Nelson, R.R. (1987). Understanding Technical Change as an Evolutionary Process. Amsterdam: Elsevier Science Publishers.

Nelson, R.R. (1995). "Recent Evolutionary Theorizing About Economic Change", in *Journal of Economic Literature*, vol. 33 (1), March, pp. 48–90.

Nelson, R.R., and Winter, S.G. (1982). *An Evolutionary Theory of Economic Change*. Cambridge, Mass.: Belknap Press of Harvard University Press.

NIFT (1998). *Indian Garment Exports: In The New Millennium*. National Institute of Fashion Technology, New Delhi

Nishi, Y. (1993). "The Japanese Semiconductor Industry" in Wellenius, B., A. Miller and C. J. Dahlman (eds). *Developing the Electronics Industry*. The World Bank, Washington, D.C., pp. 123–130

NCRPB (2000). *National Capital Region Directory*, National Capital Region Planning Board, Ministry of Urban Development and Poverty Alleviation, New Delhi, July, 2000.

O'Brien, P., and Y. Karmokolias (1994). *Radical Reforms in the Automotive Industry: Policies in Emerging Markets*. Discussion Paper No. 21, International Finance Corporation, The world Bank, Washington, D.C.

OECD. (1974). *Transfer of Technology for Small Industries*. Paris

Papola, T. S. (1989). "Restructuring in Indian Industry: Implications for Employment and Industrial Relations" in Gus Edgren (ed). *Restructuring, Employment and Industrial Relations: Adjustment Issues in Asian Industries*. Geneva: ILO (ARTEP), pp. 29–79

Patel Pari and Keith Pavitt (1995). "Patterns of Technological Activity: Their Measurement and Interpretation" in Stoneman, Paul (ed). *Handbook of Economics of Innovation and Technological Change*. Oxford: Blackwell, pp. 14–51.

Patvardhan, V.S. (1985). "Role of Small Scale Industries in the Process of Industrialisation in Pune and Aurangabad Districts of Maharashtra State" in *Arthavijnana*, Vol. 27, no. 3 (September), pp. 195–271

Pepper, R. and Bhattacharya, H. (1994). "Changing Trends in Global Textile Technology

and Trade" in Meyanathan, S.D. (1994). *Managing the Restructuring in the Textile and Garment Subsector: Examples from Asia*. EDI Seminar Series. The World Bank, Washington, D.C., pp. 31-58

Piek, H. (1997). *Development and Acquisition of Technology in Rural Collective Industries: The Case of China's Hinterland*. Tinbergen Institute Research Series. Amsterdam: Thesis Publishers

Piramal, G. (1996). *Business Maharajas of India*. Penguin

Porac, J.F. (1997). " Local Rationality, Global Blunders and the Boundaries of Technological Choices: Lessons from IBM and DOS" in Garud, R., Nayyar, P.R., and Shapira, Z.B. (eds). *Technological Innovation: Oversights and Foresights*. Cambridge, UK: Cambridge University Press. Pp. 129–146

Radosevic, S. (1999). *International Technology Transfer and Catch-up in Economic Development*. Cheltenham, U.K: Edward Elgar

Raffaeli, M. (1994). "Some Considerations on the Muti-Fibre Arrangement: Past, Present and Future" in Meyanathan, S.D. (1994). *Managing the Restructuring in the Textile and Garment Subsector: Examples from Asia*. EDI Seminar Series. The World Bank, Washington, D.C., pp. 59–82

Ramachandran, R. (1989). *Urbanisation and Urban Systems in India.* Delhi: Oxford University Press.

Ramaswamy, V.K. and G. Gereffi (1998). "India's Apparel Sector in the Global Economy: Catching Up or Falling Behind". *The Economic and Political Weekly*. Vol. 33, no. 3 (January 17-23), pp. 122–130

Ramesh, D.K. (1991). "How Successful are Industrial Estates?" *The Hindu*, Tuesday, September 3, p. 17

Richardson, H.W. (1995). "Economies and Diseconomies of Agglomeration" in Giersch, H. (ed). *Urban Agglomeration and Economic Growth*. New York: Springer, pp. 107–116

Robinson, R.D. (1988*). The International Transfer of Technology: Theory, Issues, and Practice*. Cambridge, MA: Ballinger Publishing Co.

Romijn, Henny (1996). *Acquisition of Technological Capability in Small Firms* in *Developing Countries*. Centre for Economic Research, Tilburg University.

Rosenberg, N. (1969). "The Direction of Technological change: Inducement Mechanisms and Focusing Devices" in *Economic Development and Cultural change*. Vol. , no. (October), pp. 1–24.

Rudra, A. (1995). "Field Survey Methods" in Bardhan, P. (ed) (1989). *Conversations Between Economists and Anthropologists*. Delhi. Oxford University Press. pp. 218–237.

Sachs, J.D., A. Varshney and N. Bajpai (eds) (1999). *India in the Era of Economic* Reforms. Delhi: Oxford University Press

Sakuma, A. (1995). "The Dynamics of Innovation and Learning-by-Doing: The Case of the Integrated Circuit Industry" in Minami, R., K.S. Kim, F. Makino and J.Seo (eds.) *Acquiring, Adapting and Developing Technologies: Lessons From the Japanese Experience*. New York: St. Martin's Press, pp. 165–190

Sarkar, J. (1996). *Technological Diffusion: Alternative Theories and Historical Evidence*. Discussion Paper N0. 134, Indira Gandhi Institute of Development of Research, Mumbai

Saviotti, P.P. (1996). *Technological Evolution, Variety and the Economy*. Cheltenham, U.K: Edward Elgar.

Saviotti, P.P., and J.S. Metcalfe (eds). 1991. *Evolutionary Theories of Economic and Technological Change*. Paris: Harwood Academic Publishers.

Schmookler, J. (1962). "Economic Sources of Inventive Activity" first published in *Journal of Economic History*. Later reproduced in Rosenberg, N. (Ed) (1971). *The Economics of Technological Change*. Baltimore: Penguin Books. Pp. 117–136.

Schumpeter, J.A. (1976). *Capitalism, Socialism and Democracy*. With a New Introduction by Tom Bottomore. London: George Allen and Unwin Ltd.

Sharma, S.K. (2000). "WTO & Some Vital Issues For SSIs" in *Laghu Udyog Samachar*, vol. XXIV (6-8), Jan-March, 2000, pp. 40–45

Shukla, Madhukar (2000). *Understanding Organisations : Organisational Theory and Practice in India*, New Delhi. Prentice - Hall of India.

SIDBI (1999). *SIDBI Report on Small Scale Industries Sector*, Small Industries Development in India, New Delhi.

SIDBI (2001a). *SIDBI Report on Small Scale Industries Sector*, Small Industries Development Bank, Lucknow

SIDBI (2001b). *Technology for Small Scale Industries: Current Status and Emerging Needs*, Small Industries Development Bank and Tata-McGraw Hill, New Delhi

Solow, R. (1966). "The Capacity to Assimilate an Advanced Technology" first published in *American Economic Review*. Papers and Proceedings (May). Later reproduced in Rosenberg, N. (Ed) (1971). *The Economics of Technological Change*. Baltimore: Penguin Books. Pp. 480–488.

Spiegel, M.R. (1972). *Theory and Problems of Statistics in SI units*. New Yoork: Mc-Graw-Hill International

Srinivasan, T.N. (2000). *Eight Lectures on India's Economic Reforms*. Delhi: Oxford University Press

Staley, E. and R. Morse. (1965). *Modern Small Industry for Developing Countries*. New York: McGraw-Hill

Stewart, F. (1979). I*nternational Technology Transfer: Issues and Policy Options*. World Bank Staff Working Paper No. 344.

Stiglitz, J.E. (1975). "Information and Economic Analysis" in Parkin, J.M., and A.R. Nobay (eds). *Current Economic Problems*. Cambridge: Cambridge University Press, pp. 27–52.

Stiglitz, J.E. (1985). "Information and Economic Analysis: A perspective" in Conference Papers Supplement to *The Economic Journal*, vol. 95, pp. 21–41.

Stiroh, K.J. (2001). '*Information Technology and the U.S. Productivity Revival: What do the Industry Data Say*?' Staff Research Paper no. 115. New York: Federal Reserve Bank of New York.

Stoneman, Paul (1995). "Introduction" in Stoneman, Paul (ed). *Handbook of Economics of Innovation and Technological Change*. Oxford: Blackwell. Pp. 1–13.

Stoneman, Paul (ed) (1995). *Handbook of Economics of Innovation and Technological Change*. Oxford: Blackwell

Teece, D. (1988). "Technological Change and the Nature of the Firm" in Dosi, G., Freeman, C., Nelson, R., Silverberg, G., and Soete, L. (Eds) (1988). *Technical Change and Economic Theory*. London: Pinter Publishers. Pp. 256–281.

Teece, D.J., and Gary Pisano (1998). "The Dynamic Capabilities of Firms: An Introduction" in Dosi, G., Teece, D.J., and Josef Chytry (eds). *Technology, Organisation and Competitiveness*. Oxford: Oxford University Press.

Teitel, S and L.E. Westphal (1984). "Introduction" to the Symposium on Technological Change and Industrial Development in *Journal of Development Economics*, vol. 16, nos. 1-2, (September-October), pp. 1–12.

Teitel, S. (1984). "Technology Creation in Semi-industrial Economies" in *Journal of Development Economics*, vol. 16, nos. 1-2, (September-October), pp. 39-62.

Tendulkar, S.D. (1993). "Industrial Planning in India: Institutional Environment and Regulatory Regime" in Ahuja, K., H. Coppens and H. Van der Wusten (eds). *Regime Transformations and Global Realignments*. Indo-Dutch Studies on Development Alternatives. Vol. 11, New Delhi: Sage, pp. 279–293

Tendulkar, S.D. and T.A. Bhavani (1997). "Policy on Modern Small Scale Industries: A Case of Government Failure" in the *Indian Economic Review*, vol. 32, no.1, January-June, pp. 39–64

Thomson, R.J. (1993). "The U.S. Electronics Industry" in Wellenius, B., A. Miller and C. J. Dahlman (eds). *Developing the Electronics Industry*. The World Bank, Washington, D.C., pp. 93–110

UNIDO (1995). *India: Towards Globalisation*. Industrial Development Review Series, UNIDO, Vienna.

Vaidyanathan, A. (1989). "Macro and Micro Approaches to Studying Rural Economic Change: Some Pointers from Indian Experience" in Bardhan, P. (ed) (1989). *Conversations Between Economists and Anthropologists*. Delhi. Oxford University Press, pp. 13–31

Varadharajan, S and S. Kannan (1998). "Brimming With Challenges" in *The Hindu Survey of Indian Industry*, Chennai

Vepa, R.K. (1988). *Modern Small Industry in India*. New Delhi: Sage

Watanabe, S. (ed) (1987). *Microelectronics, Automation and Employment in the Automobile Industry*. New York: John Wiley & Sons

Wellenius, B. (1993). "Electronics and the Developing Economies: Introduction and Overview" in Wellenius, B., A. Miller and C. J. Dahlman (eds). *Developing the Electronics Industry*. The World Bank, Washington, D.C., pp. 1–14

Wellenius, B., A. Miller and C. J. Dahlman (eds) (1993). *Developing the Electronics Industry*. The World Bank, Washington, D.C.

WTO (1998). *Trade Policy Review: India 1998*. Geneva: WTO.

WTO (1998). *Trade Policy Review: India*. A Report by the Secretariat

Yule, G.U., and Kendall, M.G. (1958). *An Introduction to the Theory of Statistics*. London: Charles Griffin and Company

Author Index

Dosi 44, 70
Dosi and Nelson 63
Galbraith 50
Garud et al 44
Hicks (1932) 51
Mansfield 51
Mintzberg (1979) 54
Mowery and Rosenberg (1979) 50
Nelson and Winter 44, 47
Rosenberg (1969) 51
Sahl 44
Schmookler (1966) 50
Schumpeter (1935, 1942) 50